CAN I come out from behind the settee now MARCUS.

Anyway Here is your MAIN course

ersoy

D1493666

McCoy

xx

INTRODUCTION TO PART TWO

'Mally - The Rebel Without A Pause' provides a stunning 'middle' to the fascinating story of Mally Welburn's remarkable and troubled life.

At the beginning of Part Two, Mally has escaped from his abusive Father, but only to be confronted by a new set of problems. Running away doesn't provide Mally with the freedom he was dreaming of. Quite the reverse in fact as the troubles he suffered as a child are merely replaced by new, self-inflicted ones.

A combination of drinking, fighting and gambling - problems that he finds impossible to solve - become his new way of life. When he's away fishing, Mally is a conscientious, hard-working individual who is always willing to learn and eager to improve himself. But when he's ashore and flush with money, the self-inflicted demons take over and he descends to the deepest depths of human existence.

Fighting with anyone who gets in his way, he unwittingly plots his own individual course to self-destruction.

Time spent in a Detention Camp and finally imprisonment follow with an almost inevitability. But even then, Mally recalls these potentially traumatic experiences with a certain amount of affection and humour...

Finally, as Mally descends into an ever more shocking lifestyle, he loses, in different ways, the two people who provide his main chance of returning to some form of normality.

Without them, how can he hope to survive?

MALLY

PART TWO:

THE REBEL WITHOUT A PAUSE

RIVERHEAD
PUBLISHING

MALLY WELBURN

First published in Great Britain in 2007
by Riverhead Publishing

A CIP catalogue record for this book is
available from the British Library.

ISBN 0-9550237-3-4

Typeset in Times New Roman by
Riverhead Publishing, Hull, HU1 1PS.

Designed by Riverhead Publishing

Printed by
John Boland Print, Hull, HU9 1NW.

You can find out more about future books by
Mally Welburn on: www.riverheadonline.co.uk

CONTENTS

DEDICATION

This book is dedicated to my dear late Mother, Ada,
without whose love and care I undoubtedly wouldn't still be
here to tell this story.
Also to my two daughters, Tammie and Keelie,
my son, Peter, and my four grandchildren - Kailem, Aydan,
and twins Ethan and La'tia Mai.

ALL BUT THE STONIEST OF HEARTS
WILL BE TOUCHED

This is Mally Welburn's second book in an autobiographical
trilogy.
It is written in an inimitable and conversational style, and the
wit, great humour and vivid imagery of his story quickly leads
the reader to understand how his early years in fear of a harsh
and violent Father plotted the path to his rebel years.
Alcohol-fuelled violence and consequential spells as a guest of
H M Prison Service are recounted, as are the hard lessons
learned, but not before he had touched rock bottom and lost his
marriage and much else.
The closeness to his family shines through, and the concluding
Chapter, 'Pal of My Cradle Days', is testament to his undying
love for his late Mother. As you read Mr. Welburn's last
Chapter, tissues will not suffice. Get out the sandbags!
All but the stoniest of hearts will be touched.

Beryl Urquhart, O.B.E.
Former Principal Officer for the Parliamentary Labour Party

CHAPTER TWELVE
SMOKE GETS IN YOUR EYES

It was hot and smoky in the betting-shop as I studied the runners and riders for the next race. I didn't give the sound of the passing fire engines a second thought at first. The sirens just blended into the background. As far as I was concerned they were nothing unusual.

I'd been out drinking since opening time that morning and no doubt the beer-induced haze had something to do with my lack of concern. Another reason was undoubtedly the winning start I'd made at my local bookmakers. I was enjoying one of my 'lucky streaks'.

I'd already had two winners from my first two bets. And the task of choosing a third seemed far more appealing than finding out what was causing the commotion in the street outside. All that changed seconds later though when a bloke who was obviously out of breath and already coughing, rushed into the bookies.

'Bloody hell! Haven't you seen what's going on?' he shouted. 'The street's full of smoke and the flat above the taxi office is on fire.'

That altered everything! The flat above the taxi office was where I lived! And where my brother Trevor was currently sleeping off the effects of five pints of beer and a couple of rums. I threw the newspaper in the air and charged out of the half-open door...

We'd lived in the flat for nearly a year. I'd got it just after I'd started on the trawlers. When I got home after my second trip I'd heard there was a flat for rent above the 'Ken Kabs' taxi office in Gipsyville. It was only three shops away from my local, the Gipsyville Tavern and four shops away from the betting shop. On top of that it was just five minutes walk to my loving Mother's.

Perfect! I thought.

MALLY - THE REBEL WITHOUT A PAUSE

My Mother used to go out on Hessle Road shopping every day, so I'd get to see her. She could even come to the flat for a pot of tea. When I came home from sea I'd make sure she got her little treats. I'd buy her some hair spray and some hair colouring, my Mother loved her hair. We couldn't really give her money because she was the most honest lady you could ever meet. She'd just go and buy the old man some cigs and tell him where she'd got the money. We couldn't let her get into trouble off the old man as he was now working ashore. But I'm sure he didn't mind when I used to send him some 'bacca' round as well.

I went to see the joint owners of Ken-Kabs, Billy Burrows and Billy Hames at their office. They were both ex-trawler skippers but they'd got out of the fishing game to set up the taxi firm, it was big business. They knew who I was, they knew I was a fisherman, even though only a galley-boy. I had to work in the galley peeling spuds, scrubbing berths out, and doing all the shit jobs for my first two trips. Billy Burrows said he'd keep the flat for me until I got home from my next trip. He said he'd have to put an electric cooker in it and tidy the place up a bit.

I told two of my brothers, Trevor and Bobby about the flat and the benefits it had for us - the most important one was that we'd be near our loving Mother - and I asked them if they wanted to move in? They did!

There were two flats above the taxi office but one had already been taken. The other one was basically just one big room on the first floor. You had the main door to the building and then up a flight of stairs was a bit of a landing. If you then went straight ahead you'd get to the back flat where a young woman lived. But do you know? I never saw her all the time I was there.

On the landing was a bathroom, which we shared with the mystery woman. We'd then go up another small flight of stairs to get to the 'fortress', which was our flat. The flat had a big bay window overlooking Hessle Road. Trevor soon had it spotless - well, he always had a girlfriend to impress.

As you walked into the flat there was a fridge on the left-hand wall and then next to the fridge was this old three-ring electric cooker which took about half an hour to warm up. It then took nearly an hour to cool down after I'd done my fry-up in a morning. Our kid was always telling me to make sure I turned the cooker rings off after I'd finished cooking.

'And don't forget to keep the place tidy,' he'd always say.

Also in the room was a big double bed and next to the bed, a three-seater settee with a little coffee table next to it. I think everyone had the little coffee table in them days. I think most of my brothers still do. There were a few cupboards on the wall for the grub and the pots and pans - and a couple of wardrobes to hang our clothes in. There wasn't much more we could fit in the flat apart from our record player and the old Redifussion telly. But the telly was nothing to brag about. Every time we switched it on, all we heard through the speakers was,

'Car six can you go to so and so. Car eight, where are you now?' It was run off the same bloody aerial as the taxi office! Billy needed a month's rent up front which I paid him using my wages from the three weeks I'd just done at sea. At the time Trevor was living with one of our older brothers, Raymond, and Bobby was living at his girlfriend's Mother's house.

The flat was in a poor state, a bit of a dump in fact but as I say, Trevor soon smartened it up. I'll say this about Trevor, he's a very clean and tidy person and he always avoided trouble.

The master, Jack 'Sensei' Cochran, was teaching him the art of karate.

'Self discipline' was Jack's motto.

Our Bobby was on his way to two hundred amateur boxing fights. And Mally? I was well on the road to two hundred fights without gloves on! To be honest, I just didn't care in them days, I'd chosen the life of a 'fisherman' - and everything that I thought went with it. My brother Bobby was one fit lad, he was well into his boxing, I tell yer, he's in the record books for the fastest knockout in boxing. He was boxing at the City Hall and on the night of the fight me old man said to him, 'I want you in for nine o'clock'.

I think our kid got in the ring at twenty to nine and when the bell went for the first round he came out and just landed the Bobby 'bomb' - his right hand!

His opponent went down straight away. The fight only lasted

thirteen seconds, including the ten-second count. He then ran the three and half miles home. He walked in through the front door on the stroke at nine, he didn't want turning into a pumpkin did he?

Bobby used to run everywhere. His girlfriend lived eight miles away and he would run there and back. As our Bobby keeps reminding me in his Marlon Brando voice, 'I could have been somebody. I could have been a contender.' I for one know he should have been a champion, but he was mismanaged, most probably the same as another champion from Hull, Ricky Beaumont was.

It was agreed that I would pay the rent and Trevor and Bobby would live in the flat rent-free. They'd get the grub in and pay for the electricity. We were all excited to be living together - even though I was away at sea most of the time - but it was to be a real home and the big plus was that we got to see our loving Mother. Me old man had got a shore job, working on the tugs as a 'steam raiser'. Don't ask me what that was because I haven't got a clue. I think some ships had different engines and the new modern engines were coming in so it was out with the old, in with the new. It was sad to see the old man thrown on the scrap heap after nearly forty years with the one firm. I was glad to hear he got his compensation for his service to the fishing industry, it was a long drawn out battle but in the end the fishermen got what they deserved.

Every day when he went to do his job on the tugs, Mother would be round at our flat, for about ten o'clock. She daren't stay too long just in case the old man came home for his dinner. And while Trevor and Bobby were at work fish filleting I would spend time with the 'Pal of my cradle days,' my ever loving Mother. Oh, how I miss her to this day. I only have two photos of my Mother. I've included one of them on the back cover of this book as a lasting memory.

Unfortunately Bobby only stayed for a short time because when he got the chance to move back in with his girlfriend, he jumped at it. I couldn't blame him, that sixteen mile run every time he wanted to see her must have worn him out!

On the day of the fire, Trevor had been out drinking with me since opening time. Now bear in mind Trevor wasn't a big drinker. He never has been. He only drank at the weekend as he was into all his 'karate stuff'. And as soon as he started on the shorts, he was gone! He was absolutely smashed, hammered, out of the game! As we left the pub and the fresh air hit him, it simply knocked him out!

Getting him back to the flat wasn't easy. I carried him up the first flight of stairs, then after a little readjustment, up the other flight and then I had to get his six keys out of his pocket, to open the 'fortress' door. I often made fun of Trevor's 'over the top security system' but I admit the six locks did serve their purpose one day when the big bad wolf, my Dad, big John, came a calling looking for my Mother. The old man huffed and he puffed outside but he couldn't blow the door down. And all the time my Mother was just down the road at Raymond's house...

I got Trevor inside and threw him onto the bed and tucked him in. I guessed he'd be there for quite a while! It was about half past two in the afternoon and there was no point in going back out, so I thought I'd make myself a nice fried-egg sandwich.

I like a bet on the horses and I always got a morning paper and had a bet when I was home from sea. I still like a bet now but I'm not a big gambler anymore.

There I was digging the frying pan out of the cupboard and at the same time turning the knobs on the cooker. I didn't know which electric rings worked and which ones didn't. So I banged all three on at once, cut up some lard and put it in the pan.

Our kid was just laid there, snoring his head off. I shouted to him to see if he fancied an egg sandwich. He just mumbled something about feeling sick so I told him to get his head down and he'd soon be okay again. While I was waiting for the electric rings to warm up I started to have a look at the horseracing page in the morning paper. I noticed a horse I'd backed before and it had been unlucky not to win. I still had some money in my pocket. The horse was running in the 2.45 and it was only about twenty to three at the time. I shouted to Trevor that I wouldn't be long - that I was just going to the betting shop - and for him to keep an eye on the cooker. I was only going to be five minutes. I shook our kid as I went past him and told him to leave the door open.

'Okay,' he mumbled.

MALLY - THE REBEL WITHOUT A PAUSE

I ran out the door not knowing our kid had actually got up and slammed the door shut after me with all six locks, locking at the same time. Then our kid had just gone back to the 'land of nod'.

I got to the betting shop, which was only a few yards away, got my bet on and yes, the horse won! I think it was 10/1. I know I had a fiver on it so it was an easy £50 back - a good week's wage at that time. As I was on a lucky streak, I decided to have another bet. And then another! I was having a great afternoon at the bookies until that guy ran in, shouting about the fire...

'Fucking hell - our kid's in there,' I thought as I ran down the street towards the flat - and what about my eggs?

There were two fire engines already there and about half a dozen firemen were running into the entrance of the flats. They ran upstairs in their breathing masks. The smoke was billowing out of the big bay window. All I could hear was our kid screaming, 'Get me out of here!' He was being overcome by smoke and couldn't open the locks on the door.

I started to run up the stairs but the firemen told me to go back and get out of the building. I told them my brother was in there, as they pushed me back and tried to bang the six lock door down, but with no success. Our kid was screaming, 'Get me out, I can't breathe!' And the firemen were shouting back to him, 'Stand back, lay on the floor, we're trying to get the door open!'

One fireman then told me in no uncertain terms to get out of the way! I sneaked into the bathroom but the place was filling up with smoke. And the next thing I remember was our kid coming out of the flat coughing and spluttering and gasping for air. The firemen had finally banged the door down and the black smoke just followed our kid into the bathroom, where I was hidden behind the door. Our kid was coughing like mad over the sink as the black smoke filled the room. He turned the cold water tap on and was splashing his face and rubbing his eyes. He then threw some water on the mirror and wiped it so he could see himself. While he was rubbing the mirror with one hand and his eyes with the other, he looked like one of the black and white minstrels. I was still hidden behind the door. He then gave the mirror an extra rub and caught sight of something moving behind the door.

Well, the room exploded as he spun round doing all his karate noises and moves. It was just like the time in Part One when I hid behind the couch when he was eating his fish and chips, watching the horror film. I even asked him the same question.

'Now then Trevor. How are you?' I said.

'You bastaaaaaaaaaard - I'll kill yer,' he shouted back.

Oh, that still makes me laugh. I know it's not funny really but it still makes me laugh. And those six locks on the door - that makes me laugh as well...

That was the end of the flat as far as our kid and me were concerned. We'd lost most of our stuff through smoke damage and needless to say we were 'asked to leave' - immediately!

Trevor went back to stay at brother Raymond's house and I went back to sea for a ten-weeks trip on the St Jason...

My first trip to sea had been on the St Dominic - as a seventeen year-old in 1975 - when that brave man threw himself over the ship's side. The St Dominic was a sidewinder trawler. The skipper of the Dominic was the legend, Pete 'Greybo' Greyburn, he was a real 'daddy'. A 'daddy' was a nickname we used for a good skipper. Arthur Ball was the 'daddy' of them all as far as I was concerned, I was with him later on the St Jason.

For every week you did at sea, you got a day at home, and the first day would be the day you tied up alongside the fish docks. It was usually by mid afternoon so that the bobbers could unload the catch ready for the market the next day.

Our catch would be sold and we always hoped there weren't a lot of other trawlers landing at the same time as us. The more fish that was landed, the cheaper it was - and the less we got for ours. We got paid the day it was sold, this was called 'settling day', and it was always party day. I think the saying 'live for the day' may have come from the fishermen. You never knew if you were coming back after you let go of them ropes at the quayside as you cast off, heading for the Norwegian coast or Bear Island, but it was always an adventure.

My second trip was also on the St Dominic, still peeling spuds from five in the morning and doing all the berth cleaning until seven at night. But then it was 'my time'. The time when I loved to go down to the fishroom with one of the top den-house men I ever sailed with, Jimmy McCoid. Jim taught me a lot. He was another very, very hard man. You didn't mess with Jim. Saying that, the skipper, Pete, was also a hard man, but he was never hard on his men.

The skipper's nephew, who was a 'deckie learner', a snacker, was Ian Rouse, the same Ian Rouse who'd been at Stockton Hall School with me. The same Ian Rouse who did the Lyke Wake Walk with me. And the same Ian Rouse who played in the football match and joined in the brawl after them two long-haired wankers had started throwing pebbles at me. I met Ian again recently and we couldn't stop laughing when we started to relive it all. He'd been on three trips before I'd got on the St Dominic. The times we spent together in the mess deck playing crib will be a lasting memory. 'One for his knob', we used to say. That's a cribbage term.

My second trip was to the Norwegian coast where we had to trawl our nets for about six hours. We could catch up to about 100 kit - ten stone to a kit - of granddad cod, some of them were as big as me and I'm six-foot. Then after we got our nets in we'd steam back over where we'd just towed our nets. That could take about two hours. In that time the men would gut all the catch what had just been caught and throw it into the washer, which cleaned the fish before it was dropped down to Jim in the fishroom. He would store all the fish in ice. Ian's job was to shovel the ice to Jim to keep the fish fresh. By the time the deckhands had cleared the decks it was time to drop the nets again and the skipper would ring the bell. The engines would slow down and the magic words, 'down trawl' would echo through the ship. Then the herbs, the deckies, would shoot the trawl away - and they'd have six hours playing cards, dominoes, reading, or whatever else they wanted to do...

If Ian wasn't playing cribbage with me on the night, he'd be in his pit! I kept telling Ian I wanted his job when he was ready to go up the ladder in the fishing industry. He had to go to fishing school for about six weeks to get his deckie/spare hand's ticket. To get up to the next level it was all about how much time you did at sea, and you first had to do three trips to sea in the galley. You got all the shit jobs and on the sidewinder trawlers you did three weeks away at a time. It was like nine full weeks in the galley. I hated it in the galley but it had to be done. To compensate, I used to love going down to the fishroom and throwing the ice about. After I'd done my day's work in the galley it was workout time in the fishroom. On my second trip I was dead jealous of Ian because he was in his bunk more times than I was working. He told me he was due to go for his spare hand's ticket when we got home from that trip.

He said, 'The skipper likes you, Mally - ask him if you can have my job while I'm at school.'

He also said he'd have a word with the ship's runner, Renee, to see if I could go as a 'deckie learner'. It meant I'd get an increase in wages and a small percentage of what we made from the catch. So when we were steaming home from the fishing grounds and we all knew we'd had a good trip in, I asked the skipper if I could do Ian's job for him while he was at school. This, bearing in mind, was only my second trip to sea and you had to do three trips in the galley before you could go on deck.

Pete Greyburn replied, 'Leave it to me', as he handed me a forty quid back-hander for cleaning his berth. It was like getting two weeks wages and on that particular settling day I was the richest galley boy in Hull. I got back-handers off every member of the crew, even the chief engineer gave me a treat, and that's rare in the fishing industry, as oil and water don't mix. This particular settling day for me was like getting five numbers - and the bonus ball!

When I got home I went to see Billy from Ken Kabs and paid him his month's rent up-front. I then went out and got a telly, some curtains and a carpet. I also got whatever Trevor wanted, after all, I was the king, the 'King of the Road'. I remember Roger Miller sang that song.

We were only at home for about forty-eight hours, then we were back on board the St Dominic. But before I was due to go back, the ship's runner called me into his office. I had to go to sign back on the ship. Renee, who was a really nice man said to me, 'Listen here son. We've had some really good reports about you and we know you want to go on the deck, don't you?'

'Yes I do,' I said.

He then said to me, 'Listen, it's a hard job where you're going on this trip and it won't be like the last trip, we're only allowed one trip to the Norwegian coast for each ship we have. We're also only allowed to catch so much cod and the Dominic has caught her quota for the year. You can go on deck but I'll warn you, it'll be very hard work. It'll be freezing cold where the St Dominic is going as its next trip is to Greenland to catch flat fish - plaice and halibut. So, do you want to go as a snacker? The skipper has asked for you.'

'Yes please, anything to get me out of that galley,' I replied.

So I signed on the dotted line to sail on the St Dominic for the third and last time. I then got a 'stores ticket' so I could go and get my sea gear i.e. duck suit - waterproofs, gutting knives, gloves, cap etc. We also had a muffler, which was like a scarf that stopped us getting boils on our necks from the sea water. Oh! And don't forget the thigh boots. They were like big Wellington boots that went right up to our thighs, hence the name. We also had our 'clumpers' - small Wellington boots. Our thick woolly jumpers, boot socks and our cloth gloves for gutting fish. So there I was with my heavy bag sorted, all paid for by the firm, ready for my first trip as a deckie learner.

I'll never ever forget that trip to Greenland - seeing the stars at night - it took the best part of five days to get there.

We then put the trawl into the sea and hauled our first catch in. It was three hundred baskets of flat fish.

Well that was it, I was never off the deck for my full 18 hours because flat fish are so small and take longer to gut.

You need about 500 of them for a ten stone kit compared with two of the granddad cods.

As you can imagine, with it being minus 20 degrees most days, the ship's rigging used to freeze up and we'd be chopping ice away from it constantly. We couldn't feel our hands and the fish were frozen solid by the time you got to gut them. It was so cold, the snot from our noses would even freeze up. And the skipper would let us go into the galley to get warm. A new kid got my job in the galley but he didn't like it. He was always in his bunk crying and he wanted to go home. We were twenty-eight days, dock to dock on that trip and we did 18 hours on the deck every day when we were fishing. It took us a long time to get into our five hours sleep, because it would take us half an hour to defrost and half an hour to eat our three-course meal. Then we'd try to get to sleep before they called us back out again, to do another 18 hours on deck.

We were eighteen days in the fishing grounds, then it took five days to get home and for two of them days we were still gutting fish. It was piled up on the deck and we couldn't wait for the skipper to go to sleep so we could dump it over the side to save us gutting it. The trouble was, the skipper never seemed to sleep!

Our reward for that trip was that we landed in debt - nobody wanted our catch. In the end it went to a factory where unsold fish was sent to be turned into fishmeal for the farmers.

'Some you win - some you lose,' was the fisherman's saying, because on that trip we didn't pick up a penny! But we were always ready to go back to the unknown and give it another go.

When we got home we were told the St Dominic would be laid up for a while because there was nowhere it could go fishing. The 'Cod War' meant we weren't allowed to go fishing off Iceland due to the Icelanders extending their fishing limits round their tiny island from twelve to two hundred miles!

There was a lot of conflict over it with some trawlers getting their warps chopped by the Icelandic gunboats. There weren't a lot of places left to fish for cod and haddock and the places we could fish were further and further away from Hull.

It also wasn't worth it for the sidewinder trawlers to go fishing because the fish wouldn't stay fresh. They had to keep going into foreign ports to pick up ice, fuel and more food. So it worked out that they were going away for nothing. In the end the trawler owners had to invest in bigger trawlers that could freeze the fish within half an hour of it being caught. You can't get fresher than that!

The company I was working for got four of the new super trawlers. They were called stern draggers, which meant they fished from the stern instead of the side like sidewinders. By, you learn something new every day don't you?

With the laying-up of the sidewinders there were a lot of men

out of work. It was the time when they said; 'You'd better get another pair of shoes cos you could be on a long walkabout.'
While they were getting the four new stern draggers ready we were kept waiting for about six weeks. This was the time when we found out if we were one of the lucky ones, chosen to sail on these so called, super trawlers. If we were successful we'd be sailing on the St Benedict, St Jason, St Jasper and St Jerome and each ship needed 25 men. But while we waited we had to sign on the dole...

After a couple of weeks I was called to Renee's office. Renee signed the crew on but nine times out of ten it was up to the skipper if he took you or not. I was in Renee's office when the top skipper Arthur Ball walked in. He was going to be the skipper of the St Jason.

Renee said to skipper Ball, 'Here's a good snacker for you, skipper. He did that trip to Greenland on the Dominic and earned nowt, but he never missed the boat.'

'Missing the boat' meant you never got out of your bunk to do your work. Remember you can't let your ship mates down!

Skipper Ball said to me, 'Can you do ten weeks away son?'

My reply was a definite, 'Yes skipper.'

'Sign him on,' said Skipper Ball.

Renee then said to me, 'Listen son, I'll sign you on when the ship's ready to sail, now keep out of trouble and don't be getting into any fights. Keep popping in to see me two or three times a week and the deckie learner's job is yours. Even though you haven't been to deckie learner's school, you can go when you've done a couple trips on the St Jason.'

'Thank you, Renee', I said.

His parting words as I left his office were, 'And don't forget, keep your nose clean.'

Up until then I'd only done three trips on the St Dominic and if you totalled the time spent at sea on the Dominic it would equal only one trip on the St Jason. Those four weeks couldn't pass fast enough. In the meantime, the St Jason arrived at St Andrews Quay and everyone who was due to sail on her went down to the dock to get the ship ready. The nets needed putting aboard along with all the wires, bobbins and the ship's stores. We were under the watchful eye of one of the best trawler mates I've ever sailed with, the late Brian Ridsdale.

He was another hard man but one with a wicked sense of humour. Nothing ever seemed to bother Bri. He was in the same mould as Dave Lilley. Do you remember Dave, the bosun of the Arctic Corsair who I talked about in Part One? The guy who was swept up and down the deck in that gale? The guy who climbed up the bridge ladder, bollock-naked? Well Bri Ridsdale was in the same mould as Dave, but he was only half of Dave's weight. And with all due respect to Dave, Bri was also twice as fit...

The St Jason was a really big ship. I tell yer, she was that big, she had two massive fishrooms, where we stored the ten stone blocks of frozen fish, which came out of twelve freezing machines. We packed the fish after it had been gutted in the factory - there was no gutting on open deck like on the St Dominic. The fish we caught was tipped down a ramp. Below deck we would stand at a bench and gut the fish. Unwanted innards would go down the 'shit chute' and straight into the sea to feed the seagulls. You could always tell if a ship had caught a lot of fish, you just had to look for the seagulls, we called them mollies, nobody can tell me why!

The fish livers would be put down another chute, where they dropped into a basket. It was then one man's job to boil the livers for cod liver oil. That was a nice bonus for us as we sold it when we got home.

When we'd gutted the fish it went on a conveyor belt to the big washer and then onto another conveyor belt that led into the packing area. This was where the fishroom men would pack the fish into the freezing machines. Each freezer held twenty individual blocks of fish, each weighing from eight to ten stone, depending on the size of the fish. The smaller the fish, the heavier the block - and when the freezer was full it would hold around a ton in weight. There were twelve of these freezers aboard the St Jason, which would freeze the fish solid in four hours. So every four hours we'd have to go and knock out the frozen fish that came out in these frozen blocks. We'd push these frozen blocks down big chutes which led to the fishrooms where men were waiting, in minus 20 degrees, to store the blocks of fish. I swear, you could play a full eleven a side football match in them fishrooms. When I saw an empty fishroom I thought I was at Wembley, that's how big they seemed. They could hold 300 tons of fish each.

We had to catch at least 500 tons of fish before we went home so it was down to the skipper and the mate to find the best fishing grounds. Sometimes we'd catch ten ton of fish for a four-hour tow, sometimes we'd only catch three.

We used to work twelve and six when we were fishing, twelve hours work and six hours sleep. The crew would be spilt up into three watches. The mate would have five men, the second mate five men and the bosun five men. When we were fishing there were always twelve men on the deck, with the other six, below deck, off watch in bed. The deckie learner - which was me, was always on the mate's watch.

The fishroom man didn't come on the deck to haul and shoot the nets. He had a new name - 'factory manager' - well he *was* in charge of 'the factory'.

The huge trawler I was on was like a hotel compared to the St Dominic. And the skipper's berth was like a room at the Ritz in London, very posh! The crew's berths were mainly two man berths, apart from one four man berth. The cook had his own berth, the factory manager had his own, the bosun had his own and the second mate had his own berth. Well, we were away a long time so some of us had to have a bit of comfort.

As well as the fishing work we also had to do what we called 'inside cleaning'. This happened twice a week when we had to clean all the alleyways and berths from top to bottom.

We had showers and big baths, even a washing machine to wash our clothes, but saying that, some men never changed their clothes for weeks on end. Most of us never got a shave till we had passed a certain milestone e.g. 250 tons in the fishroom.

One of my jobs was to take skipper Ball a nice cup of coffee, no sugar. He used to shout out on the tannoy, 'Tell the deckie learner to fetch me a pot of coffee please.' He always said, please, and I never once saw Arthur Ball lose his rag, never, he was a gentleman. And when I used to take him a pot of coffee, he'd ask me questions about my life and what I wanted to achieve. I told him I wanted to be a skipper, if not, then a taxi driver. He would show me how to steer a ship, he taught me how to read a chart and how to navigate. He told me, if I was willing to learn, he was willing to teach me - and I was willing to learn.

Bri Ridsdale, the mate, would teach me how to splice rope and wire but my main job was to grease all the shackles. There were hundreds of them and woe betide me if we had to put a shackle on something very quickly and there was no grease on it, he'd have me greasing all the shackles for twelve hours.

I didn't like the net mending side to the fishing industry as I was classed as a 'grafter' more suited to physical work. I loved splicing wire and rope but more than anything I loved being on the bridge, learning from the master.

When we were on the deep-sea freezer trawlers we got a lot of time on our hands and the crew was like one big family. And after we'd got the gear and the nets all ready, there were always plenty of parties in the berths as we were sailing to the fishing grounds. The skipper didn't mind people drinking, as long as they didn't come onto the bridge with a drink down their necks. And as long as they never 'missed the boat'.

If anyone ever 'missed the boat' through drink, skipper Ball sacked them. I didn't blame him. There was nothing worse than when there was work to do and someone was pissed-up and couldn't get out of their bunk.

On the trip we were allowed three cans of 'Long Life' beer on a Wednesday and six on a Sunday. Most of us would save them up until we reached the halfway point of the trip. We also used to get letters from home. If another trawler, regardless of which company it was from, was just leaving Hull, they'd fetch our letters out to us. They were put in a sealed plastic container with a little flashing light attached to it. When the ship came to the same fishing grounds as us, they'd call us up and say they had mail for us. It was an exciting time getting mail.

I never got letters from my brothers Trevor or Bobby but there would always be one, every week, off my dear Mother. She would always end her letters by saying, 'Lots of love and kisses' and would put lots of kisses at the bottom. I've included a very special one in Chapter 22. It was the last one she ever sent me and has eighteen kisses at the end of it - eighteen! - how spooky is that? That was the number of my box on 'Deal Or No Deal'.

We got the mail by someone on the other ship throwing the

plastic container over the side when the two ships were about 50 yards apart. We'd all be there with little grappling hooks on the end of a line. It was a buzz getting our mail. And if a ship was leaving the fishing grounds for home and we'd just got there, we'd send our own container to them so they could take our letters home to our loved ones. I sent my Mother a letter every week.

Do you know, I learnt more about the fishing game in that ten-week trip on board the St Jason, than I did doing three trips on the St Dominic. I learnt all about net mending, even though I didn't like it, but my job was to make sure all the 12 inch wooden needles were full of nylon. These had to be ready in case the net got damaged. One of the most important things were the 'sittings' which were six feet long pieces of rope which tied the plastic floats onto your net. The floats would keep the mouth of the trawl open when it was on the seabed. Sometimes, with the pressure on these floats under water, they would come adrift. We had to make sure they were fastened on securely. So, every time the trawl would come up the ramp at the arse end of the ship we would check to see if we needed our sittings and needles. I was always ready. I used to double the sittings in half so they were 3 feet long and then tie them round my waist. It looked like I had a ra-ra skirt on - or like an Indian dancing round the camp fire in them cowboy films. My Mother always wanted the Indians to win but they never did. When someone got shot or got an arrow in them on them films and died, my Mother used to say, 'Their arse will be cold now'. She was always good at summing things up!

Talking about films, when we were on the St Jason we got ten films to take away with us. They weren't DVDs or even videos. No, they were reel to reel films that we played on a film projector. We always had to ask the skipper if we could watch one. We tried to work it where we watched at least one film a week. When we were slack we'd watch a couple of the films in the mess deck after tea with the skipper in attendance. He picked the film of his choice. It was a good way to unwind when we were steaming to the fishing grounds after the day's work had been done, getting the nets ready for fishing. Everyone used to watch the film, apart from whoever was on watch on the bridge, safely guiding us to our hunting grounds.

SMOKE GETS IN YOUR EYES

You could say we were a tribe of hunters, us fishermen. We were definitely a breed of people, which was slowly dying out, just like the Indians in the films, the cowboys being the Governments of this world. A bit like the miners - a dying breed. I'll tell you later about me getting involved with miners...

One of the films I remember watching time and time again, with the fishroom manager, Bob Spicer, was 'Steptoe and Son Ride Again'. It was where old man Steptoe pretended to die and claimed the insurance. Him and Harold also bought a blind greyhound. Oh we thought it was really funny. It was the last film we got to see out of the ten we'd taken away with us and we must have watched it more times than all of the other films put together.

When we had time on our hands at sea due to slack fishing, or as we steamed towards the fishing grounds, the spare time was called 'gash'. In our gash time we were either in our bunks reading our worn out 'Playboy' magazines or watching a film, and in my case it was a bit of both.

I also liked to go up onto the bridge where skipper Ball was always happy to teach me how to use the compass.

'There are 360 degrees in a compass, Mally,' he used to say. 'Now what's the opposite of 15 degrees?' he would ask.

Well I'd be counting on me fingers and trying to work it out when he'd say, 'It's simple, just add 180 degrees. And if you're asked the opposite to anything over 180 degrees just take away 180.'

That stuck with me and it sure helped when I got 99.9% in my mock radar observer's exam later on, when I went for my bosun's ticket. 195 degrees is opposite to 15 degrees by the way. It was a lot harder to learn north, north by east, north - north east, north east by north, north east, etc. But it's easy to get the opposite course to north east by north. You just say the opposite to north is south, the opposite to east is west, the opposite to north again is south, so the answer is south west by south. There you go again, a day without learning is a day wasted. But that first trip on the St Jason wasn't wasted, I learnt a lot, including too much masturbation is bad for you.

You couldn't get to sleep, especially if you had them 'thinks' on, believe you me, you'd get them 'thinks' on after you'd

MALLY - THE REBEL WITHOUT A PAUSE

been away over five weeks with still five more weeks to go.
We just hoped the skipper would find the fish to keep us busy.
Nine times out of ten, skipper Ball was on the ball, so to speak
and when we saw them football sized fishrooms filling up, it
filled our hearts with joy. We'd go into our berth and play our
Patsy Cline cassettes, or in mine and Bob Spicer's case, watch
'Steptoe and Son Ride Again', for the hundredth time.

I really loved my first trip to sea on the St Jason and do you
know what, nobody said anything about the spots on my face.
I was able to grow a bit of a beard while I was away.
Someone did mention again that pissing in your hands and
rubbing the piss on your face would get rid of the spots - but
I can tell yer that never worked!

When a trip was over, it was great to see Trevor and Bobby
waiting at the quay for me. It was then party time with ten
days at home to enjoy ashore. Remember I got a day for every
week I'd been away and I made sure I enjoyed every second
of it...

The difference between being at home with my family and
friends or working away at sea was as different as chalk and
cheese. Fishing in the 70s was one of the most dangerous jobs
imaginable. Many men left their wives and families and sailed
to the icy waters off Greenland and Norway, never to return.

So naturally, every time a trawler made it safely back to port
the crew was always keen to celebrate the fact. And for
nearly all fishermen, settling day was party time. It was for me!
I'd meet up with me mates and family members, get
pissed-up and blow all the money I'd just earned. And more
often than not the day would end with the odd fight.

On my first trip home off the St Jason I got two pay-days. The
first was our usual settling day wage but we also received
another payment, four or five days later, according to the
tonnage we'd actually landed. The difference between fishing
on the St Dominic and the St Jason was that you got a
percentage of the money made when the fresh fish was sold
on the market from the St Dominic. But on the St Jason, you
got paid on the tonnage, so we had a rough idea what we'd be
picking up on that one.

For the St Dominic it all depended on the markets and how
many ships were landing at the same time as we did. If we had

good quality fish then it would sell - not like the last trip I did on the St Dominic, 28 days and all for nothing but landing in debt! I picked up my ten-week's wages plus the half a per cent tonnage payment from the St Jason. It meant my pockets were bulging with over £1,000 which was a lot of money for a teenager in the 70s. I was what they called us - 'A Three Day Millionaire'.

On settling day, we'd always go down to the dock to get paid wearing our suits and we'd always turn up in a taxi. After all it was 'our day'. When the cashier had paid us we'd go to see Renee, the ship's runner, to see if we were going on the next trip. We'd ask if we'd got a good report because it was at that time we were told if we'd got the sack or not. It was also the time to treat the ship's runner for getting us the job. I can honestly say, I've never given money to get work on the trawlers. But saying that, I used to give Renee cigs and bacca as a treat. So in one sense you could say I treated him - but never with cash.

Some men would pay up to £100 to get on a good ship. I called them sneaky bastards! You shouldn't have to pay for a job if you're good enough to do it, was the way I looked at it. But many fishermen did, and we always knew the ones who were 'dropping it' in to Renee because he used to shut his office door.

When we came out of Renee's office, men would be standing outside waiting for the chance to see if there was a job available. They'd wait to see if anyone had got the sack or was having a trip off. In my two years with the St Jason there weren't many changes. In fact these were the happiest days of my fishing life, sailing with a good skipper, a first class mate and a great bunch of 'herbs' - deckies. And let's not forget the engineers and the cook. Some cooks were what we called 'belly robbers'. They were gaffer's men, trying to save grub, working under instructions from the trawler owners.

Sometimes, some of the men waiting outside of Renee's office were some of my mates. Ian Rouse was one of them. He'd done his spare hand's course and was waiting for his chance to sail. We knew Ian and a few of our other mates had been home for a while so we'd give them a few quid out of our wages - a 'back-hander'.

MALLY - THE REBEL WITHOUT A PAUSE

We'd always treat our mates cos we never knew, it could have been us stood outside the office, hoping somebody had got the sack. It could have been us who had worn out our shoes walking down to the docks every day, showing our face, trying to get a job.

The competition was hot after they laid up the sidewinder trawlers and a lot of the men couldn't do ten weeks at sea. Some of them would 'miss the boat' at sea due to drink. And they knew they wouldn't be going back on the next trip when the skipper told them to pack their heavy gear. They knew they'd got the sack!

Fortunately that didn't happen a lot on the St Jason. Only when a new skipper took over, when skipper Ball took a trip off. Then the new skipper would often bring in his own crew. So there I was, pockets full of money, having just given 'back-handers' to my mates who were waiting for jobs. We then went to meet up with the rest of the crew at St Andrews Club, just off Hessle Road. All the wives and girlfriends were there, it was always a really happy day. We used to get our money at about half past eleven in the morning so we'd have a full day out. Mind you, the pub closing hours were three o'clock in them days.

Talk about binge drinking! I've never seen men drink so much in such a short space of time. As you can imagine, it used to go straight to our heads. But we didn't care. We'd sometimes even get a lock-in at St Andrews, when the landlord allowed us to stay behind after everyone else had gone. I remember one time in St Andrews Club. Four ships had docked on the same day as there were still a number of trawling companies on the go in Hull at the time. Things got out of hand and there was a massive brawl.

Massive brawls weren't unusual in St Andrews...

The Marr's Trawler Company was full of snakes, men creeping up the skipper's arse and paying the ship's runner a lot of money to get onto one of their ships. They also say their men had square eyes due to them looking up to the square bridge windows to see if the skipper was watching them. Like snakes, some of the men even had a basket outside the skipper's berth just in case he whistled for a pot of tea. Six men would rush to make one for him in the Marr's outfit!

British United Trawler owners, B.U.T. was another outfit. That was the company my old man sailed with but I didn't want to sail in that company just in case my old man did a final swansong.

Boston Trawler owners only had a couple of ships and they seemed to keep the same crews.

Thomas Hamlyn Trawler owners, the ones I worked for, were known as the cowboy outfit, rough and tough I suppose. But I believe most men who went to sea were rough and tough.

Anyway, on this particular day there were four different crews in St Andrews Club. It was quite a big place, with two rooms sectioned off, one room for the bar and one room for the disco-dancing. All the crews had just arrived home and had had a good pay-day, so everyone was enjoying themselves. Then the bell rang and the shout was 'Last orders'. Well we'd double or even treble up at last orders! My drink at the time was triple rum and I'd been drinking it from twelve o'clock that day.

Half an hour later at three thirty, the next call was, 'Let's be having you out now, please.' Most people would then drink up and leave.

We always wanted that next drink. We wanted to stay behind and carry on drinking. But no, the landlord shouted, 'No stop back today lads,' so I got up and began to leave with a few of my deckie mates.

I could see through into the other room and about 30 men and women had been invited to stay back. I could also see a couple of my shipmates in there but I didn't know the rest. I barged my way in and went to this one table where there were ten men who'd all obviously just got fresh drinks. The table was full of glasses of spirits and pints of lager.

I knew of this hard-case who was a ship's mate in the Marr's outfit, you know, the sneaky outfit. He was sat at the head of the table, so to speak, shouting out to the barman to get even more drinks in. When he saw me he shouted out, 'Fuck off - this is a private party for skippers and mates only.'

When I pointed out half the men in there were not skippers or mates he bellowed back at me, 'If you don't fuck off - you'll be carried out.'

'And who the fuck's going to carry me out, you fucking

arsehole?' I replied. He was still sitting down with me stood over him and I knew by then everybody was watching.

'Look you may think you're a bit of a hard-case, you wanker, but you're not invited in here, now fuck off before I knock you out,' he said.

'I'd like to see you try,' I said. He was built like my old man. Mountain Man! A few of me mates who'd followed me in started saying, 'Come on Mally, we've had enough, let's go.' But I'd never had enough!

'Like fuck,' I shouted. 'I want this wanker to try and knock me out. Come on big man, outside!' He then told me to go and play with my toys or something like that. I told him I never had any toys.

'Come on big man, let's have a go!' I said. He just kept smiling and goading me while he was supping his drams of rum. But then he mumbled, 'I did warn yer,' and slowly started to get to his feet.

He then made the biggest mistake he could have made though, because as he rose to his feet he turned his face away from me instead of standing straight up. So as he turned back to face me I just stuck the perfect right punch on him and he went down. To my amazement, as he was staggering to his feet, someone jumped on my back. This forced me to fall on top of the 'rising mountain' who was still trying to get up. Before I knew it I was in the middle of a mass brawl.

Everyone was at it! Women were screaming! And the only other sounds I could hear were the smashing of glasses and tables being overturned. I was on top of the guy who I'd just punched and somebody was on my back thumping me with his fists on both sides of my head.

The guy I was on top of was trying to poke both my eyes out, while I was trying to get the wanker off my back. At the same time I was headbutting the Giant on the floor whose fingers were now in my mouth, trying to rip it open!

'Get this fucker off me, I'm going to kill him,' he was screaming! As I was trying to say, 'Get yer fucking hands out my mouth you wanker.'

Somebody then knocked the guy off my back with a stool and I was left, face to face with the Giant, rolling about still trying to say, 'Let go of me mouth, you fucking wanker!'

All he seemed to say was, 'I'm going to kill yer, you bastard!' With that I dug my teeth into his finger and heard him scream. 'The bastard's biting my finger off,' he yelled, as I chewed through to the bone.

'Let me go, I give in, let me go,' he yelled even louder.

'What are you going to do?' I screamed.

'Nowt,' he yelled, 'Just let go of my finger, you're biting it off you bastard.'

With that I let go and sprang to my feet. There was blood coming out the side of my mouth where he'd ripped it open. I then felt a bit of gristly stuff in my mouth and spat it out. He stood up and ran behind the bar shouting, 'The bastard's just bit me finger end off!'

I went chasing after him but he grabbed a big bottle of Lamb's Navy Rum and said he'd smash it over my head if I went any closer!

With that, a few people got between us and all the fighting stopped. I was facing this hard-case who was behind the bar screaming, 'Look what you've done, you fucking animal!'

The best thing about it was, in them days, there were never any coppers involved. We had our fight and the next day we made up and shook hands. I never got to shake hands with that guy though because I got banned from St Andrews's Club.

I never saw him again for ages.

Our paths have crossed a few times since however, in fact we still give each other the nod nowadays. But at the time the word soon got out after the brawl - Don't fuck with the Welburns, they're all fucking mad...

That's what it was like for me back in the late 1970s, living, or should I say surviving, in the backstreets of Hull.

My life was made up of being away - fishing, or being at home - gambling, drinking and fighting!

Not necessarily in that order.

It was a lifestyle that I'd drifted into. But one that had now completely taken me over. When I was at sea and sober, I realised it wasn't any good for me. I realised I was on the road to nowhere. But back ashore, with a wad of money in my pocket, the beer would always start to flow. Followed usually by what caused my real problems - the rum...

MALLY - THE REBEL WITHOUT A PAUSE

In the next chapter I'll tell you how I tried to change my senseless existence.

How I set up home with my wife-to-be, Kerry Anne.

And about the 'house-warming party from hell', which led to me doing six months in a detention centre, after I pleaded guilty to charges of wounding a Police officer and criminal damage...

See ya soon - Mally

CHAPTER THIRTEEN
STAND BY YOUR MAN

When I got home from my next trip, Trevor had found us a new 'home' down Subway Street. It was our fourth 'home' together - if you count Brighton Street and 11 West Grove as homes when we lived with 'Big Daddy'!

Trevor also had a new girlfriend - Janice - and she had a mate, the beautiful Kerry Anne and I fell in love with her straight away. I was nearly eighteen and she was going on 'sweet sixteen'.

Her Father Dave was a trawler skipper and her Mother, Pat, she turned out to be the best mother-in-law any man could ever wish for. I still call her my number one mother-in-law to this day. She put up with some shit from me and stuck up for me on more than one occasion.

As soon as I set eyes on Kerry Anne I knew it was love.

It had to be - I started to be nice to our Trevor and even started to clean my room and not eat our kid's grub.

At the time, I was about to reach the second rung of the fishing industry ladder, going for my spare hand's ticket.

It was a six-week course and I also did a fire-fighting course, as I needed that as well before I could get my ticket. I had to know how a compass worked, how to do net mending, plus rope and wire splicing. Getting my ticket meant I could work on the deck and get the same money as all the other 'deckies'. I became one of the men, so to speak. I was on par with them 'herbs'.

On my next trip home I had to see Kerry Anne again, so I got Trevor to set up a first date for me with her in Gipsyville Tavern. I was too shy to ask her. Yes me, Mally Welburn, the man who'd fight anyone, anytime, anywhere was shy about asking a girl out on a date. But you would have been as well, with a face like mine. It was still full of spots, I still looked like that spotted dick pudding!

MALLY - THE REBEL WITHOUT A PAUSE

I'd like to thank Trevor for fixing me up with that first date. And I'll admit it if I'm honest, that I love my brother Trevor, very much. I guess that's what twins are like.

I'd no idea what our kid had to put up with as a boy, while I was away in those 'lovely' children's homes and approved schools. I just never imagined what both Trevor and Bobby went through.

When I was at home the old man showed Trevor affection, something that I often resented. But I recently found out that when I was away things were very different. The old man was almost as wicked to Trevor and Bobby as he was to me!

But I'm proud to say Trevor has turned out to be a good man. He's helped so many young kids through his karate schools and he's taught them a lot of discipline through sport. And I take my hat off to him because deep down he's a bigger man than me, in more ways than one!

I know he isn't happy about me saying he used to have all the locks on his bedroom door. I guess that's just one of the little insecurities we all have in life. But back in the 70s, there was one life-changing moment that I'll always thank him for. And that was introducing me to my second true love, Kerry Anne Milner.

She was a skipper's daughter who I'd willingly have shovelled shit for - and I did. She was and still is, a beautiful woman.

Stand by your man, well Kerry Anne did. Although I still wonder why after everything I put her through. My drinking, gambling and fighting were bound to take me further down those 'wrong roads'. I was a rebel without a pause!

I knew it was only a matter of time before I'd end up in serious trouble - or worse. And although Kerry did her best to get me off my downward spiral, I couldn't change, especially when the drink started to flow...

Before I could complete writing this part of my story, I had to send off to the Home Office for my criminal record. I had to make sure I'd got all the details of the offences I've committed. It cost me £10. I had to go to my local police station first, then I had to wait for about ten weeks for it to arrive. Mine arrived by special delivery as the envelope was that thick they couldn't get it through the letterbox - that's a joke by the way. I must stress that my criminal record is something I'm not proud of but if it helps to paint the picture, then great. My record reads like this:

Convictions: 15 - Offences: 36

First conviction: 28/04/1969 Last conviction: 28/11/1994

Offences summary:

9 offences against the person 1970 to 1994

1 offence against property 1979

7 theft and kindred offences 1969 to 1985

4 public disorder offences 1974 to 1994

4 offences relating to police, courts or prison 1977 to 1986

1 firearm, shotgun, offensive weapon offence 1974

9 miscellaneous offences 1973 to 1986

1 non-recordable offence 1986

The firearm/offensive weapon one in 1974 involved a lump of wood and a pocket-knife. I was 16 at the time and recall it was outside the youth club when two gangs went to fight each other. One onto one wasn't a problem for me, but when you're faced with a dozen or more, it was survival. I ended up in court on three charges, two of breach of the peace and one for possessing an offensive weapon in a public place. I don't know whether it was the lump of wood or the penknife.

They found me guilty and I was given a two-year supervision order, where I'd go and see a probation officer once a week. If I'd have done anything else wrong during those two years, I'd have been in trouble and back in court.

The offence against property must have been the criminal damage I did to a police van when they were trying to get me in it. When I checked my criminal record for the date, it was March 21 1979, the same date I was charged with wounding. It was when I received six months in a detention centre for my part in a mass brawl. That took place at our lovely house that Kerry Anne had put all her time and effort into, turning the run down house into a little palace.

When we bought the house in 1978 it was a run down, middle of a row, terraced house in Eastgate, Hessle. I was 20 at the time and Kerry was 17.

We bought it just after I'd passed my spare hand's ticket to be a deckhand, the six-week course. The one where I learnt my net mending, which I hated, compass, the rope and wire splicing, which I loved - and the fire fighting. I found it an easy course to pass even though I struggled on net mending.

It was learning how to make fly mashers and putting the top part of a trawl together with the lower wing of a trawl that troubled me! I just couldn't get it right, so please, don't expect me to try and explain it to you.

I was okay net mending the belly of the trawl and the cod ends, but don't ask me to mend 'round the edges', a fisherman's term. I'd gone to sea to graft, not net mend, but we had to learn it. We weren't there to be a £45 a week net hook, holding the net while others mended it. But I've sailed with a few £45 a week net hooks in my time.

'I'll make you laugh and you do the graft, Mally.'

I've sailed with them guys, but hey, I loved it.

Each to their own is what I say. Some were good at net mending, some good at splicing warp, some were good at navigating. Some were fast gutters of fish and some were just out and out grafters.

I ended up in the den house, the factory. I loved it, it was a paid workout and you got all the grub you could eat.

Like I've told you, in my spare time I would be on the bridge learning off Skipper Ball or Bri Ridsdale, about how to navigate the ship. I wanted to be the skipper. I wanted to sit in the holy chair - the chair that was forbidden for us to sit in.

The skipper's chair on a trawler is hotter than the chair on 'Deal or No Deal'. If you got caught in the chair you could be in trouble, but Skipper Ball used to let me sit in it.

I'd done a few trips on the St Jason and saved up my wages and put my settlings into the bank. It was so the mortgage company could see I was getting a regular income coming in each week. There was no pissing my money up the wall this time!

By then our Trevor was letting me stay, rent free, in the house down Subway Street. I guess he didn't want me jumping out and putting the shits up him again. It was also good of our kid to let Kerry stay when I was home from sea. Our kid was ready to build his love nest with his girlfriend, so the quicker he got Kerry and me married off and out of the way the better...

The house that Kerry and me bought needed a lot of work

doing to it. It only cost £5,000 but that was a lot of money in those days.

As soon as you walked through the front door there was a narrow passage which led to the foot of the stairs. There were two doors that led into the front and back rooms, with a long narrow kitchen off the back room. When you went up the narrow staircase, it led to a first floor bathroom and three small bedrooms. There was also an attic room, which was in the roof of the house. It was the spare room but it was nice.

The floorboards needed replacing all over the house. Kerry knocked the two downstairs rooms into one and had ranch style swing doors put in. The whole place was rewired and re-floored, the kitchen was made wider and we made the staircase open plan with a large, wooden 'rising sun' carved beneath the banister rail. It was stunning! I tell yer, Kerry should have been an interior designer.

The front room was the pride and joy of most people's houses in those days and Kerry soon had ours looking really nice. There was a brand new two-seater settee, new carpets, rugs and a top of the range record player, the type you played 45s and LPs on.

I also remember we had a really posh serving trolley with two glass shelves where we kept our drinks. We had Lamb's Navy Rum, whisky and a bottle of Baileys, my Mother's favourite. She loved her Baileys, that's when she had a drink, which was very rarely. There were the bottles and cans of beer on the bottom shelf and on the top shelf would be the glasses - pint, half-pint and dram ones, the size of an eggcup. When we had a dram it was like an eggcup full of the rum, whisky or vodka. We'd usually put the dram down our neck in one go.

The living room was where the telly and dining table were. The kitchen was fitted out with new cabinets and the whole house had new carpets from top to bottom. Every room was decorated to a high standard. I didn't know what flock wallpaper was but I knew it didn't come cheap.

In front of the house, there was a little, neat garden with a path leading to the front door. I hope I've painted a picture for you of our beautiful little house in Hessle, the posh part of Hull... Now was the time to have a house-warming party. To show all our friends and family what my darling girlfriend and me had achieved. It was a time for celebration.

I arranged it when I got home from another ten-week trip on the St Jason. We'd had a good trip and on top of our wages and settlings we got a bonus for doing 100 days at sea, it was called 'holiday pay'. I think it was something like £2 a day, so it was another £200 we could put towards the house-warming party.

I spent this particular settling day in the Gipsyville Tavern with a few of the St Jason crew, my family, friends and cousins, it was one big party. There wasn't a problem buying all the drinks for the party, after all we were 'three-day millionaires'. Mind you, in this case we were 'ten-day millionaires' because for every week we were away at sea, we got a day at home. Sometimes we'd be 'eight-day millionaires', it varied.

The house-warming party was arranged at short notice in Gipsyville Tavern. I whipped out to invite me Mam and Dad and at the same time took me Dad his bacca and cigs. To my surprise he said they'd both come, so I gave him a back-hander for the taxi as well.

My Mam was so excited to be coming to my new house and meeting Kerry again. Kerry used to go down to see my Mam, to see if she needed anything doing, and I'm glad to say my Dad never turned Kerry away.

Everyone from Gipsyville Tavern was invited.

We hit Skelton's bakery for sausage rolls, flans, cooked meats, bread and not forgetting the custard pies for my old man. I hoped I wasn't going to get them over my head that day.

We all got taxis to my house and in the end there were 10 men and 8 women in our tiny house. The women were in the back room, the kitchen and up and down the stairs as Kerry proudly showed them round the house.

All the men hit the booze trolley, each having a couple of cans of beer from the case I'd brought in from Tavern. Now you have to bear in mind we'd been drinking from eleven o'clock in the morning until 'kicking out' time, about four in the afternoon.

We were well pissed by then, apart from my old man, and we always finished a drinking session on drams. It was all about trying to beat the bell and the 'last orders' call. Usually we would get about six or seven doubles down our necks in that half-hour spell, not forgetting what we'd drunk during the afternoon as well.

It was supposed to be - come and have a look at my house, have a little drink to celebrate, then everybody would get off home. But it didn't turn out like that!

No, someone realised that right opposite my house was an off-licence, which sold everything you'd expect from a little corner shop. There was everything from bread and milk right through to cigarettes, beer and spirits!

On our way from the pub to my house, everyone stopped at the shop and bought as many cans of beer or bottles of spirits as they could carry. After all it was a one off party!

When we got to the house, Patsy Cline was blaring out on the record player, with Roy Orbison and Elvis cassette tapes lined up and ready to play next.

In the front room were five of my shipmates, with their wives and girlfriends. My Mam and Dad were there and also one of my cousins, 'the Tank' and he sure was a hard-case. With them was one of my older brothers, Raymond, who was a black belt in karate. And talking to him, was his instructor, the master Sensei, the one and only Jack Cochran. Jack was the man we all feared, apart from my old man. He was the man who could put you to sleep with just one touch to a certain part of your body. He was the gentleman who taught my brothers the art of defence, without fighting. But if you had to fight, you fought to win.

Now the Cochran family was one we got to know very well as we grew up with Pat, Colleen, Graham, Jack, Carl and Ricky. Mrs Cochran was out of the same mould as my Mother, a loving lady Mrs Cochran, Lily. The times we thanked Mrs Cochran for coming to knock on our front door at number 11 and having a go at my Dad. He wouldn't go out to Mrs Cochran - or Mrs Milner come to think of it.

What happened at the party is heartbreakingly hard to write about because of the love I have for all the Cochran family.

I hope they can find it in their hearts to forgive me for what I did to their loving Father that day.

When I met Jack Snr., after I'd done six months in a detention centre, he forgave me straight away and never did press

MALLY - THE REBEL WITHOUT A PAUSE

charges against me, that was how close our families were. After all, I think the devil got into us all on that particular day. The devil called rum...

The party was in full swing with everybody happy and singing and it was great to have my Mam and Dad there.

Someone then came up with an idea, 'Why don't we have a rum-drinking competition?' they shouted.

'£20 a head - and the first person to finish a bottle of Lamb's Navy Rum would be the winner.'

The cost of a bottle of rum was about £8. I went across to the off-licence and brought back ten bottles, paid for out of my holiday money.

Everyone was up for it - Jack, cousin Tank, our kid, the old man, the five shipmates and me.

Our wives and girlfriends pleaded with us not to play the game as it would only lead to trouble. How true those words were but they weren't heeded. The men never took any notice of the women. So the women went in the back room and the men stayed in the front. Five men sat on the two-seater settee with my old man standing near the glass trolley, using it as his table.

Sitting in a mini circle on the floor was Jack, who was opposite me. To my left was cousin Tank and to my right, big brother, black belt, Raymond.

The rules were simple. You had to drink a 'two-pint' bottle of rum faster than anyone else! You couldn't mix it with any other drink, it had to be drunk neat. You could drink it in a dram, half-pint or pint glass or if you wanted to, straight from the bottle.

There was £200 up for grabs. It was like four weeks wages for people working ashore at the time. It was easy money if you could drink rum and we'd all been well schooled in drinking Lamb's Navy Rum. Remember we grew up at number 11 with those 'parties' when the old man came home from sea.

My old man was the favourite to win the drinking competition, followed by a couple of the lads off my ship. I would then put my older brother next and me not far behind. For anyone who's never drunk rum, it's horrible drinking it neat, especially in large amounts.

Also bear in mind we'd already had about eight doubles

before leaving Gipsyville Tavern.

It was then count down, 3-2-1 - Go!

A few in the party started to drink from the bottle or out of a half-pint glass. Some were sipping it from a dram glass. We were always told the art of drinking rum was not to rush. My old man was taking his in drams, you know, an eggcup full at a time and this went on for about half an hour or so.

Someone then said, 'Let's see how many press-ups you can do on one finger and how many you can do on your wrists.'

It turned into a press-up competition. My old man never took part in the press-ups, but Jack did, and he showed his fitness by doing fifty on one finger of each hand. My brother also showed his fitness, but I wasn't far behind. I was always up for a challenge and I still am but in different ways.

The party, as they all did in those days, then got into an arm wrestling contest with the old man as always winning hands down. The conversation then turned to, who was the 'hardest' bloke in the room? This was when the women, who'd been keeping an eye on us, drew the line.

'Come on that's enough. We don't want any trouble in Kerry's house, let's all be going home now,' they said.

Two or three of my shipmates decided they'd had enough as well. They didn't want to carry on. They knew when to stop and leave the party but how could I leave? It was *my* house-warming. It was *my* house. So I never took any notice of Kerry telling us to stop. No, I wanted to win the drinking competition!

Three had gone, there were seven to go but I knew four of them weren't going to win the contest.

It then got back round to the fighting talk again and my old man said, 'We'll have none of this fighting talk or else I'll sort the lot of you out.'

'Not in my house,' I said.

With that I saw the old man put his drink down and give me 'the look'.

Oh fuck, I thought, here we go. I knew the look and I think I started to frown.

I think we all know, that look, the one where we can see it in their eyes. Well I sure saw the look in my old man's eyes that day. I was thinking, here we fucking go, as the mountain stood above me, while I was sat on the floor, opposite Jack.

Then out of the blue Jack said, 'Do you know Mally, by the time you count to three, I could put you to sleep with one touch.'

Fuck this I thought. I'd got big bad John stood near the swing doors. He was that big, he had to move to one side to let you go in and out of the room. He was bigger and wider than the swing doors, there was no way out.

Then I'd got Jack saying, 'I bet you all the money in the middle, by the count of three I could put you asleep.'

To be honest I think I'd sooner have been put to sleep by Jack than take a punch off my old man.

So my reply to Jack was, 'Go on then Jack you're on, who's going to count?' I don't know whether it was the old man who said he'd count but Raymond was telling me not to do it.

Cousin Tank was trying to cool the situation and some of my shipmates still wanted to leave - but it was too late.

ONE!

I looked at Jack. He was giving me the look and was ready to make that one-finger attack. Fucking hell, what a situation!

Here I was facing the much-feared and respected Sensei and in the same room, blocking the doorway, was the hardest man I'd ever met in my life, my Dad. Next to me was one of the hard-cases of his age group, my brother Raymond, then the Tank - fucking hell!

TWO!

I was facing Jack, with half a bottle of rum in one hand and a dram in the other. He was the one who threw the challenge out to me. I held the bottle of rum by the neck when I heard...

THREE!

As Jack reached out to give me the one finger to the side of me head to try put me to sleep, I lurched forward. I smashed the rum bottle over his head and it knocked him clean out.

I was shitting myself. I just didn't realise what I'd done, it happened so quickly. I didn't even have time to put the rum bottle down. I just didn't believe Jack was going to put me to sleep. But he went for me. It was over in a flash.

As I was getting to my feet, to go for my old man, I didn't see the glass trolley raining down on my head. It brought the lovely chandelier crashing down, the one what Kerry had got fitted instead of one light bulb. The frame from the trolley fitted me like a straitjacket. I couldn't get my arms out of it.

All you could hear were the women screaming and a voice shouting, 'Get an ambulance.' The next thing I knew, something hit me so hard and everything went black...

When I came round, the house was full of police. Our kid and cousin Tank were going at it toe to toe with the coppers.

I managed to get out of the framed cage and waded in as well. I don't know how long I was knocked out for. It must have been a while though because Jack wasn't there and neither was my loving Mother - or the old man!

The next thing I knew, I'd got four coppers trying to arrest me. I could see one of them had been through the 'rising sun' on the staircase banister and even though it was dark I could see all the front room was smashed up. I could also hear my girlfriend Kerry. She was sobbing her eyes out.

The coppers were very heavy handed, so it was punch for punch and kick for kick. Then the truncheons came out as they tried to ram me to the floor, face down, into all the broken glass. They were trying to get the handcuffs on me and by the time they got me to the floor another two coppers had joined in. They punched me, trying everything to handcuff 'this animal' but I was just seeing a red mist.

I thought, they'd no right to gatecrash a party even if we'd been fighting, it was our party. In those days if it kicked off amongst you and your friends it was all sorted and you were back to being friends the next day. There was never any involvement from the police. Or at least, there shouldn't have been.

Where were they when you needed them, when you were a young kid? Why did they come down my path but not my old man's? There's no question I resented the police - but that was hardly surprising - and now there were six of them trying to handcuff me!

Somehow one of the police officer's fingers found its way into my mouth. He was trying to pull my mouth open. But I was acting like an enraged animal and I bit down on his finger.

Then the lights went out! And the next thing I remember was when I woke up at five o'clock, the next morning. All I could hear was the sound of my cousin Tank shouting, 'Are you in the cells, Mally?'

I thought I was dreaming, but apart from the shakes, I could hardly move. I was battered and bruised, trying to register where I was?

I soon realised I was in a freezing cold, dank cell.

Then I heard, 'Is that you Tank? Is our Mally in?'

It was Raymond who'd just been arrested after he came to see what was happening to me at the police station. He'd been to the hospital with some deep glass wounds to the soles of his feet. That was because it was, 'shoes off at the front door', when you went into anybody's house in them days.

I then heard a couple of my shipmates' voices. It was like a scene from the Walton's.

'Is that you John Boy? Is that you Tank? Is that you Mally? Is that you our kid?'

Then I started thinking, what the fuck am I doing here? What have I done? Fucking hell! - what had I done?

Someone then asked what time it was? I never wore a watch in them days but I had a nice watch on in the cell that morning. I looked at it, shouted to them that I was also banged up and I'd someone's watch on and it said five o'clock.

With that I heard the clatter and jingle of keys going into my cell door and before I knew it four of the boys in blue came in waving truncheons. They shouted to me that I was a thieving bastard and I'd got an officer's watch.

They gave me a few more bruises to go with the ones I'd got the previous night. Who'd believe I'd been assaulted by the police? I suppose they were just doing their job but they were also going to cost me *my* job on the St Jason.

We stayed in the cells until they put a case together against us. I then spoke to the duty solicitor, Mr John Robinson, a no-nonsense guy who gave it to me straight.

He came into the cell and the first thing he asked was if I was alright? He then put me in the picture and told me what I'd done. They were trying to charge me for the assault on Jack but he didn't want to press charges against me. But there was a serious charge against me of wounding a police officer, by punching him and biting his finger. Also there was another charge of criminal damage not only to my house but to the police van. I'd apparently smashed the lights and damaged the door when they tried to put me in it. He told me there was no chance of getting bail and I could be looking at three years in prison. Fucking hell, what had I done?

I remembered putting the bottle over Jack's head but what could I do? I feared for my life at that particular moment in time, yet there wasn't much more I could remember.

I remembered getting the trolley over my head. But I couldn't remember who'd clouted me. I could remember the coppers in the house and the battle I had with them. Then I woke up in the cells. There was a bit of a memory loss somewhere, so I had to believe what my solicitor told me. His advice was to plead guilty so it wouldn't waste their time. They had too much evidence against me.

Mr Robinson told me I'd be up in court in the next day or two and I'd be remanded to prison until they fixed a court date. I was in the cells for about five days.

To be honest the brawl was nothing to do with my shipmates and they got away with a fine and a binding over. But my brother, Tank and me - we'd all be spending time in prison.

They took our fingerprints and our photos. I was complaining all the time of the police assault but it fell on deaf ears. I tried to tell them there was no way I could have got all those bruises on my back, belly and legs from just one punch.

Some say I deserved what I got, well so be it. I'd never get all those bruises from fighting amongst ourselves.

In those five days in the cells I was allowed visitors after seven on the night. This was after I'd been fed, with what could only be described as what looked like somebody's leftovers. And, if you were lucky, three-quarters of a cup of tea in a plastic cup. You had to ring the buzzer in your cell to ask to go to the toilet and the officer would stand and watch you 'do your business'. It was a bit like Big Brother is now.

Kerry used to come and visit me and I could see the hurt I'd put her through, her home all smashed to bits. All her hard work over the last year was gone. She told me I'd just turned into a wild animal but told me it wasn't my fault, I just got dragged into it.

She told me, 'At first you said no, to the rum drinking competition. But then you gave them the money to go buy the stuff.'

MALLY - THE REBEL WITHOUT A PAUSE

She just couldn't understand how rum could turn us all into Dr. Jekyll and Mr Hyde characters. One minute everybody was laughing and joking, the next we were all fighting amongst ourselves. She told me, just before the ambulance came for Jack was when my Mam and Dad left. Kerry told me my Mam was in tears and they wanted to walk home. Then when the ambulance came, about twelve coppers just piled into the house.

'Mally, you did nothing wrong until you put the bottle over Jack's head and then all hell broke loose.'

I asked how Jack was. She told me he was in hospital, 'He's going to be alright but the coppers are still trying to get him to press charges against you. Jack's refusing so they're trying to get you for biting a copper's finger, but there were about six of them kicking ten bells of shit out of you. They couldn't arrest you, you were like a man possessed, you were crazy Mally, and you frightened us.'

Kerry said she'd never seen anything like that in her life and didn't want to be part of this kind of life.

I begged her to forgive me.

She said she couldn't understand it, after all the hard work we'd both put in to get our little house together.

'It's when you get with your family, every time you're with your brothers. It doesn't matter which one you're with, you always end up fighting with other men. What is it with you Welburns? There's something wrong with you!'

'Too fucking right,' I said.

'Let's see what happens at court, I can't hang about for you if you get three years, I can't put up with that, Mally,' she said.

It was then back to my cell. I thought to myself, 'What have I gone and done? I'm on the verge of losing my second love, my house, my job, the lot - and all through the devil - rum!'

It's strange when I think back now to what it was like then and what I'd done. I never gave it a thought, well not until I was locked up in the cells facing a three-year prison sentence and all through booze.

Six days after the party, the time came for us to go before the court. It was held at Brough because the offence took place within their boundaries. We were taken to court, in the back of police vans, each handcuffed to two police officers.

On March 21 1979 I was charged with wounding a police officer and criminal damage.

This was 28 years ago and at the time I was 20 years of age, just a month away from my 21st birthday.

Five of the ten men who were at the party were charged with different offences ranging from breach of the peace and criminal damage, to assault on the police and wounding.

It was only a small courthouse and you'd have thought the great train robbers had come to the little village court. The whole village had turned out to see who was getting out the back of these three police vans and the two police escort cars.

We were put in different cells at the court, but saying that, I think they only had three cells at Brough. We then waited for our time to go in front of the bench.

We were told, because it was a Magistrate's Court, they had the power to send us to prison for a year. But if we pleaded not guilty we'd go to Crown Court, in front of a jury and could then face three years in prison!

The evidence they had on me and the advice I had from my solicitor meant it was a case of pleading guilty, taking the sentence handed out and doing my 'time'.

We were taken from the court cells in handcuffs and in the order they wanted us. I was placed at the far end of the line, nearest the 'going down' door. I knew as soon as I walked into the packed court, and by where they placed me, that I was going down because there was a copper on both sides and behind me. My big brother was at the other end of the five-man line up, with the Tank in the middle.

The tiny courtroom was packed with police, court staff, the press, family and friends and I looked round and saw my loving Mother. Next to my Mother was Kerry Anne, the love of my life, who gave me her loving smile. I could read her lips when she said, 'You'll be okay,' and 'I love you.'

At that moment, I admit I shed a tear.

'Court Rise,' said a voice at the front.

We were already standing as the three magistrates came into the court but the rest of the court stood up and bowed their heads. These three, retiring old magistrates didn't look like they were greeting their long lost grandkids. No, they looked more like the headmaster who always gave you the cane at school - and loved giving you it!

The Clerk of the Court then read the charges out.

'Your Honour, the five accused who stand before you are all charged separately. From your right Sir is Mr Welburn senior, who is charged with assault.' That was my big brother Raymond.

'The man to his right is charged with breach of the peace. The man to that man's right is the Tank who is charged with assault. To his right Sir is another shipmate charged with breach of the peace. And the man on the end Sir is Malcolm Welburn - my Sunday name - he is charged with criminal damage and the most serious offence of wounding a Police officer.

All the charges relate to a house-warming party, which got out of order and where one man needed hospital treatment, this was from a bottle being put over his head by Mr Welburn.'

With that, my solicitor jumped up and objected to what had been read out as it wasn't what his client was charged with. The Judge - I'll call him the 'Judge' even though he was only a Magistrate - overruled him and said he needed to know the full story. 'Which one was it who put the bottle over the man's head?' he asked.

The Clerk of the Court pointed to me saying, 'Mr Malcolm Welburn is the one on the end, Sir.'

'Just a minute, there are three Welburns here and there's one on each end of the line,' said the Judge.

He ordered my two shipmates to be put together at one end of the line. It was then the two shipmates, our kid, cousin Tank, then me, still closest to the 'going-down' door.

Anyway, the Judge gave me the look, a bit like the one the old man used to give me, so I knew I was going down. Now the Judge was happy with the line-up and he said he could now put a name to the face. He said he didn't want to be giving out the wrong sentence.

'Carry on please,' he said to the Clerk of the Court.

'As I say, your Honour, on such and such a day this house-warming party got out of hand. An ambulance had to be called and the police had also received a call at the same time.

'As the ambulance men were trying to take the injured man to hospital, two police officers turned up at the house and they

were greeted with abuse and threats, by who we don't know.
'The officers called for back-up and a riot van arrived at the
house containing another six officers. They had to force their
way into Mr Malcolm Welburn's house and this was the time
they were faced with three or four men wanting to fight them.
'It was then a mass brawl broke out with several officers
receiving cuts and bruises and one officer received a severe
bite mark to his finger, your Honour. Here is a photograph of
the officer's finger. The brawl has left both him and two other
officers still on sick leave.'

As the Clerk of the Court was passing this enlarged photo to
the Judge, all the people in the court could see the photograph,
except the Judge. It was facing the open court and it was
actually of our kid's foot. It showed all the deep cuts he'd
received in the melee and it showed the sole of his foot all
stitched up. The Clerk was passing round this photograph
telling the court it was what Mr Malcolm Welburn had done
to P.C. so and so's finger. The court erupted into fits of
laughter, even the two coppers who were sat next to me
started to chuckle. They'd uncuffed me by then but I could
still feel their bodies quivering with laughter. The Clerk then
turned the photograph to face the Judge who said, 'That's a
peculiar looking finger.'

We all burst out laughing but the court fell silent when the
Judge forcefully stated,

'You think it's funny do you? Well that's three months before
we start.'

'Frigging hell,' I thought, 'here we go.' The Clerk then passed
the right photograph of the policeman's bitten finger to the
Judge.

'Which animal did this, did you say?' asked the Judge.

'Mr Malcolm Welburn,' said the Clerk. With that, my
solicitor stood up and said, 'Allegedly your Honour.'

'Sit down Mr Robinson, you'll have your turn, I need to hear
what the prosecution has to say, you'll get your turn.'

The Judge wanted to know how the police officer had got
such a bite mark.

'We can call the officer, your Honour,' said the Clerk.

'That will be fine.' They fetched this police officer in and he
was built bigger than my Dad. He took the stand and taking

47

the Bible in his right hand said the following words.

'I swear by almighty God, That the evidence I shall give, Shall be the truth, The whole truth, And nothing but the truth.' He then relived the day, how he saw it, saying he got the call to act as back-up and he was one of the first officers into the house. My house! He said it was like going into a lion's cage. He was being attacked from all sides. It was like facing a pack of wolves. He said it had taken four of them to arrest me and the 'incident' happened while they were trying to restrain me. They wanted to force me to the floor, face down, to try and get my hands behind my back.

I was kicking and punching out and looked as though I was very drunk, that's why it took four officers to restrain me. It was when they got me face down that he was trying to stop me cutting my head on the glass. He said he had his hands on my face when his finger slipped into my mouth. It was then he felt a sharp pain and realised I was trying to bite through his finger. The officer then said he had to punch me hard on the side of the face so I'd release his finger. He was pleased to say I let go but I'd taken half his finger off.

The court went deathly quiet. The Judge asked him if he was okay and what was the extent of his injury?

He replied it was early days. They'd stitched it back together but he was still on sick and a bit traumatised by it all. He said he'd never been in a situation like it before and hoped he'd never be faced with such a situation like it ever again.

The Judge said, 'Well you won't be seeing anything like it for a while from these after I've finished with them.'

He thanked the officer and wished him a speedy recovery.

The Judge, pointing his finger at me, then asked, 'Why did you bite the officer's finger?'

'He shouldn't have had it in my mouth,' I replied. 'There were four of 'em punching and hitting me with their truncheons. It was dark, I had my face down and it didn't say 'policeman' on his finger.'

'That's another three months young man,' he said.

'I'll teach you not to fight, bite and kick the police, so that's six months for you up to now. I'll come back to you after I've dealt with the rest, now shut up and don't speak until you're spoken to.'

'What about the assault on us?' I said.

The Judge replied, 'I'm warning you.'

I looked round and saw both my Mother and Kerry crying so I shut my mouth and awaited my fate. I was hoping my shipmates didn't get 'time' as they'd done nothing wrong. They were just in the wrong place at the wrong time. They were too pissed to even stand up and luckily, all they were charged with was breach of the peace. We all knew they had nothing to do with the assault on the police but I knew our kid and cousin Tank could look after themselves. You didn't mess about with those two guys; they were two very hard men in their time.

I was glad to hear the words, 'Fined £100 and bound over for a year', for both my two shipmates. They were told they were free to go and never to return to a court again. I could see how relieved they were when they heard the words, 'You are free to go.' I was pleased for them.

It was then cousin Tank's turn and he was sentenced to six months in prison. The Judge then sentenced big brother to six months, to which our kid said something along the lines of, 'Piece of piss.'

The Judge asked for them to be taken away and for him to be left with the 'wild one.' They took our kid and cousin down, with both hurling obscenities as they went.

Now it was my turn.

The Judge looked at me and said, 'Even though you pleaded guilty to the charges against you and even though you're too young to go to prison I am still going to teach you a lesson.'

Oh by the way, we all pleaded guilty to the charges.

The Judge continued, 'No, you're not going to be sat in a prison cell but you're still going to learn the error of your ways young man and you will learn the hard way. But before I sentence you, I want to hear what you have to say for yourself.'

'All I can say is that I'm sorry to all concerned,' I said. 'I'm sorry for what I've done to my girlfriend and my Mother. I'm sorry my house got smashed up and I'm sorry I've lost my job!

'I'm sorry for being in front of you, Sir. I can't remember half of what has been said because I was knocked out. When I came to, all these coppers were in my house and the next thing I knew I had about six of them at me.

'I know I woke up in the cells with a policeman's watch on but I wanted to press charges against the police. It was their heavy-handed use of their truncheons not just on me, but also on my brother and cousin. The police had no right to be in my house, Sir.'

'Now look here,' said the Judge, 'We take it you were out of control and alcohol played a big part in it. But we don't take kindly to any assault on the police whatsoever. You're lucky we aren't charging you with the theft of the watch, which I see, was also damaged.'

'I don't remember anything, your Honour,' was my final reply.

'Before I sentence you,' he said, 'I want to hear about any previous convictions.'

My solicitor then put in an objection saying to the Judge, 'I object your Honour, I don't think it's fair on my client, he has admitted what he did was wrong.

'He maintains that it was just a rowdy party amongst friends and the sort of friends who stick by each other. He has said, he believed if the police had not attended it would have blown over, after all, they were all well and truly drunk. They all know what they did was wrong.'

My solicitor then started to tell the Judge where I was from and how I was a hard-working fisherman. He continued, 'All he ever wanted to do was show off what he and his girlfriend had worked damned hard for, their first house.

'It was a shame what had happened to his house and what his girlfriend had gone through. She says he isn't a bad man and that it was the rum-drinking which caused the problems.

'I think my client was too proud to back down in front of his Father and his peers and he knows he's done wrong. He knew this as soon as he woke up in the police cell but he can't remember being taken to the cell. He recalls four or five police officers trying to arrest him but then it's all a blank to him. My client doesn't remember biting the officer's finger, only that he took a bang to his head and was knocked unconscious, somewhere between his house and the police station. But how this actually occurred, we'll never know.'

My solicitor pleaded with the Judge to be lenient and the Judge spoke to the other two Magistrates, who hadn't said a word all through the case. They were whispering amongst themselves.

Then the Judge said, 'You will go to a detention centre where they will sort you out. You will do six months for the wounding charge and another three months for the criminal damage and they will run concurrently.

'Now,' asked the Judge, 'Can I hear his previous convictions?'

He told me to sit down while the Clerk got my previous convictions ready to read to the court. The copper next to me whispered, 'You're okay, you'll only do six months.'

I looked round at my Mother and Kerry, who could just raise a small smile, but a puzzled look as well. My Mother said she'd write to me and to behave myself and I would be okay. My solicitor came across to me and told me I'd got nine months but you'll only do six, they're sending you to Boston North Sea Camp Detention Centre.

'You'll serve the full six months, whereas your kid and cousin will only do four months in prison, that's the way it was. You don't get remission in a Detention Centre.

'It will be hard. It's running everywhere and floor scrubbing, working on the sea marshes, but keep your nose clean and you will be okay.'

I thanked my solicitor for what he'd done for me and then we heard,

'Your Honour, Mr Malcolm Welburn's record reads as follows.

At the age of eleven he was charged with theft and was given a conditional discharge for twelve months with his parents to pay a one pound fine.

In 1970 Mr Welburn was found guilty of theft of a chicken! and handling stolen goods and breach of his conditional discharge. He was sentenced to 12 hours at an Attendance Centre.'

This was a bit like going to school on a Saturday morning and doing lots of running and press-ups. Also playing football, which wasn't punishment and I even got me dinner there.

'In the same year 1970 Mr Welburn was sent to Stockton Hall

MALLY - THE REBEL WITHOUT A PAUSE

Approved School, near York, for assault causing actual bodily harm and theft.

In 1973 he was found guilty of making a false phone call to Kingston High School saying there was a bomb in the school. He was fined five pounds. These were the years of the bomb alerts in Britain. Also in 1973, your Honour, he was fined twenty pounds, which his parents had to pay, for him being charged with assault causing actual bodily harm.

In 1974 he was found guilty of two breaches of the peace and possessing an offensive weapon (a pen knife) in a public place and was fined twenty pounds.

In 1975 he was fined fifteen pounds for theft.

In 1976, your Honour, Mr Welburn was found guilty of assault causing actual bodily harm and he was fined a further one hundred pounds.

In 1977 he was found guilty of assault on a police officer and fined fifty pounds and in the same year he was found guilty of being drunk and disorderly.'

The Judge said, 'Take him down, if I'd known all that I would have given him a lot longer. Get him out of my court, get him to the detention centre and let's hope that sorts him out, get him out.'

I had one quick look round at Kerry and shed a tear for my Mother...

I didn't see my brother or cousin Tank until after I'd done my six months at Boston North Sea Camp, near Boston in Lincolnshire. I recently wrote to Boston North Sea Camp to see if I could go and make a return visit, legally this time.

It's where Jeffrey Archer did his time - you know, the Lord who is a writer as well. You never know, he may have slept in my bunk in them ex-army barracks...

They replied to my letter saying, no, they wouldn't let me go back! But not to worry.

In the next Chapter I'll try to paint you a picture of what it was like.

See ya - Mally.

CHAPTER FOURTEEN
BOSTON TEA PARTY

'I can't stop loving you' - it wasn't only Ray Charles who said that. It's what Kerry used to put in her letters when she wrote to me when I was at sea. But it was a different kind of letter I got off her not long after I started my six months in Boston North Sea Camp...

It was a long drive in the back of a police car from Brough Magistrates Court to Boston in Lincolnshire, especially with only three, burly coppers for company. They took me down the long and winding roads, in the middle of nowhere, next to the North Sea and in March the easterly winds can blow. They're cold winds.

I knew in my own mind I was going to a training camp, so to speak. It's where we had to run at double quick time, march everywhere and stand to attention. We had to call the screws 'Boss' or address them as, Sir. It felt like I was going home from Stockton Hall to number 11.

I didn't fear going there, the only thing I was worried about was how was Kerry going to cope? What had I done? What had I done to Jack? All these thoughts were going through my head on my way to Boston North Sea Camp in the back of the police car.

I was twenty years old. You start 'stinking thinking'. You start to get bad thoughts, all brought on by the devil. I tell yer, the devil comes to you in different guises and he came to me through the spirits of booze, the rum and whisky. And you don't know until it's too late. I know talking like this now may seem strange but I was twenty years of age, I feared no man, I believed I was well taught, I'd done my apprenticeship so to speak. The coppers also told me I was going to be alright because where I was going was more like an Open Prison.

'You won't be banged up for 23 hours a day but they'll work you hard. If you're into your fitness you'll be okay.'

MALLY - THE REBEL WITHOUT A PAUSE

I was thinking, it was going to be a 'piece of piss'.

In my head I was saying to myself it would be like doing three ten-week trips on the trawlers.

I knew I'd done wrong when I woke up in the cells after the house-warming party. I knew what was to come, but knew the time away wouldn't bother me. It's the effect it has on the loved ones you leave behind...

I knew I would get my three meals a day. I knew I would sleep in a nice comfy bed. I knew I would get to watch telly.

I knew I would be able to play sports. I knew I would get clean clothes every day. I knew I would get a nice shower.

But what about Kerry? What about my Mother? And what about Jack?

Look what I'd done to Kerry; she was torn apart over it.

I'd smashed up - well not just me - but everybody involved in the fight at the house-warming party had smashed up our lovely little home. She'd put her heart and soul into it.

The party had also led to Jack being put in hospital and let's not forget my black belt brother and cousin Tank who both got six months in prison, all through the booze.

I know you're probably asking the question why? But don't ask me why - I don't know the answer.

I look back at it now with a different view. I think, what a dickhead I was. When I'm putting this down now in words, I'm trying to relive it through my thoughts and memories of that particular time. I'm trying to make sense of it. But at the time, the fact was I just never thought of what the consequences would be. How times change.

I now think about the consequences of everything I do.

I've sat down with Kerry Anne on many of our baby-sitting shifts. She's told me about what things were like and how I'm now a changed man. I think she could write a book herself.

She always remembers 'the house-warming party from hell' and she's said it's something she's never, ever going to forget. She can remember it very clearly and says an argument started over a football score. When it all kicked off, all she was concerned about was my Mother. She's told me, we were like wild animals. I can't deny she was probably right...

Anyway back to the trip I was on. After about three hours on the road we arrived at Boston North Sea Camp.

'Here you go, my lad,' said one of the coppers. 'This is where it starts. This place will sort you out.'

Boston North Sea Camp was like an Army camp and where we slept was like a barracks. There were a number of dormitories, with about twenty of us sleeping in each.

I remember the first day I was there, I got marched to the Governor's office with two screws, one in front, one behind me. It was 'By the left, quick march, left, right, left, right.' I knew how to march as we'd had to do it at Stockton Hall.

The Governor laid the rules down, it was a bit like being at home with the old man. I was then marched to my 'house', they called it a house, within these barracks. There was also a housemaster who laid the house rules down.

I was then taken to the shower rooms to get showered and given my clothes issue to wear. It was plain and simple, blue and white striped shirts and dark blue jeans. They had to let me wear my own shoes until they ordered me a pair of size 14s. Do you know why we wore blue and white striped shirts? They say you never see flies on the butcher's blue and white apron. And come to think of it, I can't remember seeing any flies at Boston North Sea Camp, it was spotless.

In the first two or three weeks at the camp they put us through what they called an induction. It was two weeks of scrubbing floors with a big bar of carbolic soap and a big scrubbing brush. We had to scrub the floors, from early morning until late afternoon on our hands and knees. When we scrubbed we had to get rid of all the screws' black polish marks, which they'd deliberately rubbed off their shoes onto the floor. They then did it again meaning we had to do it all over again! At times it felt like I was cleaning out the rabbits at number 11.

Every time a screw rubbed black polish off his shoes onto your freshly cleaned floor, he would scream at you. He'd tell you to get back on your hands and knees and do it all again. I knew not to say anything, it was a case of just doing it.

They were testing us, pushing us to our limits and we'd do a full day scrubbing the floors.

The next day we'd be marched round the exercise yard in our tee shirts and shorts, even though it was March and the cold, easterly winds were blowing. We then went to the gym and did circuit training. I loved it in the gym. We had to go round the circuit three times before we could stop. There were three colours on the circuit, red was the hardest and the others I think were yellow and green.

When we did the first circuit we started on the yellow one and they timed us. I think there were about 20 different things to do. You had a 30 second time limit on each thing like bench presses, squat thrusts, press-ups, sit-ups and star jumps.

We sprinted up and down, did pull-ups on wall bars and after the first circuit we were shattered doing 30 seconds on each exercise. We had to go round three times. It got to where we felt for our fellow man. We couldn't move onto anything enjoyable, like volleyball, until the last man had finished.

I believe there were some lads who couldn't do 30 seconds on one exercise, never mind 20 of them.

To do it three times was a 'killer' and they timed our very first circuit the day we got there. They also timed our very last one when we were about to go home. I think I improved about 500 per cent in my time there and I got the job as gym boy.

But the first thing we had to do was to get through the induction of scrubbing floors every day, looking for the fresh black polish marks. We managed it once the officer knew we weren't going to crack and blow up. We were doing the same thing minute in, minute out, hour in, hour out, day in and day out!

After we'd done the induction we were given a job in the camp, mine was in the laundry. There was a civilian worker in there who had the power of a prison officer - and by hell did he let you know it!. He was a mean man. A horrible, little guy who told us what we had to do, which included counting all the dirty socks and underpants. If they didn't tally up, he'd make us count them all over again. Not once, but three times. Believe me, there were some kids in there who used to fill their pants when they were forced to do extra press-ups and running on the spot. The evil little shit got a kick out of knowing our first count was wrong. He was pushing us to see how far we'd go.

It stunk in the laundry as we had to bag all the heavily soiled pants in one big bag. They were wrapped up in the piss stained sheets to get sent away to be washed. I don't think they were washed on-site. When I was there I can remember the laundry van coming once if not twice a week.

I remember having to count the underkegs in North Sea Camp. I can smell it now - but it was the job that got me the gym boy's job.

The gym orderly was due to go home and his job, the best job on the camp was up for grabs. I think there were about four of us up for it and I'd only been there about six weeks or so. By then I'd celebrated my 21st birthday.

There was no party - just a ten-mile run around the boundary of the camp. It was all through the marshes - it was another real killer - I'm not into long distance running.

I always tried to work my visit from Kerry when I knew I was going to do the boundary run. But everyone who went to Boston North Sea Camp had to do it at least once, just to say they'd done it.

The camp routine was based around hard work and there'd be kids out working from seven in a morning until late at night. They were building a sea defence, building banks and reclaiming the land from the sea. Those lads worked hard and I got to know most of the lads who were there as we all used to love our time in the gym.

We were allowed to send two letters out each week; one was paid for by the prison, the other we had to buy the stamp for out of our wages. I think I was on about £1.20 a week, which got me my toothpaste, soap and shampoo. Saying that, I didn't need soap and shampoo when I got the gym job as the lads were always leaving theirs in the showers. Finders - keepers, in them showers.

I was settling in well at North Sea Camp when out of the blue I got the letter everyone dreaded the most - the 'Dear John' letter!

Our letters were always read before they were given to us. The nasty little bloke who worked in the laundry department, the one who made me count all those underpants, handed me my letter. The little arsehole stood in for our house officer when he was on holiday. The horrible little shit, for some reason never liked me, I don't know why. He handed me the letter from Kerry that told me she no longer wanted anything to do with me. She couldn't cope on her own and was going back home to her Mother. She told me to keep my head up, not to get into trouble and she said she was sorry it was over between us.

The little shit of a man who thought he was a screw said, 'There you are big man, your girlfriend has dumped you and run off with someone else.'

I thought it was some sick joke at first. But I could see it in his face, the little bastard was a happy man giving me the letter that day. It just blew my head, but luckily for me the two guys who ran the gym were very supportive. They made me do red circuits every day until I came to terms with it.

'Get it out of your system,' they said.

A short time after, I got my own back on the little shit when we played rugby against the screws. He didn't know what had hit him when I tackled him.

I went to see the Vicar to see if he could get in touch with Kerry to see what the problem was. I think it was the mortgage money and other debts were piling up. I have to thank the Vicar because he also got in touch with the trawler company I worked for. Word soon got round and somehow Kerry managed to pay off all the bills and the 'Dear John' letter turned back to 'Dear Mally'...

We used to have a night watchman who used to come round, on the hour, every hour through the night; he used to carry a big stick with him. But he was a really funny guy who used to come in singing and whistling.

He was a good man and there was also a guy we called 'dead eyes.' He was built like my old man, you didn't mess with him if he gave you the look.

I had a few fights while I was there, I was the oldest inmate on the camp and there were kids in there aged from 16 to 20. There were about 200 lads at the camp from all different walks of life.

The camp used to have a farm and gardens, where some of the kids worked. Some did cleaning. Some were in the laundry. Some worked in the kitchen. Others were in the officers' mess. We then had 'the Governor's boy'. He was a grass. You never told him anything or he would go straight to the Governor. The screws were hard but fair and when we got to know them and we did our job, there weren't any problems.

I got the gym boy's job, the best job in the place and I got a red band. That meant I was a trustee and allowed to go all over the camp without an officer in attendance. But it was while I was walking round the farm without an escort, that some dickhead said something about Kerry. He called me a spotty faced twat and said that one of his mates was seeing my bird. He said he knew cos he was also from Hull. There were a few lads from Hull at the camp.

He said he'd been sent a letter, which told him to tell Mally Welburn that his bird was out with 'so and so'.

I just lost it. I banged him one and they found him in a pile of pig shit...

There was an unwritten rule in North Sea Camp, you never grassed on anyone - no matter what. I was called into the Governor's office over this lad they'd taken to hospital with a broken nose.

'Do you know anything?' asked the Governor.

'No sir, I don't,' I replied...

It was the same thing every day on the camp with a kit inspection - with our kit folded to the 'nine inch rule'.

Everything had to be folded to less than nine inches. Try to do a pile of all your clothes to nine inches, socks, jeans, vest, shirts, underpants and jumper. It's not easy!

Our bed had to be folded in a special way too. Our sheets had to have the envelope fold at the corners of our bed. And if any one of the twenty in the dormitory had done it wrong, we all suffered, everyone had to fold all their clothes again.

We also had to miss our favourite TV programme which at the time was 'Mork and Mindy' with Robin Williams. He later played 'Mrs Doubtfire', but in 'Mork and Mindy' he was a guy from outer space who used to come to planet Earth and his catch phrase was, 'Nanoo Nanoo.'

I remember kit inspection one night when one kid just didn't give a knack if we passed or failed as he was going home the next day. He just wasn't bothered but we all wanted to watch our weekly Mork and Mindy.

When we heard the house officer coming to our dorm - the big room with twenty lads - we all stood at the foot of our beds with our kit ready for inspection. The kid nearest the door shouted, 'Dorm - Attention!' Everyone would stand to attention and await kit inspection. This kid who was going home the next day wouldn't shut up and didn't have his kit ready.

The house officer said, 'I'll come back in an hour, the rest of you stand to attention while he does his kit.' We all knew the kid was playing silly buggers but he didn't care. He was going home the next morning and just carried on talking and messing about - but we'd missed our Mork and Mindy. The five o'clock inspection didn't take place till gone nine that night. The wanker who was going home thought it was really funny. When we did finally pass the inspection we then had to go and get a kit change.

With me being a red band I could take up to twenty lads on the march through the canteen to line up for our kit change. When we went through the canteen we had to go through in twos as it was a narrow passage. It was also a long passage, which led past the serving hatch where we'd get our food on a tray. The trays had three different indents in them, one for your meat and potatoes, one for your pudding and the other for your bread and butter. You'd also have a plastic cup for your weak tea. I was leading the lads to the laundry room to get their kit changed and we had to go through the long corridor to the dining area. It was then through the dining room to get to the laundry room, which was across the parade ground.

We took the short cut instead of walking all the way round the dining room. The wanker, who'd been doing all the gobbing off, was at the back of the line, still shouting and not doing as he was told. He was pushing his luck so I told him to get in line.

'If you think you're hard enough, come and make me,' he replied

With that, I said to the group, 'By the left, quick march,' and they all started to march, all apart from this wanker, he was still messing about. I knew there was no screw about as it was my job to take the lads to change their clothes but I knew there was a screw in the laundry. The lads at the front of the line started to march and as they passed me I said, 'Well done lads, take no notice of the wanker.'

Then, as he strolled past me I said, 'Are you taking the piss?'

'Yeah - what are you going to do about it?' he replied.

He woke up in an ambulance and they kept him in hospital for a few days while the swelling on his broken nose went down. It was then all hands in front of the Governor and do you know what his final conclusion was?

This superman of a character had fallen at the entrance to the corridor. He'd done two somersaults and banged his head half way down the corridor. He'd got up and banged his head on the serving hatch and had then walked into three doors.

He'd slipped on the parade ground, run into another door, banged his head on the hatch again, and had been finally found in the corridor.

That wasn't quite right of course. And despite a number of other suggestions, only two people ever knew the real truth about what had happened to the 'gobby' wanker that night...

I hope you're getting a feel for what it was like at North Sea Camp. It was what you'd expect a boot camp to be like. It was very hard if you weren't used to the running, marching and floor scrubbing and some lads just didn't take to it.

I remember one lad called Browny, an apt name if ever there was one, cos he was that scared every time an officer screamed at him to do a star jump, he shit himself! And I mean actually shit himself! Don't forget I used to work in the laundry and we hated it when Browny was in the line and we had to take his dirty laundry off him. I felt sorry for him, he really was a weak lad of about seventeen. I think he was in for shoplifting.

I remember one weekend after I'd been there for about four months, I'd become one of the fittest lads there and was doing three red circuits a day. Even the prison officers couldn't keep up with me. I'm not being big headed, I just loved my training and working out, the harder the better as far as I was concerned. I was also the best goalie there, I still thought I was Gordon Banks every time I put the green goalie's shirt on. I was very fit and I must have impressed a few officers as they got me a trial with Boston United reserves on Boston's ground. I was listed on the team sheet as A. N. OTHER - another name for a trialist. I did no good though...

It was the weekend of the ten-mile boundary run and I wasn't getting a visit off Kerry. She'd sent me that 'Dear John' letter. It was to say she just couldn't cope with it all and would see me when I got out. My head was 'up my arse'. I certainly didn't want to do the ten-mile boundary run, even if I was one of the fittest there.

I overheard two screws talking. One of them was the little civilian shit who worked in the laundry, you know, the one who made me count the likes of Browny's underpants. They were taking bets on who was going to win the boundary run and the little shit even pulled me to one side.

'Look young Welburn, I've got twenty quid on you to win the boundary run this weekend, don't let me down,' he said.

'Okay Boss,' I replied, but under my breath I may have added, 'Kiss my arse!'

On the day of the race about 120 lads who didn't get a visit had to do the boundary run, all round the marshes, it was a good ten miles. There was a prison officer at every half-mile stage of the run just in case some lads decided to do a runner, in the true sense of the word.

Many had tried to escape in the past but they'd never got very far and had just added another seven days onto their sentence. Every attempt to escape would double up the extra time.

There were some lads who were doing many weeks on top of their time! It was hard for some.

But in a strange way I got to like it there. I wasn't up for this boundary run though and neither was 'shitty arse' Brown.

Do you remember Joe Beaumont in Part One - the lad who chased the rat down the hole? He had that two-inch bug in his arm and we pulled half of it out with a pair of pliers. Well Joe was at North Sea Camp as well, and believe me he could run. He was a Forrest Gump - run Joe run - and very rarely got caught at the scene of the crime. He never got caught when he did a runner - they'd always arrest him at his mum's home, back home in Hull.

Joe could really run and I knew I'd never beat him on the boundary run. At the start of the race there were a few screws saying, 'Don't let us down Welly,' that was my pet name in there.

I then heard the horrible little laundry guy screaming at 'shitty arse' Browny to, 'Get ready to run.' But all you could hear were Browny's pleas of, 'Please sir, I can't run, my stomach is upset.'

The little man said something along the lines of, 'Go shit

yourself out on the run, it will do you the world of good.'

Some of the other kids were keeping their distance from Browny, taking the piss and laughing along with that little evil man, he who wasn't really a prison officer. The whistle went for the countdown from three, and we knew we were all going to do the run. Three, two, one...

Joe Beaumont shot clear and I went with him for about two hundred yards round the parade ground. I could see Browny and I think we lapped him because we had to do two laps round the parade ground before hitting the marshes.

I then heard Browny's cry of, 'Please sir don't make me run, I can't run.'

I just stopped running, turned around, ran back to Browny and put my arm round him.

'I'll run with you, and even if you can't run, I'll walk with you, don't worry Browny, I'm with you,' I said.

You should have seen the laundry man's face and he shouted as he came running towards us, 'Welburn, leave him and get on with your run.'

I said to him, 'Go fuck yourself and pick on somebody else.'

I must stress, I was out of earshot of all the other officers. So even when the laundry man said he'd report me to the Governor after I'd completed the run - and even though I knew swearing at an officer meant another seven days was added to your sentence - it didn't bother me.

I told him to fuck off or I'd tell the Governor about him gambling on me to win the race. He told me if I opened my mouth he'd make sure I would do another month on top of my sentence. I told him, if he did, I'd knock him out and he could then explain to the Governor why I'd done it!

I then started to walk Browny round the ten-mile course and I got to know Browny on the first two miles.

On top of that, the four prison officers who were spaced at every half-mile congratulated me on helping Browny. The smell of shit started to smell sweet because, at the four-mile stage, there was a Land Rover truck with refreshments i.e. water. As you can guess, by the time we got to it, there were no refreshments left. And Browny played his part by saying he was dying of thirst. Well it was a hot day. It was decided we were too far behind the rest so we headed back to the camp

MALLY - THE REBEL WITHOUT A PAUSE

in the back of the Land Rover.

Joe had won the race and a medal but not the trophy. After everyone had done the run you had your shower. We then had to go to the gym for the awarding of medals and praise.

The Governor said it was all about being a sportsman, helping your fellow man when they are down. 'A special award goes to Mally Welburn for helping young Brown,' he declared, 'Come and get this trophy Welburn.'

I couldn't believe it. It was the inter-house trophy for 'Sportsman of the Month' - and it was some trophy.

When I went up to collect it I saw the evil little laundry man giving me a false clap.

He never did report me to the Governor for swearing at him and my threat to hit him. But he did get his own back, that evil little laundry man.

Being in North Sea Camp was just like being in Stockton Hall with the only difference being you were older, fitter and understood things a bit more. I believe they should bring these camps back, instead of just banging people up in prison...

Most days were the same at North Sea Camp, up at seven in a morning, a bit of exercise, washed and shaved, I still had my spots. Breakfast was at about eight o'clock in the big dining bunker with four of us to a table. Then it was into our work clothes and to the job we were allocated, mine was the gym orderly. I had to sweep the gym floor then get all the apparatus out for whatever we were doing in the lesson.

I loved the circuit training. I loved to play volleyball. I wasn't into weights or gymnastics but there were some champions in there. I loved the rugby and the football.

And more than anything, I just loved it when we played Rugby Union against the screws, I loved making those crunching tackles.

On top of it all you got your three meals a day. What more could you ask for? But on the night, when you were in your bed, you'd think of your loved ones at home and you'd start 'stinking thinking'. Thinking - what was Kerry up to? Was she coping okay?

We were also able to go to night classes at the camp and I chose amateur dramatics, you know acting and all that. The only reason was because the 'most beautiful woman' took the class. She was a teacher who worked in a school in Boston during the day and she also lived in Boston town centre.

How do I know? Because I went to her house one dinner time and she made me a nice cup of tea!

She was classed as a civilian officer who came and did part-time work i.e. night classes.

This lady, who shall remain nameless, was 28 years of age and one of the most beautiful women I've ever seen. It was definitely Shakespeare when she was around.

'Shall I compare thee to a summer's day:
Thou art more lovely and more temperate:
Rough winds do shake the darling buds of May.'

To smell her perfume got your testosterone levels up, oh she was gorgeous. The bromide never worked when she was in your presence at our night classes. It was the highlight of the week, knowing Miss Nightclass was coming to take the class. I never saw so many lads scrubbing their fingernails and brushing their teeth. I even think Browny got in her class on the understanding he never shit his pants. She was a very softly spoken and beautiful woman.

You had to wait while someone 'went home' out of the night class before the next on the list got into her class of twelve or so. Nearly everyone, including the screws, wanted to get on her list. The class didn't change much, as you can imagine, and there was always a long waiting list to get into her class.

I think I got into her class because I was a red band, I could take the lads to and from night class. There was a screw on the night class door, just in case some nutter lost the plot.

I can picture her now, her smiling face, her beautiful slim body with her short blonde hair and those 'lift me up' lips. When she walked into the class you certainly did stand to attention!

I was in her night class, which went from 7 until 9 o'clock. We'd make plays up and do a bit of acting, standing like a tree. I'd have been her tree any day of the week.

We got to know a bit about Miss Nightclass and asked her why she didn't have a boyfriend or husband. Her reply was, 'I'm waiting for Mr Right.'

MALLY - THE REBEL WITHOUT A PAUSE

She told us she loved what she was doing, coming up to the camp to teach us and help us out. She was a truly nice lady.

I remember having a nice cup of tea at her home in Boston.

I had about three weeks to go before I was due to go home and the Home Office brought out a new early release scheme. It was for those who the prison Governors thought should go out and do some work in the community.

I was called into the Governor's office and asked if I'd like to go and work with the geriatrics at Boston hospital. To be honest I didn't know what a geriatric was. I thought it was a German who'd scored three goals or maybe a German magician.

I was told it was 'old folk' who couldn't do much for themselves due to their age. Some of them had no families to visit them so to help cheer them up we had to push them around the park in their wheelchairs and have an ice cream with them.

I jumped at the chance but I didn't know what to expect. The Governor laid out the ground rules for us. There was no leaving the hospital unless it was with an officer and no taking the old folks around the park or the town without a nurse. Saying that, when we were in our blue and white striped shirts, our prison trousers and with our short hair, we stuck out like a sore thumb. There was no chance of me running off - and no point - I only had three weeks to do and I was going to spend two of them helping with the old folk.

When I told Miss Nightclass that I was going to be working at the hospital, she told me she only lived five minutes away from the park and the hospital. She was into gardening and had seen the nurses pushing the old dears past her house. I asked her that if she saw us, would she make us a cup of tea? 'Of course I will,' she replied.

I then asked her, on which part of the walk did she live so I could look out for her and we could get our free pot of tea.

She said if she saw us, she'd give us a shout. I just couldn't wait to take our dear old friends out on their walk.

We were taken in the camp minibus, with Boston North Sea Camp written all over the side. When we got there all the doctors and nurses were looking at us. The Outpatients' Department also gave us a few 'mucky' looks.

When us six convicts were shown into the old folks' secure ward, it was like a scene from the Jack Nicholson film, 'One Flew Over The Cuckoo's Nest'! There were old people going round in circles, some were dancing with themselves and a lot were just talking to themselves.

One lady reminded me of my loving Mother. They had a piano in the ward and this old dear was playing it in her nightie. She had all these bloodstained bandages round both her knees. We found out she had a habit of scratching her knees until they bled, but the trouble was she couldn't see what she was doing to herself because she was blind. If you said anything to her she'd give you a load of foul and abusive language until you sat down next to her and she sensed who it was. Then she spoke like an angel. But if she heard other people talking, she'd let rip with the foul language again.

She was a funny lady who'd lost her sight two years earlier at the age of seventy. She had no family but was a trained pianist and always told me she could play the piano with her eyes closed...

We spent the first week getting to know these dear old men and women, and it was a joy to walk in to the sound of the lady on the piano. She had a sweet voice, well until she heard a strange voice that is.

She wore the nightie so the nurses could change the wounds on her knees hourly. She'd often sit there scratching her knees and if you said anything to her she'd give you a mouthful. She'd shout for the nurse and say that we'd been scratching her knees. The nurses didn't worry about what she was saying as she used to blame everyone for scratching her knees. I don't think she was 'all there'.

You would then hear her in a sweet voice and she would say, 'Sorry young man,' then everything would be okay. I'll tell you what though, she could certainly play that piano and we had a good few sing-a-longs.

We were allowed to go just outside the hospital to use the public phone, to ring our loved ones up and I would use the opportunity to ring Kerry. We got something like fifty pence a day for a sandwich or an ice cream, our 'dinner money'. The weather wasn't good enough to take the old dears out in the first week but the head nurse said I could still go and make my call to Kerry.

We got an hour for our dinner and the screw who took us was a good guy. He knew we weren't going to do a runner, not with just two weeks left. He turned a blind eye to our lunchtime telephone calls.

It was a joy looking forward to my last week working at the hospital, as I knew that when the week was over I was going back home. I could then start to sort out all the mess I'd left behind. Kerry was living 'on the edge' but thankfully she got some help from the Fisherman's Mission. She had cleaned up the entire house and with the help of her Mother Pat, had managed to hold off the bailiffs.

I was getting all this information from my daily lunchtime calls and I even got Kerry to ring the phone box at a certain time. This was just in case I never had my ice cream money.

Things were okay until the Governor got wind of the calls and stopped the 'dinner money'. Most probably, 'the Governor's boy' had had his ear to the ground!

If us inmates wanted a sandwich or an ice cream the hospital had to pay for it and send the invoice to the camp. It meant we had no money to make a call, which also meant we had no reason to go out at lunchtime. I guess it made sense. But I knew Kerry was having trouble at home with the bailiffs and I had to make a call just to see if she was okay...

It was a hot summer's Monday morning when we went to the hospital to take the gang out in their wheelchairs. And when the nurses asked who wanted to go to the park, you should have seen the change in some of those old folk.

You'd have thought it was Christmas. They all wanted to go but we could only take a maximum of eight, one each for the six 'cons' and one each for the two nurses.

I then heard, in a softly spoken voice, 'Would you take me out please, Mally?' It was the blind, piano-playing lady, she knew my name and I told her it would be a pleasure.

At ten thirty we left the hospital in a convoy, a nurse at the front, then us six and another nurse at the back.

'Wagons roll,' we shouted and we started to sing. 'Sixteen wheels on our wagon and we're still rolling along, the Cherokees are chasing me, but we're singing a happy song.'

We got some strange looks as we went through Boston town

centre and a few snide comments as well. But we were bigger than that and we were doing our bit for the community. We had a lovely morning in the park but I didn't see Miss Nightclass.

We had to be back at the hospital for twelve thirty to get the old dears ready for their lunch. As we were passing the phone box at about 12 o'clock, the phone started ringing and I knew it was Kerry.

I told the leading nurse my story of using the phone box and that I believed it was Kerry on the phone. The nurse told me to answer the phone and if it was her, to tell her to ring back at twelve thirty. They needed help to get the old dears back to the ward and then I could take my dinner break.

The phone stopped ringing and the nurse told me not to worry as I would still be able to come and use the phone and she'd give me the ten pence. I thanked her, we got the old dears back onto the ward and I got my ten pence.

I marched out of the hospital and headed towards the phone box. I was halfway there when a nice sports car pulled up beside me. It was Miss Nightclass!

I told her I was going to ring my girlfriend as I was allowed an hour before I had to go back to the hospital. She offered to let me ring Kerry from her place, I could have that cup of tea she'd promised me and then she'd drop me off back at the hospital for one-thirty.

The 'five minutes from the hospital' to her house might have been possible on foot. But by car, around the one way system, it took about 20 minutes! It was worth it though, she had a lovely house. She let me use her phone and it was really nice to be in her company. She smelt beautiful. I made the cup of tea last over ten minutes. She said she'd drop me off just before the one way system on the way back so it would only be a short walk back to the hospital.

'No problem, Miss,' I said and thanked her for her help and for listening to me. She was a good listener.

We got back into her sports car and she dropped me off about twenty past one where I could see the hospital.

She dropped me off outside a petrol station and I gave her a peck on her cheek, a thank you peck. As I got out of her car, guess who was filling up at the petrol station?

MALLY - THE REBEL WITHOUT A PAUSE

Yes, you guessed, the laundry guy, the little shit who made me count the underpants. The little shit that had a side bet on me winning the boundary run. The little shit who said to me, 'I'll get you Welburn.'

The little shit who saw me get out of Miss Nightclass's car. The little shit who, when he saw me, shouted, 'Welburn, what the hell are you doing here?'

'Nothing Boss,' I replied. 'I was lost and Miss has just dropped me off,' I said. 'I've got to get back to the hospital, Boss.' He shouted at me to stop exactly where I was. I shouted back I couldn't as I had to be back at the hospital for one thirty and I started to leg it as fast as I could. I got back to the hospital for one thirty without any problems. Or so I thought. At three o'clock in the afternoon, four policemen and two officers from the camp turned up. They came to take me back to the camp for attempting to run away and being out of the hospital without an escort.

You'd have thought I was the Great Train Robber, Ronnie Biggs. I was put in a solitary confinement cell from five o'clock in the evening until the following morning, when I went in front of the Governor.

Word got round the camp I'd been at Miss Nightclass's house. Some officers thought I'd been to her house on more than one occasion. The head nurse gave me a glowing report as she even said she trusted me to go use the phone. She knew we had an hour to ourselves.

I was up in front of the Governor for absconding and not stopping when told to. I was marched into the Governor's office by two officers, one in front of me and one behind. It was by the left, quick march, left, right, left, right. I then faced the Governor, giving my name and number. As I glanced to the side I noticed there was someone else in the room. It was the laundry man!

The first thing the Governor asked me was, 'What were you doing in Miss Nightclass's car? He didn't say Miss Nightclass of course, he used her proper name.

'Nothing sir,' I replied.

'Why were you kissing her?' he asked.

'It was only a goodbye peck on the cheek, Sir,' I replied.

'I'll ask you again, what were you doing in Miss Nightclass's car?' he said more sternly.

'Nothing Sir', I repeated.

'Then what were you doing at Miss Nightclass's house?' he shouted. I tried to tell him I'd gone to make a phone call to my girlfriend and Miss was passing by and asked if I was lost.

I realised I might have been digging a hole because I didn't actually know what Miss Nightclass had said about the incident. The Governor told me Miss Nightclass had told him what I'd just said had happened, but he was having none of it. His next question was, 'Have you ever slept with Miss Nightclass?'

I said I never had and I didn't know where he'd got that idea from. But I guessed as I looked across at the smirking laundry man. The Governor said he didn't believe me and I'd serve another seven days - and to go tell my girlfriend why!

'Now get out! - And make sure he doesn't go back in that class!' he shouted.

Fucking hell what had I done? I thought. I honestly didn't know what I'd done wrong but I guessed it was all down to the laundry man. He hadn't known I was on the scheme. He thought I'd escaped from the camp when he saw me in the town on me own. I can understand in a way, with me not stopping when he told me to, so it was another seven days up me arse to do. They took my red armband off me and stopped me going to Miss Nightclass's class. They were going to take my gym orderly job off me as well but the gym officers stuck up for me. I even heard Miss Nightclass had put a word in for me as well. I was very grateful to Miss Nightclass and glad she didn't lose her job teaching the inmates amateur dramatics. But there were some nasty rumours going around the camp after our lunchtime cuppa. That I'd gone to her house and we'd had sex in that hour. But it wasn't true. I was in love with Kerry and I would have only had one week to go before we were together again. But now it was two weeks...

Those last two weeks really dragged.

No night classes. No visits to the hospital. No walks in the park with the old dears. But then the day I'd been waiting for finally arrived. And I can't tell you how happy I was to hear the four little words, 'It's now or never.'

That's what the prison officer said to me as we waited to board the minibus on my final day at North Sea Camp.

'It's now or never,' he said again.

'It's now up to you, to make your mind up, never to come back here again. It's a decision you should make when you step on the bus. If you feel you're going to miss this place and the people you've met, you'll be back. But, if you can get on the bus and say, I didn't like it, I hated it, then you won't be back. It's now or never, make your mind up whether you'll be back or not when you step on that bus.'

To be honest, I met some really nice people at North Sea Camp and made some good mates. In a strange sort of a way, it was sad to leave. Does that sound strange to you?

Fair enough, I'd been sent there, I'd done what they'd asked of me and I'd done my time. But there are actually some nice people about in this strange world we live in and I met some of them at Boston Camp.

I knew I'd never be going back there though, as at the time I was the oldest inmate in there.

I'd had my 21st birthday at Boston and they only took lads aged between 16 and 20. I had just scraped in, so I knew whatever happened in the future, I was never going back!

My last day at North Sea Camp, the day of my release, began at six in the morning when I was woken up an hour before everyone else. Saying that, I didn't need much waking, I never slept properly whenever I knew it was my time to go home.

It was the same at sea. I could never sleep on the last day, knowing I was going home to my loved ones. It was like being a kid on Christmas Eve, I was always so excited.

After breakfast I went to the laundry to hand in all my prison clothes. These I exchanged for the slacks, shirt and tie I'd appeared at court in.

This though was usually the moment when I found out the clothes were either too big for me or I was too big for them. In my case it was a bit of both. My trousers were too big as I'd lost weight round my waist but my shirt was too tight with all the weight training and exercising I'd done. The only things which still fitted me were my shoes - my size 14s - and of course my tie!

They had to rig me out with some trousers, a shirt and a jacket. I think it was called a 'clothes grant'. You then had to sign for all your personal belongings and they checked what you were taking out. All I had to sign for were the letters from my loving Mother and my girlfriend Kerry. Thankfully the nasty little laundry man wasn't on duty that day...

I'd done my time in Boston North Sea Camp and they took me to the coach station to catch a bus.

That took me to Barton On Humber and then to New Holland from where I caught the ferry across to Hull Pier.

Funnily enough, I now only live round the corner from where I got off the ferry in September 1979.

It was 28 years ago because, as you know, I was just 21 when I came home from the detention centre.

As I was getting off the minibus in Boston, along with another four inmates who were released at the same time as me, one of the screws asked me a question.

'Did you sleep with Miss Nightclass, Welly?'

If I'd said, 'Yes,' he could have taken me back to the camp for lying to the Governor.

So with a broad grin on my face I just said, 'No I never.' But this officer, who was one of the nice guys, kept pleading with me to tell him if I had.

He'd had bets with a few of the other screws as to whether I had or not.

'If I tell you I did, how much do you stand to win?' I asked.

'A couple of hundred quid,' he replied.

There were another two officers on the minibus so I kept saying, 'No, I'm not telling you until I know I can't get re-arrested.' They assured me as soon as my feet hit the bus station platform, they'd turn round, head back to the camp and I was free.

'I'll tell you when I'm getting on my bus to Barton to catch the ferry,' I promised.

They waited until my bus turned up, but when it did turn up it wasn't due to leave for another ten minutes. The officer who had made the bets kept asking me all the time, 'Did you Welly? Did you do Miss Nightclass? Go on Welly, tell us.'

I could see he was getting worked up about it so I spun him a load of shit saying how, every day while I was working in the hospital, she would come and pick me up.

It was outside the phone box, near the hospital, at the same time, five past twelve. We'd drive back to her house and I'd throw her all over the place. She was mad for it. She couldn't get enough of it and we'd be at it for three-quarters of an hour. Well I was only 21.

She'd then drop me back off at the garage so I could get an ice cream and walk back to the hospital.

We knew we'd been caught that day so we lied to the Governor.

'Is that what you wanted to hear?' I asked the screw.

'Tell me more Welly, I swear I won't say anything,' he pleaded.

A second later, the bus conductor told me to get on as we were about to set off for the ferry. Just as I jumped on the bus, I shouted to the screw, 'Go and collect your money!'

You could see him jumping up and down as though he'd just got five and the bonus ball on the lottery.

Some people will believe exactly what they want to believe, I guess. But I hope he got paid because he wasn't a bad screw. And for the record, all that I told him wasn't true of course - and he should have known.

I couldn't do it for three-quarters of an hour, even in those days...

CHAPTER FIFTEEN
RADAR LOVE

There were now more important things to sort out, my life for one. I got to the ferry and the mile crossing over the Humber brought me to Hull Pier. The Humber Bridge hadn't been built then, it wasn't opened until 1981.

Waiting for me at the pier was Kerry, the most beautiful girl you'd have wanted to meet you after being away for six months. I only did six months, I got nine months but three months was to run concurrent.

So six months had passed and while I was away the debts had mounted up on the house we'd bought. Kerry had done her best to hold the bailiffs at bay but we were deep in debt. I had to get back to sea, to pay back the people who'd helped us while I was away.

There wasn't much work going on the trawlers and you had to wait your turn. The St Jason had just set sail on a ten week voyage but with my reputation not many skippers were going to carry me. It was getting like a closed shop, you had to know the skipper or the mate of the trawler, just to stand a chance. Or you went to sea for the Christmas trip when the regular crew had Christmas off. You'd stand in for them for the one trip and you were then known as a 'Christmas cracker' and I've sailed with a few Christmas crackers in my time at sea.

By now Kerry had restored the house to its former glory. This was with the help of Charlie Platten and Kerry's loving Mother, Pat. She was another lady out of the same mould as my Mother - a very caring and loving lady. Do you know, she never ever turned me away from her door. But not even she could help me when I got out of North Sea Camp!

The first thing I had to do was to find work...

I went down to the dock to see Renee, the ship's runner of Hamlyn's and the only ship available was the St Jerome. It was another ship that was sailing for ten weeks and yes, I was the 'Christmas cracker'!

I had to take the work as the money went towards helping Kerry with the mountain of debts, at least she'd be getting my wages sent to her every week. She also got a little job working in a clothes shop. I didn't like Kerry working. I think it was another time in my life when I thought I was turning into my Dad again, not liking Kerry going to work. I believed in those days that it was the man's job to do the graft. It was up to him to support the woman at home. Call me old-fashioned, but it's just what we were brought up with.

I was also very insecure in those days. I was a jealous guy. I wanted my woman to stay in and run the house. It was how it was then but how times have changed. It makes you think doesn't it? When both parents have to go out to work today just to get the basic things out of life.

I did the Christmas trip of 1979 on the St Jerome, which was the same class of ship as the St Jason and the St Jasper, with the three ships built the same in every way. But they were very different when it came to their skippers and mates!

I tell yer, why some skippers turned into the devil when they left St Andrews Dock in Hull, I'll never know!

Hamlyn's only had four trawlers, the biggest being the St Benedict, so as you can guess, getting a berth aboard any of them, was like finding rocking-horse shit. There was a rumour that Hamlyn's were getting four more modern-day trawlers for 1980, so that would hopefully mean more opportunities of work for me.

I did the Christmas trip in 1979 and I got home early January 1980. The St Jason was in dock and due to sail at the end of the month.

As I was picking my trip money up for the St Jerome I bumped into skipper Ball, the daddy of all skippers. He said I could go back on the St Jason with him and I jumped at the chance. I was only home a couple of weeks or so, then it was back on the ship I loved, with the skipper and the same crew. Skipper Ball signed me on the St Jason and Renee, the ship's runner, told me if I did another ten week trip, I'd have my sea time. That would allow me to go for my bosun's ticket and to be a ship's officer - he was expecting big things from me.

Skipper Ball had put my name forward to go for my ticket, it was a three month course, and it would give me time at home with Kerry. On top of that, the company paid you well for going for your ticket.

Things were looking up for me, so much so that before I left, I proposed to Kerry - and she said, 'Yes!'

September 25 1980 was the date we set to tie the knot.

Mind you, what Kerry saw in me I'll still never know? She told me she loved me and I sure loved Kerry Anne.

In March 1980 I was booked into training school to go and study and try to get my bosun's ticket. But first I did the second ten weeks trip on the St Jason. It flew by and I also learnt a lot off skipper Ball with regards to navigation.

I spent all my spare time learning the 'Rules of the Road', which is every mariner's bible.

'Learn the Rules of the Road,' skipper Ball would say.

'The Rules of the Road', is a bit like the 'Highway Code' - the high sea code, a book of rules i.e. 'red to red, perfect safety go ahead.'

Instead of watching films and reading the 'mucky mags', I was getting my head into learning the Rules of the Road. I also had to learn the 'buoyage' system, Morse code and the flags.

We only did eight weeks on this trip - I think the fish must have been jumping aboard - the time flew by. We must have been in Norwegian waters, which had plenty of fish for the time of year and we caught some big cod on that trip.

By the middle of March I was back home again and ready to go to training school.

There was no pissing it up after *this* trip, it was study time. I couldn't afford to let down skipper Ball, Renee and not forgetting Kerry.

Kerry by the way was three months pregnant and believe it or not, her delivery date was the same date we'd booked for our wedding. In the end we cancelled the church wedding and booked in at Hull Registry Office for May 17 1980.

I started training school, where we had to have all our schoolbooks. There was a book on logarithms. I didn't even know what they were until I'd been at training school for two months. Just to tell you, they are navigational books and we had to go through these books to find the answer to where we

MALLY - THE REBEL WITHOUT A PAUSE

were on the fishing charts. They're a bit confusing so I won't dwell on them, if you don't mind. There were twenty-five of us at this training school, and some were 'sailors' from the nautical college. They were doing their radar observer's course and there were some very clever kids on the course.

I remember one day the teacher was giving us a lesson about switching the radar on. He was teaching us about the clutter on the radar and said if there was too much precipitation on the screen just turn the clutter down.

'Excuse me Sir, what is precipitation?' I asked.

A few of the sailor boys looked round at me as though I was daft, but I also saw the puzzled look on the faces of these two Chinese blokes next to me. They couldn't speak much English.

The teacher said, 'Precipitation Welburn, is rain.'

'Why don't you just say rain then?' I said.

We would have to be at a building on the dock for our radar observer's training for nine o'clock every morning. It really was a hard course but I had a few mates on it with me like Charlie Waddy, Darrell Taylor, Steve Barker, Julian Stevens, Colin Dennett and John Musgrave. We would all work together as I think we were the only trawler men on the course.

I don't know whether Kenny Offen was with us. But I know that Darrell, Steve and me would all meet up at my house every night and go through what we'd learnt that day.

It was great because the love of my life at that time, Kerry, would do all the sandwiches, tea and coffee - but always with the golden rule - no booze!

We studied really hard because if you don't really get your head into learning, you're not going to learn anything.

On top of all the learning both Kerry and me were planning our marriage which had had to be brought forward.

It was set for May 17, which would fall two months into the three months bosun's course.

You could say we all worked hard on studying to pass the course, cos even Kerry would help me with the Rules of the Road.

She would say, 'What's Rule 23? What does a red buoy mean? What flag is this and what does it stand for?'

I really got into learning and do you know, all of a sudden it all came to me, very much so, and after seven weeks into the course we had a mock exam.

We were told the pass rate was 65%.

So there we were, twenty-five of us, no talking. We all had a chart in front of us plus a question and answer sheet. We had to do the exam in three hours and the questions were something like this.

'A ship sets sail from point A, in a northeast by east direction. You're doing ten knots, the wind and tide is this and that, how long will it take to get to point B?'

You had to check on the chart, taking into account the set and drift, and calculate how many miles you would have travelled.

'And when you were a given distance from a certain light ship, what would your course be to get to point C? How long would it take you to reach the light ship? And then after travelling for two hours, where would you be?'

I got straight into it. I had my pencils sharpened, you always used a pencil on sea charts because you could rub it out. I had my parallels, dividers, compass and my book of logarithms, all navigational aids which were used on ships in them days.

Believe it or not, after about two hours, I'd completed the exam well in front of everyone else. It all came to me in the exam and I just flew through it, I was off like the clappers and everything just fell into place.

I checked my chart work; I checked my answers and then went to the front of the class to hand in my work. The teacher told me I could go and to come back at two in the afternoon.

It was eleven o'clock in the morning so I waited outside for the rest to finish. It came to twelve o'clock dinner time and most of the other lads came out. We compared our answers. We all had different answers to certain questions, and I was thinking, have I rushed it? We all went back into the classroom at two o'clock where half a dozen were still stuck on the chart work, they just never got it and their time was up. They had to hand their unfinished work in at two o'clock, after all, it was only a mock exam. The teacher said he would read the mock results, in reverse order, bearing in mind the 65% pass rate. He said that of the twenty-five who were on the course only six people had got 65% or over.

MALLY - THE REBEL WITHOUT A PAUSE

He got to the second to last name on his list and said so and so got 85%, but there was one person's result he didn't read out, mine. He said, 'I've been training for over 20 years and have never seen a 100% paper but one student here has come very close.

The person I've left until last has reached the best mark I've ever seen and the mark is 99.9%. The reason he never got 100% was because he was half a degree out on one question. I can only blame it on him rushing and not sharpening his pencil. That person is Mally Welburn.'

I screamed with joy and said, 'You're having a laugh aren't you, Sir? You're winding me up!

Surely it must be one of the nautical lads, or my fishing mates, Charlie Waddy or Johnnie Musgrave, after all, *they* were going for their *mate's* tickets.'

'No Welburn, it's you,' said the teacher. 'And for the record, I've never seen such work as this before.'

I was so excited, I was jumping up and down and all the lads were really pleased for me.

I only had one week to go before I was to get married, so the teacher said,

'Take the week off, go and get married and enjoy your honeymoon in Blackpool - and when you come back it will be exam time for real.'

They all knew I was going to Blackpool for the weekend.

We all went on the piss in St Andrews Club but I never stayed out and got drunk because I was due to get married in six days. It was back to pick Kerry up. I took her out for a meal to celebrate, it was such a buzz...

After my mock exam, I was told to forget things and to go and enjoy my wedding to the most beautiful girl in the world, Kerry Anne. She was five months pregnant by the time we tied the knot.

I'd like to thank Kerry's Mam and Dad, Patricia and Dave, they really dug deep to give us a memorable day, what I can remember of it. I know I came out with one of the biggest boils I'd ever seen on the cheek of my face. It was one of them you couldn't squeeze. I'm not kidding, it was the size of a boiled egg stuck under my skin. It just didn't come to a head but God I tried to squeeze it the night before the big day, but to no avail. I had the biggest plaster on my face ever seen. I looked a right twat so I'm glad there weren't many at our wedding. Kerry looked absolutely beautiful, stealing the whole show and she brought tears to her loving Mother Pat's eyes on our wedding day. It was a real pity about me!

I honestly can't remember who was my best man at the wedding, Kerry thinks it was my brother Michael. But I think it was my best mate from school and my early fishing days, Terry Milner.

We had our reception at the Station Hotel in Hull, a real posh place and they even laid out the red carpet for us. It was a 'testing' time for all of us because I invited all my brothers to my wedding. And believe me, when everyone learned that all the Welburns would be there, some people decided not to attend!

I'm not quite sure who turned up in the end. I know Trevor did because he had set me up on my first date with Kerry - there were times when me and me brother Trevor got on. I also remember Raymond and Mike being there. I don't know whether David was at sea, I know Richard was away somewhere but Bobby, the baby of the family, was also there. The biggest surprise of all was my Mam and Dad being there. Apparently Kerry's Mother Pat had been round to see me Dad. She asked him if he and my Mother would attend, or if he didn't want to go would he let my mother attend on her own?

To my surprise they both turned up, it was absolutely brilliant to see my Mother there. Pat had bought my Mam a really nice dress and she looked beautiful.

A few people were on their toes when all or at least most of the Welburn family got together but I can tell you there wasn't an ounce of trouble. As it happened, the Welburn clan were on their very best behaviour for my wedding and I thank them for that. The reception at the Station Hotel was perfect.

Kerry and I were due to catch the two o'clock train to Blackpool to begin our honeymoon. But as it was a sunny afternoon in May and everything was going so well, Kerry's Dad had a word with the hotel manager and extended the room hire until six o'clock in the evening. Everyone from Kerry's side of the family mixed well with my side of the family and I have to say I was really proud of my family on 'our' day.

It turned out to be such a fantastic day that I didn't want to go to Blackpool. But as soon as the drams of rum started to appear, I knew it was time for me and my new wife to leave.

I'm told Pat paid for everyone to go onto the platform at the railway station, which is next to the hotel, to wave us off as we caught our train.

My wedding day to Kerry was one of the happiest days of my life and I thank everyone who attended my wedding to the most beautiful girl in the world.

As the song goes, 'If you happen to see the most beautiful girl in the world, tell her I'm sorry.'

That was Kerry. They were happy days!

We went to Blackpool for a week and stayed in a nice bed and breakfast place, I forget the name. Well we'd planned a week but came home after four days as a precaution.

We went on either the Big Dipper or some other big ride and Kerry started to lose a lot of blood. There was a fear for our unborn baby so we didn't stay for the full week.

The people who owned the B & B said to us as we were leaving, 'If you want to come back after the baby's born we'll throw in an extra four days free of charge.'

We thanked them but couldn't wait to get home. At least Kerry would be nearer to the hospital and her family if anything went wrong, which thankfully it never did. And as soon as we got home Kerry went straight to the doctors.

I went straight on the piss in my local, the Gipsyville Tavern with a couple of my brothers. I've had a few fights in there!

I can remember going into the toilets one day when one of Hull's very own hard-cases, Pete Thundercliffe was around. Many a grown man in the fishing industry feared him. They say he was even harder than my old man. You didn't mess about with the Thunder - they said he was like lightning.

As I walked into the toilets he had one of the Rudd family by the neck and when I say by the neck I mean it. He had one hand round young Rudd's neck and he'd just lifted him off the floor.

Rudd must have only been about eighteen at the time and the Thunder was in his late forties, but still a very fit man. At first

I didn't take any notice because I thought Thunder was only messing about and giving him a warning for something.

It was then that young Ruddy said to me, in a squeaky voice, as though he was choking, 'Help me, Mally.'

'Hey Pete, leave the kid alone, you're nearly choking him,' I said to Thunder.

'Mind your own fucking business or else you'll get it instead,' he replied.

'I don't fucking think so,' I said.

Well he dropped the choking Ruddy who immediately ran out of the toilets crying. Now the toilets were very narrow in Gipsyville Tavern and there was no way out for me because Thunder was blocking the door. Everyone knew Thunder. He was part of the folklore of the sea.

He used to be a skipper and mate on the trawlers and it is said most of the crews feared Pete Thundercliffe. I'd heard of the Thunder and knew he was very fast with his fists.

But as he let his grip go on young Ruddy and turned to me I just punched him right in the face. He went backwards towards the toilet door so I followed through with another left, then a right.

Then with all my might I hit him and he flew backwards through the toilet door into the bar, landing flat on his back. Well I wasn't going to let him get back up, so I jumped astride of him, sitting on his chest and continuing to rain punches, non-stop.

He shouted he'd had enough so I screamed at him, 'Say sorry you bastard,' as I carried on punching him. He mumbled, 'Sorry', as five or six blokes started to pull me off him. I just wanted to carry on but he was out cold. I knew if I hadn't hit him first he would have hit me, it became hit first, ask questions later.

The next day I went to his flat above the DIY shop in Gipsyville and his wife/girlfriend at the time, Ida, let me in to see what I'd done. But Pete just stuck his hand out and said, 'Sorry Mally, it was my fault.'

I said I was sorry for what I'd done but he told me,

'I'd have done the same to you if you hadn't got in first.'

Nothing was ever said again after this as we knew where we stood. That's what it was like in those days. You didn't involve the coppers in your disputes, you had a fight and that was it. Sometimes there wasn't a chance to say, 'No coppers', it was just, BANG!

Long after our little scuffle, I became a friend of Pete Thundercliffe. I'd always have a pint with him when I went in the Tavern - and it was a sad day when I found out he had a bigger fight in life. It was a fight against cancer. But I know Pete will face it with his usual bravery. And I'd like to wish him all the best and hope he makes a complete and speedy recovery...

There were plenty of times when men came looking for the Welburns in Gipsyville Tavern. And there were also times these men would get carried out - but it was always, 'No coppers'.

Another incident I recall in Tavern was when four big blokes came in and I mean *big* blokes, each standing over six foot and weighing over fifteen stone. You'd have thought they were all wrestlers. They picked the wrong day though, because there were *two* Welburns in the pub on that day, me and my big brother, Raymond. You didn't mess with a black belt, 4th Dan. And you also didn't mess with the Welburns when they'd been on the shorts - the rum and the whisky. For no reason at all these four came over to our table and enquired, 'Who are these Welburns?'

'Who wants to know?' we asked.

'We do - We've come to sort them out!' they replied.

With one nod to our kid we leapt to our feet and it was, BANG! BANG! - two down. The other two started edging towards the door and you could see in their faces that they knew they'd picked on the wrong two that day.

As their two mates were getting back to their feet both me and our kid gave them another left-right and it was good night for them. They were flat out and the other two ran out of the pub. I ran after them. They were running for a waiting taxi but unluckily for them I knew the driver. He was one of the Ken Kabs drivers and after all, I lived above their office, in the bed sit, at least I did before I left the frying pan on.

These two blokes jumped into the back of the taxi screaming at the driver to pull away.

Even with the doors closed, you could hear them shouting,

'Get us out of here!'

I got to the taxi on my own and screamed at the taxi driver not to pull off. I wanted these two windy bastards to come back and get their mates and I called them, 'Fucking cowards'.

One of the guys then shouted to me, 'I'll fucking kill you if I get out of this taxi.'

I screamed back to him, 'Come on then you fucking wanker.' I was pulling on the door handle but he'd locked it from the inside.

The poor taxi driver just didn't know what to do. In the end he refused to move and these two guys in the back were left sat there, shitting themselves.

I was banging on the windows and the guy in the back, the one giving me all the gob, told me to stand away from the taxi, let him get out and then we could have a scrap.

I took two paces back saying again, 'Come on then you fucking wanker!'

As he opened the taxi door and started to get out, head halfway out, I ran up to the taxi and booted the door. He was halfway out of it and it took his breath away so there he was slumped and hanging out of the back door.

I grabbed his hair and then slammed the taxi door on his head and it really connected. I just kept slamming the door on his head with his mate screaming at the taxi driver to get fucking going.

With that, the taxi started up and began slowly pulling away but I still had hold of his hair. The head of this Giant was still half hanging out of the taxi as I had him in a headlock. I was punching fuck out of his head as I screamed at him, 'You came looking for us but we don't even know who you are, you bastard.'

The taxi then sped off with his mate pulling him inside and I went to go back into the Tavern. The other two were staggering through the front doors after our kid had continued to give them a good hiding.

I got started, punching the bigger of the two but our kid pulled me off him as he was really in a bad way. They both were and we never did find out who they were and never saw them again.

I think someone rang an ambulance and the police came and

asked everyone in the pub what had happened but nobody said anything. And there were no charges made against us that day which made a change. But that incident just summed up what life was like for the Welburns.

You could almost guarantee that when I got home from sea and I went out with my brothers, some arsehole would always try and pick a fight with us.

I got into a lot worse trouble than that later on when I did nine months in prison for three fights in two days!

But on my wedding day there was no such trouble and I thank my brothers for being a big part of our special day.

Do you know, some people actually say that the Welburns are a really nice bunch of polite lads and they sure were on my wedding day...

Thankfully Kerry got the all clear after the ride on the Big Dipper at Blackpool on our honeymoon.

I then had to go back and sit my radar observer's exam for real and do you know what, I failed. I only got about 45 per cent! It had to be that week away from the observer's course, everything just went out of my head. They gave me another week to get my head into it again and I passed with flying colours with a mark of 85%.

At that time Kerry was my rock and didn't deserve all the shit I put her through. But I just couldn't stop the booze.

I'd say I was only going out for an hour but it never turned out like that.

Some people ask why I didn't stop drinking when I knew I'd had enough?

All I can say to that is, knowing when I'd had enough beer wasn't the problem - it was knowing when I'd had enough rum and whisky! Spirits just did something to me and got me into loads of trouble, as you'll find out.

How any woman could put up with what I put Kerry through, I'll never know.

In the end I lost everything I had through booze.

I even got pissed out of my head when I got my bosun's ticket!

CHAPTER SIXTEEN
SAILING

The fishing industry was changing big style. We weren't fishing off the Norwegian coast trying to catch cod and haddock anymore. The cod wars in Iceland had depleted the fishing industry and some brave men lost their lives on the trawlers, but for what? To be shit on by the trawler owners - yes the trawler owners!

The company I was with received a big contract to catch mackerel off the west coast of Scotland. When the ships had taken on board their full catch they'd go and discharge their catch in Hirtshals in Denmark. You also went to IJmuiden in Holland near Amsterdam and you could be away from port for up to four weeks at a time. You had to do three trips, then after that you got time at home. While you were away you did twelve hours on and six hours off. The work was pretty easy really, once you got into the swing of it. Don't forget, you got your three big meals a day and you sailed with some really good lads at Hamlyn's.

Once I got my bosun's ticket I was home for about four weeks before I got a call out of the blue off Renee. He asked if I wanted my bosun's start on the St Jason. Skipper Ball was having a trip off and fat Fred, who was the mate at the time, was going to be the skipper of the St Jason

I knew fat Fred didn't like me but I couldn't miss this opportunity for my start and it was only going to be for the one trip, then skipper Ball would be back. At the time I signed on, I wasn't sure if the best mate in the fishing industry, Bri Ridsdale, was still the mate of the St Jason.

Unfortunately Bri passed away at home at an early age later on and this was a big loss to the fishing industry. He was an inspiration. Nothing ever got him down and he was always laughing and joking while we were away at sea. I learned a lot from him and to this day I still have happy memories of the guy, God rest his soul.

Anyway, I jumped at the chance to go back on the St Jason, even if fat Fred was taking her for one trip. I could handle any shit he was going to throw at me, no problem.

Well, it was nearly a complete change of crew because the ship had already done her three trips. Renee got all the crew into his office and told us we were to sail on the North Sea ferry, Norland, which would take us to Rotterdam in Holland. Waiting there for us would be a coach to take us to join the St Jason in IJmuiden.

The company had paid for our seats.

'Seats?' somebody questioned.

We were to sleep in what they call 'aeroplane seats' on the ferry. If we wanted a berth and a bed we had to pay for it ourselves as the company would only pay for a seat.

We were given five pounds in travelling expenses and the person in charge of the expenses was to be - Mally Welburn. I was also put in charge of the men to make sure they behaved themselves and didn't get pissed or miss the coach at the other end. It was like being at school and they all said to Renee, 'Yes Sir.'

Renee told everyone a taxi would pick them up and we would then all meet at the ferry's booking-in desk at 4.30 in the afternoon, two days later. Somebody asked when would we be paid our expenses and was told, when the ferry set sail.

Renee asked me to stay behind and laid the law down to me saying, 'Now look young Welburn. This is your chance to prove to everybody you've changed. You'll be looking after sixteen men and need to get them safely to the St Jason.

They'll each be given an extra five pounds which you, as you're the officer, will give them once the ship has sailed.'

I thanked Renee and told him I wouldn't let him down. And I said goodbye to Kerry as the taxi was bibbing its horn.

Remember that you never looked back when you walked out of your door when going away to sea and your woman didn't do any washing on the day you sailed.

'Wash you away,' was the old wives' tale...

We all met up at the booking office of the superferry at King George Dock in Hull and some men were already the worse for wear, drink-wise, which was normal really. When I say normal, in them days nobody said anything if we turned up to join our ship with a drink down our neck. It was okay as long as we weren't legless, because all we had to do was let go of the ropes that moored our trawler to the quay. We had to stow the mooring ropes down the hatches and if we knew the weather was going to be bad, we just battened down the hatches. This was until the next day when we had to work on the deck ahead of three days of steaming towards the fishing grounds. There was time to recover but most men could hold their beer.

Catching a ferry to get to work was a whole new ball game for us. It hadn't happened to any of us before, sailing to another port at the other side of the North Sea. It was like going on a little holiday, waiting to board this superferry, but even though we were going abroad, we didn't need a passport at that time. You could travel on your fisherman's book. That was like a work permit and Renee was there at the booking office just to make sure everyone had turned up. Believe me, there were some bonny sights to look at and you could say there were a few 'Christmas crackers' amongst them and they'd turned up half pissed.

It was then time to board the ferry with about another two hundred paying passengers but before we did, Renee gave us all the gypsy's warning.

'Any trouble on the ferry and you will need a new pair of shoes.' He meant you wouldn't get a job with the company again. It was something I couldn't afford to let happen and on top of it all, I was the officer. I was the one in charge of these men, a good half a dozen of whom knew they were only going on the one trip. You can imagine what it was like when you have sixteen hairy-arsed fishermen, half pissed, going on this deluxe ferry. I was in charge of these lads, 'the pride of the fishing industry'!

When we boarded the ferry we were greeted by the ship's steward and he showed us where we'd be sleeping. These were those 'aeroplane seats', like reclining seats, but I knew the lads would just hit the bar, get really pissed-up and enjoy themselves.

Everything was going really well with people playing on the roulette tables and there was a disco going on. And as expected, there was plenty of drinking going on in the bars and the lads were really enjoying themselves. I made sure I didn't get on the rum but I had a good drink. I wasn't a dancer but some of the lads did hit the dance floor. It was fun mixing with all the other passengers and I was a proud man to be in charge of these men. When it got to the end of the night we hit our so-called beds - the 'aeroplane seats' - but you couldn't get any sleep during the night.

It was pretty quiet, well as quiet as you'd expect from sixteen drunken men trying to sleep in reclining chairs. Some of the lads were in high spirits and singing and kept getting told to keep their voices down.

I had a couple of mates on the journey with me, big John Mays and Gibbo, they were my drinking buddies on the night. Well, about three in the morning, the three of us decided to try and find an empty berth so we could crash out properly. As we were going up and down the passageways we kept trying all the cabin doors, hoping one would be empty so we could get our heads down, but none were open.

I remember going down one passageway and as we passed one cabin the door was open and there were four Dutch guys in there having a drink with music on. They said something in Dutch, but we couldn't understand what they were saying, though I knew it wasn't, 'Hello, come in and have a drink.'

It was more like, 'Fuck off, you English bastards!'

Outside their cabin were two boxes of what I thought were Walkers crisps, you know, the boxes which hold forty-eight packets each. On the side of each box it said, 'Cheese and Onion.' I thought, I could just eat a packet of those, they're my favourites. So I stuck my hand into what I thought was a box of crisps, but it turned out to be something rather different. Because as soon as I put my hand in the box, something started to peck at it!

Shocked, I quickly pulled my hand out thinking, 'What the fuck's in there!' For all I knew it could have been a live snake. As I pulled my hand out, four pigeons flew out the box.

Two of the Dutch guys came bouncing out of their cabin screaming some Dutch crap and running at me with their fists flying. Before I knew it, big John had put one of them on his arse and was rolling about with him in the alleyway.

This other guy came for me, screaming in Dutch and you could see he wasn't bothered that I had my hands in the air, I was surrendering. I was sorry for what had happened but it all happened so quickly as he tried to headbutt me. Our heads met and he went down and left me thinking, 'Oh fuck, we're in the shit now.'

I dragged John off this other guy and said, 'Let's get back to the aeroplane seats.' I just couldn't believe what we'd just done - and on my first trip as an officer! I'd been thinking of getting myself a new pair of shoes anyway but I also knew I'd be out of a job! Well nothing happened until seven o'clock in the morning when we were getting our continental breakfast - you know them fancy buns and that.

These Dutch guys, four of them, were with three or four stewards, looking and pointing at us. One of the Dutch guys had a bandage round his head; he looked like an Egyptian mummy. He had blood stains on the bandage and blood still dripping down his cheek. The other guy had a black eye and the other two Dutch guys kept pointing towards me and big John.

Big Johnnie Mays is about six foot four, built like a barn door and with his short, blond hair he stuck out like that sore thumb. I don't know about the Dutch guy, I suspect he must have had a sore head.

Well nothing happened at breakfast but when the ship was ready to dock in Rotterdam, we heard, in broken English, over the ship's tannoy, 'Would the crew of the St Jason please wait at the disembarking desk. Could Mr Welburn please gather his crew together, thank you. To all other passengers, thank you for travelling with North Sea Ferries, we hope you enjoyed your journey and hope to see you again soon.'

Well, as we gathered at the disembarking desk, there waiting for us were four Dutch police officers and four ship stewards. There was also the Dutch guy who looked like the mummy and his three sidekicks with the two boxes of Walkers crisps which had his re-caught pigeons in.

One steward told us that the police wanted to question the people who had assaulted the two Dutchmen for no apparent reason. As soon as they found out who had done this we could all get on our way.

MALLY - THE REBEL WITHOUT A PAUSE

He added nobody was going to get on the waiting coach to join our ship until they had the man or men who had done it. Well, we had a code of honour amongst fishermen in them days and you didn't grass on your fellow man. Nobody said anything. One of the Dutch coppers then said,

'Will the person or the persons who have done this to these men please step forward.'

Nobody moved.

'Okay I will ask once again, will the person or persons who have done this to these men please step forward. If nobody does then you will all be arrested, as we do know who has done it.'

'If you know who's done it, arrest them now and we can get on our way, we've a ship to catch,' I said.

He called me John Wayne, I don't know why.

'Listen John Wayne, you're in charge of these animals and if you don't tell us who has done it, you will be arrested,' he said.

'I don't know, but surely *they* should know who had done it,' I replied.

'Okay Mr Wayne,' said the copper, 'I will ask them to pick out the men who have done it and we will take it from there.'

The one who looked like the mummy obviously didn't know who'd hit him. He looked puzzled and a bit confused. His mate had a big black eye so he could hardly see straight and the other two had still been in the cabin at the time it happened.

None of our crew stepped forward and to be honest a few of our lads could hardly stand, let alone step forward as they'd been on the piss all night. The Dutch copper went back to the mummy and his mates and they started whispering amongst themselves. I looked across at big Johnnie Mayes and Gibbo, giving them the wink, as if to say, keep yer head down and don't say anything.

The next thing I knew, the mummy and the black-eyed guy were walking in front of us. They stopped in front of each and every one of the crew, it was like an identity parade, you know, like you see on the police television programmes.

They stopped in front of me and one of the Dutchmen said, 'He was one,' pointing me out to one of the coppers. I was asked to go and stand with the other policemen.

They carried on down the line and yes, they stopped at big John and Gibbo, why they didn't just pick us out at the start I'll never know.

The coppers said to the rest of the crew that they could leave the ferry to go and join their ship. But to my surprise the rest of the crew refused to leave the ferry until we joined them.

The copper told us three we were going to the Customs Office, which was ashore and there was no point in the rest of the crew waiting for us as we could be a while. So the rest of the crew were led to the coach, under a police escort and unbeknown to us, as soon as the crew got on the coach it left without us.

The Dutch police led big John, Gibbo and me to the Customs building and all the time I'm thinking, fucking hell I'm in shit here. I've just got my first start as a bosun and here I am on the verge of getting deported and looking for a new pair of shoes. We were put in this office which had a big see-through window, a big table and four chairs. We sat in the chairs and talked amongst ourselves. Big John was so laid back, he didn't care what was happening and put his feet on the table. He was shouting at the mummy and the black-eyed guy every time they looked through the window. It was as though we were fish in a fishbowl.

We were in the office and we realised they didn't know who had hit who so we did a deal amongst ourselves. Whoever got done for the clout on the mummy and the black-eyed one would take the rap. And if they got sent home the other two would give them a big back-hander.

Big John said, 'Don't fucking worry. They started it and they shouldn't be carrying pigeons on board and they haven't got a clue who hit them.'

The 'Chief' of the Dutch police came in and spoke to all three of us.

The Dutch guys had admitted they told us to fuck off and when the pigeons were let loose, the bandaged guy, admitted hitting one of us. He then asked us to say in our own words what had happened, then we could get things sorted out and we could rejoin the ship.

We all said together, 'It was them who started it.'

MALLY - THE REBEL WITHOUT A PAUSE

I added, I thought the boxes contained bags of crisps and I didn't know they had pigeons in them. Then before I knew what was happening this big guy came towards me throwing punches and he headbutted me. The copper said he knew all of this but wanted to know who hit the other guy? Nobody said anything.

The copper went out of the room and the next thing we knew they were all at the window again pointing at us.

I said to John, 'It's either me or you who's going home.'

John said, 'It won't be me Mally,' as he pulled a few faces at the audience who were looking at us. Throughout all this Gibbo was very quiet. Then after about an hour the copper came back in and told us they'd decided who they would be sending home and reporting for assault. My arse was twitching but to my surprise they picked big John out.

He was taken straight out of the room shouting and screaming but to this day the code has still never been broken. As we agreed, John was well looked after when we got back home.

He ended up running his own pub and the trip proved to be his last one to sea I believe. John is a good man and I was only on the phone with him a few weeks ago. John said to me,

'Mally when you write your book don't forget to tell the story of the ferry, you owe me big style.'

I look forward to visiting John and his family and taking them out for a well-deserved meal.

They took John away and Gibbo and me were told we could go join our ship. I asked where the coach was and was told it had left over an hour ago. We had to get a taxi to where our ship was berthed. We were told, after a phone call to Renee, to go and see the ship's agent and he'd pay for the taxi but it would come out of our wages. Believe it or not we got there before the coach, the taxi drivers drive very fast in Holland...

Skipper Fred wasn't a happy chap and I knew he'd got the perfect excuse to sack me when we'd done our three trips. Don't forget we did the three trips in one and each trip might be for four weeks. But we fished for mackerel and if the fishing grounds were rich in mackerel you could be at sea less than twenty days on each trip.

My job as bosun was like being a charge-hand in a factory because that's all it was, you were just working in a factory on a ship. We'd catch up to fifty tons of mackerel for one hour's fishing, we called it 'dip and fill'. We fished off the North West coast of Scotland, not far from the Outer Hebrides, it was a popular place called the Minch. We also caught fish off Cape Wrath and the Kyle of Lochalsh. There is some beautiful scenery around the coast of Scotland and I've also been to the Scottish port of Ullapool a few times.

When we left Holland for the Scottish fishing grounds it would be a good couple of days steam even if you had a back wind. We always seemed to hit bad weather off the Shetland Islands or going through the Pentland Firth.

My job was to be in charge of the men in the factory and also to take a steaming watch on the bridge. This was when we were steaming to the fishing grounds and I used to love it on the bridge. I took watch with two watch-mates, I just couldn't beat being on the bridge, watching the shooting stars at night and doing all the navigation. I loved it and I'd take the midnight to breakfast watch. But once we started fishing it was work, work and more work but I loved that as well. It made life easier if you had a daddy of a skipper like Arthur Ball. On this trip it was fat Fred who did his best to keep you at work on the deck, even when there wasn't anything to do. I was glad he was only going to be the skipper for this one trip, I guess I could put up with him until skipper Ball came back.

When you are fishing for mackerel you used what was called, mid water trawl. It was called a pelagic trawl. You never fished for mackerel on the seabed as they always swam mid water. The net was very long and you fished from the stern of the ship, hence the name stern trawler and the trawl could be as long as a football pitch. You then had your two big trawl doors, which weighed about a ton apiece. You were pulling all this lot on the end of your two, half mile long wire warps. Then, when it was time to get your nets in, it would all be winched in on one big drum, which was operated from the bridge.

The factory was the same as for fishing for cod and haddock but these freezers had a divider in them. Instead of having twenty, ten stone blocks you'd get forty, four stone blocks.

When the freezers were full they were left to freeze for four hours and then it came to 'knocking out time'. That was where one man would knock the blocks out of the freezer. The blocks used to lift up out of the freezer and the same man would put a plastic bag on each individual block of mackerel. He then turned round with the block in his hand to where a man would be waiting with a cardboard box. The box then went onto a conveyor belt to another man on a strapping machine and from there down to the men in the Wembley Stadium-sized fishroom.

Four men were in the other factory where the freshly caught fish would be stored. We called it 'the ramp' and it could hold anything up to twenty tons of fish.

So as one freezer was emptied two men would follow you, filling it up again. It worked like clockwork and if we had the fish we could process fifty tons a day.

All the cardboard boxes were stored in the Wembley size fishroom - and at the end of every watch we had to go in there and get enough boxes for the next watch - and they then did the same for us. We had two teams of ten men on each watch. It was the young deckie-learner's job to make up the flat pack cardboard boxes ready for the frozen blocks to go into.

It was very much like working in a factory when we were packing frozen mackerel. But the difference was when it was rough weather, the job was a hundred times harder! Skipper Fred cared little about his men even if we were in storm force conditions. He'd fish in any weather, even though his men were getting thrown around in the factory - to him it was part and parcel of the job.

While we were searching for mackerel down the west coast of Scotland it was reported that ships were catching up to seventy tons of mackerel for a ten minute tow - dip and fill. This was in the English Channel, just off Lizard Point and not far away from Land's End.

The reports of the amount of mackerel told of a shoal stretching twenty miles long by fourteen miles wide. They also went down twenty fathoms and there are six feet to the fathom. I'll let you work it out, but there was well over a million tons of mackerel on the move, it was birthday time.

It was a two or three day steam down to Land's End and on the way we developed engine trouble. The Chief Engineer said we had to go into port to get it sorted out.

The nearest port was a place called Cobh which is near Cork in southern Ireland and what a beautiful place that was to visit. Just a piece of history for you as well, Cobh was the last place the Titanic stopped off at before it sailed to America, it stopped for ice, how spooky is that?

I've been to some lovely places when we were fishing on the trawlers. It makes me smile when I think of the thousands of pounds people pay to visit some of those places today. We got to visit them for free and southern Ireland is one of the friendliest places I was able to visit.

We got tied up in Cobh, a really beautiful little fishing village where the experts came aboard to check the engine problem. We were told it could take up to two weeks to repair the engine and to get the St Jason ready for sea again.

It was decided to send the crew home, only a skeleton crew would remain to look after the ship. That basically meant to slacken or tighten the mooring ropes every twelve hours for the rise and fall of the tide.

Fat Fred asked for volunteers who had to consist of an officer, a deckhand, two engineers and someone to knock our grub up for us. I drew the short straw for the officer to take the watch. The chief engineer I think was Harry Williams and the second engineer was the legendary Jack Spinks, who must have been seventy at that time. But old Jack was one of the characters of the fishing game. He was a flyweight boxing champion in his days in the Navy and he was very quick-witted and very fast with his hands even at the tender age of seventy. He suffered with poor eyesight. So we thought. He had to come nose to nose to see you but that was when he'd give you that double-quick, twice as fast as lighting, clout round the lugs. And as he took a quick step back after he gave you the quick one-two he would do the 'Ali shuffle'. He'd then remove his glasses and say, 'Don't be fooled by the glasses, I can see better without them!'

Oh I do miss old Jack Spinks - he was a lovely man - and taught me a few moves in my time.

I can't remember who the deckie was that stayed behind with me but I recall that no cook stayed. So there were only four of us altogether staying behind as we said our goodbyes to the other sixteen or so members of the crew who all flew home from Dublin airport. I also remember Fat Fred's parting words to me were, 'I know what gear we have down the hold so don't be selling it all.'

Well to cut a long story short we were there for a good ten days - and we only got £5 a day expenses - and beer was about two quid a pint! But we made sure we got more than that from the ropes, shackles, wires, cables, engine oil, big tins of coffee, meat - and other things that we thought the rest of the crew wouldn't notice had gone when they came back.

I made enough money to send home to Kerry to pay the mortgage and put towards a fish van and a fish round that I was going to buy with my brother, Mike.

The fish van and round was going to cost about eight hundred quid. I know the chief got a good holiday out of that time spent in southern Ireland.

I think we maybe overdid it a bit! Because some of the stuff we sold for a bit of pocket money came to light when all the crew came back. We made sure that each and every member of the crew received two cases of long life beer and a bottle of rum in their berth, ready for a welcome back party. But the party turned into a brawl while we were steaming to the gold mine of the fishing grounds. And three or four of Fred's mates got a good hiding after going on the bridge and telling him how we'd sold a lot of the ship's gear.

I sailed with some sneaky bastards, they were okay drinking the booze but they then went and told tales to the skipper...

The biggest surprise we got during the trip was when we lost all our nets and wires fishing amongst this massive shoal of mackerel. And when it came to replacing the nets and wires the skipper found out he didn't have any! That's when Fred put two and two together...

I knew then that I was going to be on a big walk about and get a new pair of shoes when I got home. But luckily for us one of our sister ships, the St Jerome, was leaving the fishing grounds full up. And they passed all the gear that we required for us to carry on fishing and within two weeks we were steaming back to IJmuiden in Holland full up, with five hundred tons of frozen mackerel to be exported to Africa.

When we used to dock in IJmuiden there used to be about eighty men waiting to unload our catch. They didn't mess about. Within two days our catch was unloaded and new cardboard boxes were put down into the fishroom and we were ready to go back out to sea again.

During the two days 'turnaround' we were allowed to go to see the 'sights' in Amsterdam. As you might guess, we certainly had some adventures! I'll explain later about the 'Green Door' in the famous Red Light district. But for now, back to the St Jason...

Luckily for me the daddy of all daddies, Arthur Ball, came back to skipper the St Jason and Fred had his trip off, so I kept my job that trip. I loved it when skipper Ball was on the bridge. We never heard him. He never screamed out of the bridge windows and he never treated his crew like dogs. He commanded the utmost respect, not like some of the arseholes of skippers I sailed with.

I did my three trips on the St Jason and skipper Ball was the master at just catching the edge of the shoal of mackerel and just catching the forty to fifty tons which was a day's work. Some skippers would get greedy and think it was clever to catch seventy tons in one go and end up dumping thirty tons down the shit chute. I thought it was criminal to dump dead fish but all the time I was with skipper Ball very little went through the shit chute, unlike some of the ships I sailed on.

They say that at one time in Newlyn Bay where we used to anchor and process our catch, along with anywhere up to another twenty or thirty trawlers, the dumped fish was anywhere from six feet to eight feet deep on the sea bed - all dead, rotten mackerel.

It was disgraceful to dump fish but if we refused we would have been out of work! That's the way it was! Skippers ran the show and did anything they liked, within reason.

We even had one skipper who when we were at anchor in Mount's Bay just off Penzance, would get on the little pilot boat and go play darts for a pub in Newlyn. He would make sure we always had enough fish by Tuesday, so he could play darts. That was skipper Tom on the St Jerome. We used to love it when he donned his trilby and we'd see him leave the ship with his darts in his top pocket.

Do you know, it got to the stage in the fishing industry that to save money for the trawler owners, when we'd finished our trip, instead of all the crew going to Holland and flying home, we'd get dropped off just outside the seaside resort of Bridlington. When I say dropped off, I mean a couple of little fishing boats would come alongside our ship and we had to climb down the rope ladder and jump onto them.

It was the same going away. We'd have a coach waiting outside our ship's office on the day we were due to go away.

It would take us to Bridlington bay where we'd climb back up the rope ladder and onto our trawler for another trip. How no one got killed getting transferred from one small ship to a massive ship, especially when the weather was a bit rough, I'll never know.

I think 'the health and safety' people finally got wind of the trawler owners' antics and the way they were transferring their men. They were made to go and tie up in a port so that the crew could get aboard safely. It got to the stage where we would catch a coach outside the office and travel all the way down to Milford Haven in Wales.

The skipper, mate, a couple of deckies and the chief engineer would take the aeroplane backwards and forwards to Holland to fetch the ship to Milford Haven. That was the cheapest way of doing it.

By this time, they wouldn't let anybody travel without passports - and in those days it could take up to six weeks to get a passport. On top of that I don't think the trawler owners liked the idea of twenty drunken fishermen going round Amsterdam. Plus, that ever-decreasing shoal of mackerel had moved round to the Irish Sea, so it was quicker to pick the crew up at Milford Haven. That became the way of life for the next five years or so, until it got to the stage where we were spending more time looking for the mackerel than we were processing it!

A vast number of nations were 'attacking' the mackerel shoals. The Russians had the big factory ships, which stayed at sea for up to a year, some of them. Honestly - some of them mother ships were as big as the QE2. They would have all these little ships that would catch the fish. They would lift a little ship out of the sea and discharge its catch aboard the mother ship. Then lift it back over the side and some of those 'little' ships were half the size of St Jason - and St Jason was a big ship then. And there could be up to six of those big Russian mother ships anchored off Mount's Bay when we were there! God only knows what amount of mackerel the Russians took from our waters!

The Spaniards were known to be the pirates - they would always be seen in the non-fishing zones. We always wondered how the other fishermen from the other nations lived their lives aboard their ships and what life style our fellow fishermen had?

A mackerel fisherman's life for us was: We would get signed on by the ship's runner, Renee. We didn't need much sea gear. We were only working in a floating factory really. There wasn't much deck work but we still needed our duck suits - waterproofs - and wellies, although it wasn't the same as fishing in the sidewinder trawlers and sailing off Iceland, Norway, Greenland etc.

We couldn't escape the storm force gales in them days but with this mackerel lark, if the weather got too rough, we would only be about twelve miles off land and we could always go and drop anchor in Mount's Bay, so that skipper Tom could go play his darts. It really was an easy life.

It got to the stage in this mackerel game where we didn't need to be fishermen anymore. After all, we were only working in a floating factory and that's something I never set my stall out for in life. I wanted to be that hunter. Where we went out in our fishing boat in storm force winds and tried to find the fish, hunt it and catch it. It was the thrill of the chase. It's a bit like life really isn't it? How many times do we go chasing something we want. But when we've caught it, the thrill goes until your next catch, unless we're happy with our catch!

Well the cod and haddock were like the women I've chased and loved - which now, like the cod and haddock, are getting harder and harder to catch! But the mackerel gave itself up.

We didn't have to go far. We didn't have to hunt - and the thrill was not there. It was too easy. The mackerel was too easy. There was that much of it - and in life we can sometimes get too much of a good thing can't we?

The mackerel game was like that - it was an easy way of life. Don't get me wrong, when the fish was there you did your twelve hours work but it was factory work, just packing the

MALLY - THE REBEL WITHOUT A PAUSE

freezers with full body mackerel. There was no gutting. Any 'wooden top' could do it - and this was sometimes proved when men came to sea for the very first time in their lives, just to work in the factory.

We used to say, 'Real fishermen used to be made of steel and the ships were made of wood - but nowadays the ships are made of steel and the men are made of wood'.

I was heading towards being one of them 'wooden tops' but I had one thing that most of the 'wooden tops' never had - a bosun's ticket - and every ship had to carry a bosun.

The Board of Trade made all trawlers over a certain size carry four officers. On each ship there had to be a skipper, a mate, a second mate and a bosun. My bosun's ticket therefore came in very handy because without bragging, factory workers were ten a penny.

My ticket got me on a few trawlers even if the skipper didn't like me. But he would have been told to take me, simply because I was the only one available at the time - just like the time I sailed on the Arctic Corsair in Part One. Sometimes even if I didn't sail as bosun, I would get the same pay as a bosun. But I didn't want to be just a factory worker, so if I wasn't bosun, I'd be factory manager - that's what I liked. I like to be in charge. I need to be the captain, so to speak.

I need to be in charge of men and I would lead by example. But I would work alongside any 'wooden top' and put them to shame because I was a grafter first and foremost and so were a lot of ex-deep sea trawler men. All the older men had known was hard work, but us young uns would make sure it was *us* who did all the hard work. Like knocking the frozen blocks of fish out of the freezers and doing all the heavy lifting. We'd make sure the old sea dogs only got the push button jobs in the factory. But I could still see in some of these old sea dogs' faces, like my old mate Terry Platten, that they also didn't set out in life to be workers in a factory.

I could see the sadness in their eyes and Terry would say, 'What the fuck are we doing out here Mally? We could be working at Birds Eye, packing fish fingers and getting more money than what we're getting for the hours we're doing! And you could be in your own cosy bed cuddling up to your lass and I could be in the betting shop, putting a bet on every day. We're doing eighteen hours a day in a factory when we have the fish. Work out how much we'd get at Birds Eye for all the hours we do, Mally.'

Terry was right. We used to go down to Milford Haven to join the ship together on a freezing, fucking bus. We got our pack-up off the company for the ten to twelve hour journey - sometimes when we had a new driver, it could be a lot longer. We'd tell him to call in at a country pub and then stay there drinking for hours. Or we'd get him to stop in Birmingham so that we could have a hot meal and a pint because the apple, orange, pork pie and chocolate bar was not enough to fill us up. Not if we were to sail as soon as we got to Milford Haven. We knew there would be no hot meal because the cook would be on the bus with us and God help him if he was a belly robbing bastard. The company also gave us £5 travelling expenses but we would use that five quid for playing cards at the back of the bus and Terry would always be in the school. Terry was the life and soul of the party for a sixty-year-old. He came from a family of fishermen and I'd sailed with most of Terry's sons.

Terry was everybody's Dad. He was a man of steel who didn't like this new way of fishing and it was the young kids' job to make sure the likes of old man Terry Platten got an easy job like pushing the on and off button on the conveyor belt.

I'd say to Terry as I was sweating after a good workout in the fishroom, storing four hundred blocks of frozen mackerel,

'Terry, I don't think Birds Eye would allow you to sit on yer arse for twelve hours a day smoking non-stop. And don't forget the pot of tea you sneak into the factory and how every four hours you go and watch a film or play cards for a couple of hours. Then all you do is press that button for another four hours and you always get a good eight hours sleep. You can't beat that can you Terry?'

'Oh, but you can't beat the good old days, Mally,' he'd shout. Then I'd say, 'Don't forget to press that button now Terry because the fish is piling up at the other end of the belt - we don't want you bending your back now.'

'I'll throw *you* on the belt, Welburn, I'm not scared of you,' he'd reply as he gave me that playful slap on my head.

Happy days! I often still see Terry in the betting shop

MALLY - THE REBEL WITHOUT A PAUSE

nowadays. It was nearly twenty years ago since I sailed with Terry but to me it only seems like yesterday. He still has that quick wit about him although he must be about eighty now.

And when I ask him, 'How's life Terry?' he always says 'Fine', but then he usually continues, 'We had some good times Mally didn't we? I'm really proud of what you've done for yourself but you can't beat the good old days, can you Mally?'

In some ways, I agree with him. I can still see that 'man of steel' in his eyes. Terry Platten was everybody's daddy when I sailed with him. I loved him...

But where were we?

I was telling you about my way of life as a mackerel fisherman from Hull in the late 70's and early 80's. It was the same, trip in, trip out.

Sign on, get the freezing bus down to Milford - and don't forget my apple, orange, pork pie - and a Kit-Kat if I was lucky. Stop off on the way to Milford, anywhere there was a pub would do. Have a fight with a few locals.

Get back on the bus, get to Milford Haven and sail as soon as we got there. And if the fish was there to give itself up, we'd be doing factory work for up to twenty-one days!

Come home on the bus. Then pick up five or six hundred quid - if we were lucky. Because if you lost playing cards on the way home you paid your dues as soon as you picked your money up! We would still have a settling day, where all the crew and their wives and girlfriends would meet up. Then we had a day at home and again, before we knew it, we would be back on that bus!

We got a day at home for every week we were away. They stopped that 'three trips in - one away' business.

Some men refused to do non-stop, boring factory work - unless they needed the money. There was always a 'wooden top' ready to jump in your place but as I said, I was pretty safe having my bosun's ticket.

I knew I was never going to be a skipper if mackerel fishing was going to become the way of life. A skipper on the mackerel was never going to have a trip off - it was the best job they could've had - and vacancies for skippers were going to be few and far between.

I don't know whether skipper Tom actually got to the Embassy darts final but he did have a look of Jockey Wilson, the great darts player of the time!

I was at sea when my darling first daughter, Tammie was born on October 3 1980. I was sailing on the St Jason at the time; we'd just left Ullapool in Scotland when I got the news of Tammie's birth. I got really pissed when I heard. I think it was the first time I missed the boat - I didn't get out of my bunk for work - but skipper Ball understood.

In them early days of the mackerel game we had to do three trips at sea and then had 'one trip' at home. But we didn't get any wages when we were on our trip off. We had to sign on the dole and then wait a week to get our money. And that wasn't much. When we sat down and worked out the hours we did for the pay we picked up - we'd certainly have been better off working at the Birds Eye fish finger factory!

I was looking for something else to do work-wise because it was right, I could earn more working in a factory ashore than I could on the mackerel trawlers.

It might have been possible to earn the money on the bigger, more modern ships but Hull never had them at the time. To be fair, the St Jason, St Jasper, St Jerome and St Benedict were ten years behind the modern day trawlers of the time.

Those modern trawlers were called purse net trawlers. They were big ships - not quite as big as the QE2 - and maybe the biggest purse trawler at the time was the St Lorman.

Its nets were like a big purse and the nets would cover the new Wembley football pitch! They could catch up to a thousand tons of mackerel in one go and land it fresh. The crew were on a percentage of the catch sold on the fresh fish markets of Holland and Denmark and the word was that the deckhands were picking up anything from two to four grand a week. I naturally wanted a bit of that - and I got it!

Yes, our company had bought it - and it was a memorable day when I got to sail on the biggest modern-day purse trawler, the St Lorman.

That was just after I came out of prison in July 1984 after getting fifteen months in November 1983 and serving nine months for a wounding charge and two assaults in less than two days...

MALLY - THE REBEL WITHOUT A PAUSE

You've got all that to come yet. But I've got to get us to the events that led to my spell in prison, so allow me to tell you about that later, I promise I will.

That trip on the St Lorman really pulled Kerry and me out of the shit, money-wise. We were on the bones of our arses with me doing that spell in prison, because before I got to sail on the St Lorman I was one of them 'wooden tops' and it was not for me. I just couldn't see me doing that for the rest of my life. Most of my mates were leaving the fishing industry to find work on the oilrigs or on the rigs' standby boats - that was good money then.

You did a month on and a month off on the standby boats - and you were on the same pay when you were at home. It worked out better than working on the out-of-date factory ships but you had to go up to Scotland to do more schooling. And you had to pay for the course yourself and most of us fishermen did not believe in saving money.

We were the 'live for the day' breed because we never knew whether we'd be coming back from what Mother Nature threw at us! She'd really test us with severe gale force winds and those mountainous seas off the coast of Greenland and Norway, with nowhere to run for shelter.

Oh, those were the days. Terry was right - you can't beat the good old days. The good old days meant the thrill of the chase and the adventure.

You can't beat the thrill of the chase - and going on that adventure...

See ya,
Mally the 'Wooden top'

CHAPTER SEVENTEEN
IT'S FOUR IN THE MORNING

That's the time I had to set my alarm clock at - four in the morning! That's the time I had to get up when I bought this fish van round - when I was having one of my trips off from sea in late 1980. You remember, after you did three trips you had one trip off.

It was while I was having a trip off, baby Tammie was having problems, as she couldn't keep her milk down. She was always in pain, crying every hour of the day and night.

We knew there was something wrong with our six-week old baby but the doctor and the visiting nurse just put it down to wind and baby problems.

As you can gather, it was a testing time having baby Tammie crying in pain, twenty-four hours of the day, but Kerry was the most patient and loving Mother any child could ever have.

We used to take it in turns during the night to get up and give Tammie her bottle. It could take up to an hour just to get a two-ounce bottle of baby milk into her. Then as soon as we got the two ounces down her she'd start crying all over again. We knew there was something wrong with Tammie, but we were dismissed as being over-protective parents. We were first time parents, though I'd already had a baby boy, Peter, with the first love of my life, Karen.

I'd been told Karen had moved on and she didn't want me banging on her door pissed up anymore. I couldn't go demanding to see my baby boy every time I came home from sea in the early days of young Peter's life.

What an arsehole I was then, but it wasn't until Peter was six years of age that we went to court over maintenance payments. To be fair, I wasn't there for Peter growing up. And when I look back on my life, it's one of my biggest regrets.

I vowed I would never lose contact with my two girls even when I was going through my marriage break-up with Kerry.

MALLY - THE REBEL WITHOUT A PAUSE

I take all the blame for my marriage breakdown to one of the most beautiful women you could ever meet and she hasn't changed in looks at all. Kerry didn't deserve all the shit I put her through in the time we were together.

I also need to tell you it was the love of my two daughters, which kept me going later, when I was going through the dark days in the business world. They were my light and it's now my job to try and secure my children's and grandchildren's future. Let's not forget my son Peter, he's in his 30s now. I've met up with him a good few times and I know the bond is still there and the bridges are being built. People tell me he's the spitting image of me and has the same mannerisms and characteristics as me. And before you say it, I know - they must be two huge burdens for him to have to carry through life. There was never any doubt Peter was my son but I still had to have the blood tests done to prove he was mine. This was before the judge would award the maintenance payments of £5 a week when I was working and five pence a week when I wasn't - yes five pence!

I think I got into arrears paying the five pence over the years when I was out of work. It was when Karen moved out of town for a while and I lost contact with her.

There comes a time when you have to let go - and it took me quite a while to let go of Karen and young Peter.

Well Tammie was six weeks old and couldn't take the manufactured milk, you know the powdered stuff. The four scoops or something like that, with boiled water, and then waiting for the water to cool. Not forgetting to test the temperature of the milk by squeezing it onto your wrist - a bit like testing the bath water with your elbow. But poor Tammie was in agony and Kerry had the doctor out more times than enough and for good cause in the end.

It was while I was on my trip off from St Jason, the mackerel-catching trawler, and the money we were getting, for the hours we were doing it, wasn't worth it. Was it really worth going to sea for less than £1.50 an hour?

Work it out for yourself - 24 hours a day at sea for three weeks picking up £500 when you finally got home. Where was William Wilberforce when we needed him?

What was the point in going to sea as a fisherman when all

you did was factory work?

Gone were the days when we went to sea, fishing for cod and haddock and earning good money. The days when we were three-day millionaires when we got home from sea. The days when we were at least earning more money than the dustmen. By the mid-80s dustmen were earning more money than us mackerel men! It was time for me to look for another job!

Thankfully the opportunity came along when I saw an advert in the local paper. An old guy was selling his 'established fish round' which was reportedly earning £600 for two days. He stood outside a chemist selling fresh fish from the back of a nice little van that was all lined out with stainless steel shelves. There was some top of the range weighing scales to weigh the fish and the round was a bargain at £800. He was making £300 profit for two days but he was paying way over the odds for his fish.

I checked all his books before we bought the business, we, being my brother Michael and me. Michael is three years older than me and is one of the best, if not *the* best fish filleter in Hull. Put him and other brother Richard together and they're unbeatable. They were born to fillet fish and to this day Michael still does.

I can't be doing with standing at a freezing tub of water, filleting fish eight hours a day and ending up with a hump on my back. That's not for me, I like to be on the go. I want the challenges in life. I can't do a mundane job with no prospects. I was going into business, buying this fish van and fish round...

I had a bit of money put away from my time in Cobh in southern Ireland - when me and the rest of the skeleton crew sold a lot of gear while the St Jason was laid up.

The plan was that Mike would fillet all the fish we bought from the market and I'd stand and sell the fish outside the chemist. We bought it for half the price the old man got it for so we knew we were on a winner.

The £300 profit was soon turned into £400 for just two days work. I'd have had to work nearly a full trip at sea on the mackerel trawler for that amount of money!

We'd only had the fish round about three weeks and in that time we acquired two disused garages. We set up our own little fish-filleting place with Mike being so fast with a filleting knife. We used to get other fish sent to us for our kid to fillet so we were earning money both ways. Mike was filleting the other people's fish and ours and I was going out selling. I even found another pitch where we could make another couple of hundred quid profit.

But then out of the blue, I got the call to go second mate of the St Jason with skipper Ball, the daddy. It meant more wages and more money on the tonnage we landed, and instead of me picking up £500, I could easily pick up £1,200 for basically being in the factory.

After talking with our kid and Kerry, it was decided I would go and do the three trips at sea. It meant our kid could drop at least £150 a week off to Kerry, this on top of the £100 I was allowed to send home in wages each week whilst I was away. I couldn't lose, I was on a good thing, in fact I was on more money than the mate of the trawler. I could be a three-day millionaire again, when I got home from sea!

I knew our kid would be down at the dock for four in a morning to get the amount of fish we needed for the two days on our pitch. He could get the fish off the docks and within four hours could have earned us £200. He could also be at home for dinner most days.

Kerry said she would be okay with Tammie as she could always rely on her loving Mother Pat. I'll say again, Pat's one of, if not the best mother-in-law you could ever wish for. I still call her my mother-in-law to this day as I may have divorced Kerry but I never divorced Pat! Pat is more than a mother-in-law, she's a friend and has helped me out more times than I can remember over the years. One occasion was when one of the managers from Reckitt and Colman, the makers of Dettol antiseptic, went knocking on her door.

It was about me selling my 'Dettol-like' antiseptic door to door. The leaflet I was using to advertise it had Pat's address and phone number on it. I got 10,000 leaflets posted out and I was selling nearly 400 one gallon bottles a week.

I was making a pound a bottle profit and he wanted to take me to court for using the Dettol name but Pat came to my rescue, with her ladylike charm. But that, as they say or as I sometimes do, is another story...

Now let me get back to the fish round because it was that which later on stopped me going back to sea for another three years!

The prospects were too good to miss selling fresh fish, but I really had to do the three, three week trips on the St Jason. I was just thinking about how much we could earn. With me sending wages home and our kid dropping off £150 a week to my wife, nothing could go wrong, could it? You bet it could! There was me on the St Jason, getting thrown all over the place in storm force winds, searching for the mackerel. It didn't bother me because all the time I was saying to myself, 'At least our kid will have dropped some money into my wife and it'll keep us going.'

I did one trip and when we went in to land our catch, I rang home to see if everything was okay. One thing you were never told was bad news. Everything was always okay at home. Even if it wasn't okay, your wife or girlfriend would always tell you it was, unless there'd been a death. That was different. No, everything was okay with baby Tammie, she was sleeping for two hours now and Mike had been round, said he was busy and everything was going well.

He told Kerry to tell me he'd give me the money he'd made when I came home.

I asked if Mike had been dropping off the £150 a week and the answer she gave me was, 'No.' He said it was because of the bad weather and there not being a lot of fish around. Mike said he was busy trying to get more customers to build the fish round up ready for when there was some more fish about. Kerry told me Mike had even took a job being a bouncer in a nightclub in Whitby with Raymond and two of his mates.

I told Kerry to tell Mike not to use the van for going to Whitby, it wasn't insured for that, but did he listen?

While I was on my second trip of the three, skipper Ball called me to the bridge and told me he'd just had a phone call from the office at home. He'd been told to tell me Tammie had been rushed into hospital and the ship was taking me into the port of Ullapool in Scotland. From there a taxi would take me home, yes a taxi all the way from Scotland to Hull, it's about 200 miles!

I was allowed to use the ship's phone to ring mother-in-law

MALLY - THE REBEL WITHOUT A PAUSE

Pat to see what was wrong. I found out Tammie had been rushed to hospital because she still wasn't keeping her milk down. They thought she may have a bug or something so they'd rushed her in and she'd been in hospital for two days. Fucking hell, Tammie was in intensive care. I panicked.

Why wasn't I told two days earlier?

Pat had rung the office but some clown hadn't passed the message on to Renee. That made me even madder because I knew he would have sorted things out there and then.

Sometimes the trawler owners were a bit slow in sending news unless it was a death. After all they didn't want to stop their ships from fishing, did they?

Just when I thought things couldn't get any worse - they did! While I was on the phone to Pat I was also told Michael had been involved in a bad accident coming home from Whitby.

With the country roads not being lit up, and with black ice on the roads, he'd skidded and lost control of the van!

He'd gone off the road and piled the van into a tree putting two men in hospital, it was a serious accident. Mike was okay but there was a worry over one of the blokes who was in the back of the van, he was in a very bad way...

Twenty-four hours later I was at the bedside of my darling daughter Tammie.

They were doing tests on her to find out why she couldn't keep her milk down. We were in the hospital for 14 days, even sleeping in the ward alongside Tammie's bed.

On the very first day of the fourteen days the police came and arrested me for dangerous driving, driving a van with no insurance, endangering people's lives - and criminal damage to a tree! They took me to the police station and read the charges out, that on such and such a date I was driving a white Escort van. I had no insurance and dangerously drove off the road. The van went into a tree endangering another person, namely one of 'my' passengers, who was, as a result, now in intensive care. They then asked me, 'What do you have to say for yourself?'

My reply to them came in no uncertain terms, 'How could I drive a van and at the same time be on a deep-sea trawler in the middle of the Irish Sea, you wankers? I can't be in two places at once.'

The police rang the shipping office to confirm my story and I was then off the hook.

The story I was told was that our kid had smashed the van into the tree and the only thing the coppers wanted to know was who the van belonged to?

The police took the names of the people at the scene of the 'tree felling' - one of them was a certain Mr M Welburn - our Mike. With the van being in my name the police thought I must have been there, I'll accept this story unless someone else tells me different. I don't think anybody would have given my name do you? But I wouldn't have been bothered if they had as long as they'd told me, but nobody did.

There was no way I was going to say, 'Yes officer it was me who drove the new fish van I'd just bought, without insurance.' I checked in the mirror that it didn't say 'Silly Twat' across my forehead.

I was fuming - and I was angry with our kid for taking the van. I was released without charge and you probably won't believe it, but *nobody* actually got charged!

The only trouble was I was £800 out of pocket and was also going to be at home for a while. I wasn't going back to sea until I knew Tammie was 100 per cent right.

We found out Tammie was allergic to cow's milk and every time she drank it there was a problem with the dried powder. Every time she drank cow's milk it burnt her insides, like having a fire in your belly - but for the wrong reason. The solution was to change her onto Soya milk, which is very high in protein. And do you know what? We never heard a squeak out of Tammie after that! She'd sleep right through the night...

Michael brought a bag of money round to me - it contained about six quid in loose change. He told me he was sorry for what he'd done and he would get me the £800 I'd laid out.

I'm pleased to say that Mike did give me back my £800 - about four years later, but he did at least give me it back. Michael and me were not in business very long, about eight weeks, and the only thing I got out of it was a smashed up van. Luckily for me, Kerry's brother Dave was a dab hand at motor mechanics and said he'd soon get it back 'up to scratch'.

And he did! Within a month of being handed the smashed up van, thanks to Dave, it was back on the road. It was ready for selling fish from but there was one big problem - I'd no money to buy the fish I wanted.

Also, would I be able to get back the customers I might have lost, due to me not being there for about six weeks? I even found out someone else was selling on my pitch.

He only needed telling once that this was the pitch I'd paid for, outside the chemist, and he straightaway decided he didn't need a bandage from that chemist.

With no money in my pocket, a van ready to sell fish from and no call to go back on the St Jason for at least six weeks, I decided to go it alone.

I needed to get some fish on credit, you know, until the fish was sold and there was only one man I could go and see - Wally Simpson, one of Hull's top fish merchants. I was there when Wally started out from - and he won't mind me saying - a very humble background. He started his 'empire' with very little in his pocket and what an empire he has today.

I have to say he's one of the most generous men you could meet, he'll help anyone. He's never forgotten his roots and I don't think he ever will. The man has been magnificent in his support of numerous charities in this town and for local sport and in particular, amateur Rugby League.

Wally has never forgotten the times when I slept on the old fish docks - and when I wasn't at the youth club, I'd be helping Wally.

He would still be working at ten and eleven o'clock on a night having started at five o'clock in the morning. But he was building his business up and he put a hell of a lot of hours in. I'd keep him going in tea and coffee and I'd help him to ice and box his fish. Wally was one of the men who taught me how to roll a ten stone kit of fish with one hand, it was an art. When Birds Eye used to buy all the fish on the market you could earn a bit of pocket money by helping the Birds Eye lads to clear the fish market. If you could spin a ten stone kit of fish with one hand it meant you had a free hand. This came in handy for stealing the odd fish or two out of a ten stone kit. Everybody was milking it, and there were times when I was the highest paid barrow lad on the fish docks in 1974.

Wally worked very long hours on the old docks in the mid 70's and seeing where he has got in life now shows what can be achieved through sheer hard work!

In those days the order book was worth a few quid, an order book was a book with loads of contact numbers of fish shops all over the country. As you can imagine, over 100 fish merchants all had a little office next to each other.

You always knew where they'd leave the key to their office lying about, so it was pretty easy to go into their office and get the telephone numbers of their customers.

The numbers were worth a few quid in the right hands because all you had to do was ring a number and undercut the price they were paying for their fish.

It was simple, the more phone numbers you had, the more customers you could get and I used to love working with Wally in the mid 70s, he was and still is, a good man.

So I went to see Wally in December 1980, the time I got my van back, ready to sell fish. He was a very busy man, selling fish all over the country, and he employed a lot of men.

He was well on his way to building his empire, yet his embrace was as welcoming then, as it is today. He told me I could have whatever fish I wanted, as long as I paid him what he'd paid for it.

I couldn't believe the price I was getting my fish from Wally for. I was going to be able to treble my money - and I did. Then as soon as I had Wally's money I went straight to him and paid him. Wally Simpson helped me big style and he always said, 'Keep going Mally, you'll make it.'

Those words of encouragement, coming from Wally, kept me going for a very long time.

He even gave me one of his orders, it was for forty to fifty stone of haddock every fortnight which I had to take to Armley Prison in Leeds.

I was to buy the fish from Wally for say £6 per stone and sell it to a screw at the jail for £10. He'd then sell it to the other screws at anywhere from £13 to £15 per stone, so he was also on a good screw, so to speak. Wally couldn't be arsed to drop this fish off at Leeds prison's main gates on a Saturday dinner time bang on one o'clock. He was too busy so he passed it to me and it was a good little earner for me. It also helped me when I was sentenced for assault and wounding and I did some of my time at Leeds. The first screw I bumped into on my reception at Leeds prison was the one who'd bought the fish from me.

He was really ripping his mates off by overcharging them and he even had the cheek to make sure they were there on the Saturday to pick the fish up straight from the van. He would say to me, 'If anyone asks, the fish is £12.50 a stone. I want them to know I only make 50p a stone instead of £3.'

What a robbing bastard he was!

He was as bent as a nine-bob note but you should have seen his face when I walked through the reception room, it dropped a mile. He couldn't wait to get me on my own and said if I said anything about the fish prices he'd make my life hell.

I just said to him, 'If I could just eat a Mars bar and smoke a nice cig, you won't hear nothing from me Boss...'

The following day, I went back to my cell to find two Mars bars and a packet of Benson and Hedges cigs on my bed. There were also times I fancied a fresh orange and there it would be under me pillow. A Mars a day helped me work, rest and play during my ten-week stay at Her Majesty's Hotel at Armley Jail in Leeds, before I was moved to Preston.

When I got out of Preston Prison, I had another eighteen months of selling fish and I built my fish round up to where I had two vans. My mate Terry Milner jumped on board with me and he'd stand outside the chemist selling from the back of the van.

Terry owes me big style, as I always say to him, if it wasn't for me, he'd never have met his beautiful wife. She used to work in the chemist so you could also say I'm a matchmaker. It was nice to see Terry at one of my book signings; he was my best mate at school.

I can still see the glint in his eye and Terry has done really well for himself. In fact all the Milner's are lovely people. Vonny, Terry's Mother, what a lady, you don't mess with Vonny Milner!

So I built the fish round up to where Terry was doing the two days outside of the chemist and one day outside of a big factory every Friday, it's fish day is Friday.

Kerry, Tammie and me sometimes went into South Yorkshire, to the coalmines, to sell parcels of fish. I went to the library and got the addresses of all the coalmines still working in

South Yorkshire.

There weren't many, if any, fish merchants supplying coal mines with fish when I was sleeping on the old docks. Put it this way, I never saw any of their names in the order books.

I would get Kerry to write a really nice letter to the manager of the coal mine asking if we could sell fish to the miners. Five mines said yes, so I set it up with the canteen managers. They got a good fry of smoked fish for free. They love their smoked fish in South Yorkshire, they call it finny, and we call it smoked.

We say, 'Now then,' and they say, 'Hello duck'. They also use the word 'love' a lot in South Yorkshire.

Even the blokes would say to me, 'Two stone of finny old love,' and I'd ask myself, are they gay? But it's just the way they talk, it's different all over isn't it?

The canteen managers would ring me with their order on a Wednesday and I would have it all parcelled up and delivered to them on Fridays and Saturdays. The one thing they weren't doing was, like the bent screw, adding any money onto the fish prices.

All the canteen managers at the pits were the most honest people I could have possibly wished to meet. They were just happy with a good parcel of finny and I always gave them more than they were expecting.

I'd also drop them off some fresh boiled crabs when they were in season. They love their crabs in South Yorkshire. I'd say to the canteen managers, 'What do you call a baby crab? A little nipper!'

Or I'd ask them, 'How do you tell the sex of a crab?'

Do you know, a lot of people don't know how to tell the sex of a crab?

Just take a bit of time out, yes you, the person who is reading this book. Just think for one minute, close your eyes and I want you to tell me - how do you tell the sex of a crab?

Now before you read on, I want you to really think - how do you tell the sex of a crab?

Don't read on yet!

Did you close your eyes and think about how you tell the sex of a crab? Shall I tell you?

This is what I was like with the canteen managers before I

gave them a crab. I would say,

'How do you tell the sex of a crab?'

'By the colour of its shell?' some would say. 'No,' I'd reply.

'By the size of its claws?' another would try.

'Nearly right,' I'd say.

'Males always have one claw missing?' would be another guess.

'Nooooooo!!!!!'

'The answer is - lift its claws up. Ha Ha - Got You! - Oh forget it,' I'd say as I handed over their nice boiled crab and a big parcel of fish. It was only a joke and I know it sounds corny but some of them loved it and it helped me sell £400 or £500 worth of fish every week! £250 of that was profit, apart from twenty quid in petrol. It worked out at over two hundred quid for one drop off. I'd do two on one day and three on the next, I was earning some good money and my parting words would be, 'Why do crabs walk sideways?'

'We don't know,' they would say quickly as if to try and speed up my exit.

I'd then start walking out sideways and sing at the same time, 'Oh I do like to be beside the seaside. Oh I do like to be beside the sea. See yer next week!'

This went on for about six months before they started to close the mines. I met some real 'salt of the earth' people at those South Yorkshire coal mines. I even supported them when they went on strike. I went and took them a load of fish for nothing. They were always good to me so why couldn't I give them something back?

It was a good year and a half with us selling the fish but when we lost the mines it was a decent chunk of our money gone. I know I still had the chemist but sometimes the takings were down. Maybe it was because Terry was getting to know his girlfriend better and obviously wasn't putting the hours in.

I always had the 'bent screw' every other Saturday, although sometimes that became a Friday. And I tell you what, but don't ask me why, I started to turn to the booze again!

I'd go and deliver my fish, get the money and then go on a two-day bender and go gambling. I always made sure I had the money to buy the fish but every bit of money I made, I just pissed it up the wall. It even got to the stage where I would spend Kerry's housekeeping money and only go home with twenty quid and say, 'There's your wages!'

When I look back, I was a twat. I don't know what it was, maybe it was because I was earning easy money, buying and selling fish.

You could be up at four in the morning getting on the fish market, amongst the hustle and bustle and to see if there was any fish on the ghost train. Get your fish, get someone to fillet it for you and then you were away. But it was quicker to go and see Wally and to buy the fish straight off him.

You also didn't have to get up at four in the morning.

The challenge wasn't there for me because it was a lot easier to pick the fish up at nine in the morning and go stand at your pitch until three in the afternoon. I'd make a quick hundred quid, then get on the piss and not go home.

I was like that for nearly two years and I was treating the love of my life, Kerry, like a doormat.

How did she put up with it?

How did she put up with a drunken arsehole coming in at all hours of the morning, getting his dried-up dinner and throwing it at the wall.

'Come and make me a fucking dinner, this one's burnt,' I used to shout at the top of my voice.

I was turning into my old man again!

I started to frighten Kerry and Tammie when I came home pissed out of my head.

There were times, when I got in and she wasn't there. She'd either gone to her Mam's house or the women's hostel.

I don't know what it was. I don't know why I didn't go home when I should have. I don't know why I stayed out on the piss all the time. Was life too easy for me, working ashore? It wasn't hard work to buy and sell fish, not like it is now...

From 1980 to 1983 I really did hit the booze! I'd go and get my fish off Wally at nine in a morning and I'd have it sold by 3.30 in the afternoon. I'd then be on the booze, which wasn't as easy as it sounds. Just finding a pub that was open was sometimes a problem because in those days the pubs closed at half past three. There'd always be a back street club that was open though, if you knew where to look. And you could drink in there round the clock.

There was no buying booze from the supermarkets in those days. But there were always plenty of parties going on, especially if one of your mates had just got home from sea. You'd get a back-hander off them and go on the razzle all day. Sometimes I'd go on a three or four day drinking bender, which always seemed to involve the odd scrap or two. They'd usually happen in places like St Andrews Club or Rayners pub on Hessle Road - and not forgetting the famous Gillett Street Club.

I remember one time being in Gillett Street after I'd just done a stint selling fish outside the chemist. Terry and me would take it in turns to sell fish outside the chemist, after picking the fish up from 'Uncle Wally' - that was our nickname for Wally at the time.

There I was, with money to burn from the day's takings, going up the narrow stairs to the first floor bar. It was a small place. I think you could probably only get about fifty people in at one time.

You had to get past the little old guy on the door before you were allowed up the stairs. He would always ask for a membership card but this was overlooked when you slipped him a couple of quid. You could get three pints for that amount of money then, so it was a good little treat for the old guy. He'd always say to me, 'No trouble today Mally.'

'No probs,' I always replied. But on that day unfortunately there were. That was the day I got a lifetime ban from Gillett Street Club...

As I got to the crowded bar, squeezing past everyone to get my first pint of the afternoon, I noticed a few army men in uniform. They were in high sprits and must have been on the booze all day. They were really loud and throwing their weight about a bit.

I got to the bar and was waiting to be served by the one and only bar staff who needed at least another four pairs of hands to deal with the madding crowd.

On my right I noticed this big army sergeant was trying to push his way to the bar shouting his order.

'Six pints of lager and six drams of rum,' he bawled. 'We were here before most of these arseholes.'

'Who the fuck are you calling an arsehole?' I shouted back at him.

'Who do you think I'm calling an arsehole? You, you arsehole,' he replied, in his loud army sergeant's voice, as he shoved his way to the bar right next to me.

As he got to my side I turned to face him and out of the corner of my eye, saw my brother Raymond walk into the room. Believe me, Raymond was one hard man, you didn't mess with Raymond, a black belt, 4th Dan, in karate. He'd learnt his skills off the master, Jack Cochran.

Well, this army sergeant shoved his face right into mine, eyeball to eyeball, nose to nose - and I've got a flat nose! Then, in his 'on parade' army voice he shouted,

'What the fuck are you going to do about it, you fucking...'

But, before the word 'arsehole' left his lips again I flipped my head back very quickly and headbutted him right between his eyes. It was right on the bridge of his nose and he went out like a light.

He fell backwards and landed flat on his back as all hell broke loose. It was a total free-for-all. Everyone was at it!

The army lads were up for it big style, it was a real bar room brawl. It got to the stage where the army sergeant eventually got to his feet and ran at me across the small pub floor. A few friends, who thought it best to get me out of the trouble, started to drag me away.

There were these army blokes knocked out and laid all over the place. The room soon emptied apart from about a dozen people. This sergeant came running after me again screaming for me to have a go with him, one on one.

I was quick enough and sober enough to do it, as I hadn't even had a drink. I knew exactly what I was doing.

I got out of my mates' grip and just let go with the perfect right hand punch, which split the sergeant's nose from top to bottom and he slumped unconscious into my arms. I just dragged him across the floor to the top of the stairs and threw him down a flight of steep steps.

He knocked over about ten people who were already fleeing the club, as I hurtled down the stairs, chasing the large but very limp body of the sergeant.

It was like a scene from a tenpin bowling alley and I definitely got a strike that day!

I knew when I reached the bottom of the stairs he was out for the count, so I grabbed his uniform jacket and I screamed at him, 'Don't call me a fucking arsehole, you fucking fat bastard!'

Now don't get me wrong, I've got the utmost respect for the men and women who fight for our country. But I wasn't going to have this dickhead of a sergeant treating me like a new recruit in the army.

I'd had all that, 'By the left, quick march' stuff and running on the spot when I was in the North Sea Camp. And before that, living at home with my Dad was like a little army camp of our own!

As I was leaving Gillett Street Club, the boys in blue were waiting for me and I was quickly frog-marched into the back of a waiting police van. As usual I protested my innocence, but when you have four coppers grappling with you, to get the handcuffs on your wrists, the animal instincts kick in. You refuse to be captured, but you were eventually always over-powered.

The outcome was that there were no charges against me for the brawl in Gillett Street Club because the police got the full story of how the brawl started.

I think the army guys got into more trouble than I did when they got back to camp.

They could have been charged with fetching the uniform into disrepute. After all, they were in full uniform, pissed up and were throwing their weight about.

I don't think the army would have liked some of their lads appearing in a civil court and I heard they dealt with it in their own way. Maybe they had to do running on the spot and by the left quick march, but I thank them army lads for a right good brawl...

Although that particular scrap wasn't the result of too much drink, I admit I was always going off the rails due to the booze. There was no help available for people like me in those days. The authorities' answer was to bang us up in jail, and when we sobered up we knew then that we'd done wrong.

Go on tell me, where was the help?

I mean you only have to look around you today, as I believe

drugs are the new 'booze'.

Nowadays, if you have a drug problem there seems to be help available. I'm just puzzled by it all really...

On November 2 1981 I was up at court for seven offences.

And before I forget, there were three courtrooms in the Hull Magistrates Court.

If you appeared in Court One, this usually meant there was a good chance - about nine times out of ten - that you'd get sent down and end up in prison. I was in Court One...

The seven offences I was up for were: Four minor road traffic offences, no insurance, and two charges of obstructing the police.

I'd bought a wagon, a Ford Transit flat back, a pick-up truck.

I needed the wagon for going into my next venture, which combined selling washing-up liquid, door-to-door, and clearing gardens and household waste.

My motto was, 'Leave the skip out, we'll shift owt. Mally's yer man in the waste disposal van.'

Terry was running the fish side of our venture and I got a good door-to-door round built up, selling washing-up liquid. I also did house clearances and not forgetting selling a bit of fish door-to-door as well.

I'd have the young kids off the estate, going door-to-door with leaflets for me, and they got so much money out of every order I got. It didn't matter whether it was the gallon tubs of washing-up liquid, bleach, disinfectant, and not forgetting the Dettol-like antiseptic.

The lads also got good money if they got me any rubbish-removing job. Some of the lads would also help me to deliver the washing-up liquid and clear the garden or household rubbish. We were earning a small fortune as we'd charge anything from £30 a wagon-load for clearing the rubbish, £4 for going to the local tip and we could do up to five rubbish trips a day.

I'd have a little army of lads knocking on doors all over Hull touting for the work.

The cream of these lads were Billy and Nina Pougher's lads, Stu, Shane and young Gary. Also in my team were Dougie, Steve England and the grafter of the bunch Paul Ako - by, we earned some money.

We'd do the 'rubbish' jobs during the week and finish off on a Friday delivering the washing-up liquid and bleach. I realised I was earning more money at that time than I'd ever earned going fishing on the trawlers. The trouble was I just couldn't handle money.

I was still living in the 'live for the day' lifestyle. Only now, you could say I was a 'seven-day millionaire' instead of a 'three-day fisherman millionaire'.

I had money coming in from all over the place. My fish round, my washing-up liquid round - and the big earner - the rubbish removing. I soon built the business up to where I had three wagons just for shifting rubbish and a team of eight men working for me.

But going back to the time I was in court for the seven offences, I can only think it was when I got my first wagon.

I had a pocket full of money so I went with three mates to play pool in Grimsby.

We had to cross the newly built Humber Bridge, which at the time was the longest single-span suspension bridge in the world, crossing the River Humber.

It saved us up to an hour and a half on our car journey because before the bridge was built, you had to travel 'the long way round' to get to Grimsby.

I wasn't a bad pool player but my mate, Steve England, was the David Beckham of pool. He was unbeaten in Hull and you could win a bit of money backing Steve. But in the world of pool, Hull was a small place and word got round, so we went to Grimsby in the wagon I'd just bought. Well I say bought, it was bought on the understanding that I drove it for a couple of days to check it out and see if it was worth buying. It's how we bought and sold stuff then, 'Try it and see if you like it', so to speak.

I was giving the wagon a good run out and we were Grimsby-bound to see if we could hustle a few mugs at the game of pool. But *we* were the ones who got mugged as we came across a champion at pool. He took us to the cleaners, but fair play to him. He took us for everything we had in cash, so much so, that when we were coming back across the Humber Bridge homeward bound and penniless, I drove straight past the pay-booth without paying. It was only for a laugh really but out of the blue appeared the boys in blue. One second there was nobody in sight but the next, they were right behind me with their lights flashing. I denied having been across the Humber Bridge but, when they got me to the police station, they showed me the video replay showing our wagon and our laughing faces.

We thought we'd got away without paying £1 at the pay-booth on the bridge but they had video footage. Big Brother is watching you!

I didn't see the cameras on the bridge but there was no denying it was the wagon and me. Even if the vehicle wasn't in your name, if you were pulled up by the police, it was yours!

I told the police I'd just bought it, I was giving it a run out and I didn't know you had to pay to come back over the toll bridge. I told them I thought it was £1 to go there and back but they were having none of it.

The only good thing I got out of it was that the police took the wagon and gave it a good check-over to see if it was roadworthy. They found four minor things wrong with the wagon but I still got charged for them. I also got charged on two counts of obstructing the police and having no insurance. I honestly thought I was insured through the owner of the wagon. But it came to light he didn't have any insurance either, so the outcome was a £150 fine and I had my driving licence endorsed.

The Magistrate asked why I hadn't stopped at the pay-booth.

'I never had a penny in me pocket your Honour - we'd just lost all our money playing pool, Sir,' I told him.

He was far from sympathetic and suggested we learnt a different sport...

As I say, for three years this is what I was up to - going out, doing some graft, earning some money and then going straight into the pub. I really was neglecting my loving wife and baby daughter and I honestly don't know the answer as to why I did it.

I only know that when I got into a pub or a club, I just didn't want to go home until the place closed.

I'd always look for a party to go to and it never crossed my mind to go home, not until I ran out of money.

I just never played the game with Kerry.

I'd go home and tell her I hadn't earned anything that day and I really don't know how she put up with me.

I know I'd get home after being out on the booze all day and night and Kerry would be in bed.

I'd go to the oven and see my dried up dinner, scream and throw it at the wall. I'd then shout up the stairs for her to come and cook me a fresh dinner. I'm glad to tell you she never cooked a second meal, but Kerry would never stand and argue. I asked her recently why she never argued with me.

Listening to her reply was a humbling experience.

'Have you seen yourself when you've had a drink?' she said. 'You frighten people, Mally! Even though you never laid a hand on me, you really did scare me when you came in pissed-up. You frightened the kids and me.'

Even my daughter Tammie, tells me now, she used to sleep with a kitchen knife under her pillow. It really upsets me to think she did something like that because she was so scared of her loving Dad.

But when I was drunk, she lived in fear of all the screaming and plate throwing. I still get flashbacks of me going into my Dad's bedroom with the knife I hid under my pillow. I couldn't take any more of the way my Dad was treating my loving Mother, I wanted to kill him.

Was I turning into my Dad?

Was Tammie turning into a young Mally?

It was more than a coincidence. It makes you think doesn't it? Is it in your genes?

Kerry also told me that the following morning I was always full of apologies and she always forgave me.

I think I pushed her forgiveness too far, well I did in the end, and she just didn't want the life she was living. She just couldn't put up with my ways; she didn't want my Mother's lifestyle.

How you hurt the ones you love and you don't realise you're hurting them at the time. Your head is so far up your arse; well it was in my case.

I tried to keep out of the pub by taking up a hobby.

The first one was when I joined my brother Richard's team and started to play amateur football. They had a good goalkeeper so I played up front with Richard. I was the rough, tough, but clumsy, centre-forward who did all the graft, whilst Richard was the classy footballer who seemed to score all the goals. I'm sure he used me as a decoy to put the shits up their goalkeeper and their defence.

It always took two defenders to challenge me for the ball and when they did, I'd pass the ball to Richard. He got the easy job of scoring and when we won of course, it was the perfect excuse to go on the piss again to celebrate.

We used to train twice a week but this meant another two nights on the beer, so it was a hobby that never helped to keep me out of the pub.

I had to find something else...

CHAPTER EIGHTEEN
RUN RABBIT, RUN

The next venture I tried to help keep me off the booze was greyhound racing. Greyhounds take some looking after you know, but I did it.

I got two injured greyhounds to look after. They were racing greyhounds that had been injured. But because they weren't able to race anymore, their owners simply didn't want them.

I found out that a greyhound is a good, loyal animal and if you show it love and affection you get your reward. And I certainly did from my two injured greyhounds.

I got the dogs through a friend who knew their owners. I was told they'd never race again. One of the dogs had a really bad limp, a bit like, 'Hopalong Cassidy'. It had twisted its hock, which is like a human twisting their wrist. All the dog wanted was rest and a bit of TLC.

My daughter Tammie loved the greyhounds. She was always with me when I took the dogs out and sometimes they would pull Tammie's pram. In a way, the greyhounds ensured I spent some quality time with my baby daughter.

The other greyhound had a shoulder which was very badly bruised, so it meant complete rest for both dogs.

I got a mate of mine, Kenny Grantley, to build two nice dog kennels in the small backyard we had. Kerry also loved the greyhounds, so much in fact, that she didn't mind me giving them some of the blankets off our bed. I also gave them some of Tammie's high protein Soya milk. If it was good enough for my daughter and made her grow big and strong, it was good enough for my greyhounds.

I thought it would benefit both dogs, especially on top of their Weetabix, which is what they had for breakfast. That was after they had been on their five-mile early morning walk. Sometimes the dogs got Soya milk mixed with the yolk of an egg. And never mind the greyhounds, I used to drink it as well. I needed it after those five-mile walks every day!

After they'd had their four months of living at 'Mally's Four Star Greyhound Hotel' and getting pampered, they then had a clean bill of health and started to do what they were bred for, racing!

The greyhounds were three and four-year-olds, quite old in modern greyhound racing terms, but I was determined I was going to get these greyhounds to race - and to win! That was my challenge after they said the dogs would never race again. While my injured four-legged friends were living the life of Riley for four months, they also received full body massages, with rubbing oils twice a day. I was giving the greyhounds a good rub down, working the oils into their muscles. It was good for both the dogs and for me.

I got a book from the library about greyhounds and I learnt where all the main muscles were and what to feed the muscles with. I used to get the best mince from the butchers and boil it in a pan of water. I then let the water go cold, with the mince still in the pan. If you do that you'll see how much fat there is in a pound of mince. Then I scraped the fat off with a spoon and put the mince in a bigger pan with some wild nettles. Yes, nettles, the ones that sting yer. Nettles are full of iron and it got to the stage where I could pick these stinging nettles with my bare hands, without feeling the sting. It's all about how you grab the nettle, quick and fast, then they don't sting you. Also in the pan would be half a dozen, decent sized, chopped-up tatties. There would be fresh carrots, cabbage leaves, all I needed was some dumplings and I'd have had a nice pan of stew. I bet it would have lasted a family of four for a couple of days, but I fed it to my greyhounds.

Next I drained all the nettle juice into another pan, then mashed all the mince, tatties, carrots, nettle and cabbage leaves together. I then added six raw eggs, just the yolks - I'd drink the whites of the eggs - and then I'd mash it all up together before adding some dried greyhound feeding pellets. The greyhounds were soon on the road to face anything. And the nettle juice from the pan was their last drink of the day.

So - they had the right diet. They were well rested. They were well pampered. They'd been well massaged. They'd done their walks. But above all, they were well loved.

MALLY - THE REBEL WITHOUT A PAUSE

They were more than just pets. Any animal lover will tell you that. And if you care for animals, I'm sure you know what I mean...

Within five months I had these two greyhounds who they said would never race again, contesting for the biggest monthly prize at Askern greyhound track near Doncaster.

These two greyhounds, shall we call them outcasts, these two outcasts, wounded outcasts, had been cast aside. They were down and out, injured, unloved and not getting the massage, a bit like life sometimes. We've all been injured at some time in our life haven't we? We've all been hurt haven't we? We've all had a broken heart haven't we? And there've been times we've felt unloved. When we didn't eat properly and didn't exercise like we should.

My two four-legged friends had just gone through that phase in their lives, injured and unloved! That was when Mally came along. I felt like one of them preachers, 'Praise the Lord.' There were these two outcasts who were given another chance, 'Praise the Lord.' These two poor lost greyhounds who nobody wanted, 'Praise the Lord.' These poor lost souls who had been cast aside, 'Praise the Lord.' They were thrown a lifeline, 'Praise the Lord.' They were given the love and some proper food, 'Praise the Lord.' They were given a nice bed to sleep on, 'Praise the Lord.' Now was the time for them to repay this kindness...

I'd walk them for five miles which included crossing the Humber Bridge, which is over two miles there and back. I'd walk them up and down Hessle Road, one of the longest roads in Hull, and believe me these two greyhounds had more muscle on them than Linford Christie! I was even getting into shape myself. Then came the time to see if they could recapture their former glories.

There was and still is a greyhound track at Askern, a little village just outside Doncaster, about 40 minutes away from Hull by car. This was a track called a 'flapping track', as it wasn't governed by the National Greyhound Society.

If you couldn't get a licence to race on the main tracks because of too much red tape, Askern was one place where the likes of me and other owner-trainers could race our dogs.

A day at the dog racing is a big buzz and an even bigger buzz when you've got your own dog running, especially when you know your dog's got a chance of winning. It needs a clear run but there's always a chance of your dog getting a bump when racing and if this happens your chance has gone. At Askern the first thing you had to do was to get your dog accepted on the track.

The track would hold trials on a Monday night to see if your dog was fast enough to race. One thing I never ever did was to stop my dogs from running to their true potential. But some owners would give their dogs a drink of water or feed them a couple of hours before the trial. This was so their dog would get a slow time and be put in a lower grade race with all the other dogs that had got similar times in the other trials.

The slow dogs raced each other and the fast dogs raced each other. But you soon found out which owners had slowed their dogs down. On Saturday, the day of the main races, all of a sudden some of the slow dogs from the trials would sometimes become a hell of a lot faster!

If the track owner suspected a dog had been 'doctored', the owner was banned from the track. After all, the track owner was also a bookmaker and he didn't want his pockets emptied. He was a clever man because if you were new to the track and he wasn't sure about your dogs, after your dog had done its trial, he'd put it in the high-grade races against the cream of the crop.

He was in a continuous battle with trainers to make sure racing at Askern was fair. He had to be canny because as well as being a bookmaker, he also had some top class dogs in his own kennels. So how did I beat the bookie?

My dogs did their trials, each having three races, not winning, but doing reasonably well. I was accepted onto the track.

I met up with a bunch of guys, who like myself, owned their own dogs and I got to know them pretty well. They'd tell me if their dog was up for it - so I'd know which ones to put my money on and I seldom went home empty handed.

Once a month at Askern they'd have a day where all the weekly winners and seconds were invited back to the track. They would be entered for the monthly trophy with a £100 first prize. But with two race nights a week, eight races each night and six dogs in each race, it was like trying to win the

MALLY - THE REBEL WITHOUT A PAUSE

F.A. Cup or the Grand National. But yippee, my dogs managed to finish second in their races, so I qualified for the F.A. Cup of greyhound racing at Askern dog track.

Of the 128 dogs that were in the running for the end of the month finals, the fastest sixty were invited to the Saturday morning race meeting. This was where ten races, with six dogs in each took place. My dogs were in the fastest sixty.

On this particular Saturday morning we were informed that the six fastest winners of the ten races would go straight through to the final which was to be held on the same afternoon. The next six fastest dogs would compete in the 'loser's final'. So for me, it was all about winning one of these races. But my dogs had never had their noses in front to win a race up to that point. This time I had to win and win in a fast time. It was the only chance I had of getting my hands on the trophy, the prize money and any winnings from a bet on the dogs as well.

A week before the big day, when I knew my dogs were in the fastest sixty to race for the star prize, I got talking to an old guy who'd been in greyhound racing for over 50 years. He could remember the famous Mick the Miller, a legend in greyhound racing, as famous a name as Red Rum was in horse racing. The old guy gave me a very unexpected tip - he told me to give the dogs the 'taste of a hare'.

'Get a dead rabbit from the butchers and tease your dogs with it,' he suggested. 'Let them bite into the dead rabbit but don't let them eat it. Just let them have a taste and get the feel of the kill and see what it does to your dogs.'

I followed his advice and my dogs went crackers as they fought each other for the taste of the dead rabbit. I kept them safe, gave them light exercise and light food. My dogs were lean, mean, racing machines.

At that time I knew they were in the best possible condition and ready to repay all the hard work I'd put into them. So much so, that I went into the Gipsyville Tavern and told everyone to put their money on one of my dogs, the one I believed was the faster of the two. I soon collected over a hundred pounds off different people to gamble on the dog that I thought had a chance of winning the trophy.

The big day arrived...

I ripped the shelves out of the back of the fish van I had so that there was enough space for my two dogs and my mate, Kenny. We put a load of blankets in there just in case Kenny wanted to have a nap! Kenny is a great guy. He helped me big style with the dogs. Kenny was also an old sea dog, he was known as 'the fastest fish-gutter at sea' when we were on the trawlers. He could gut three fish to most people's one! I always wanted Kenny on my watch when we sailed together in our sea days, he's a good honest friend.

In the front of our little Escort van was me the driver, Kerry with baby Tammie on her knee, and someone who I won't name, but he worked in the fish game. For this part of the story we'll call him the 'fish man' if that's okay with you.

He loved a bet and he'd gamble on which of two flies would shit first, if someone offered him a price.

He used Gipsyville Tavern regularly and knew all about my dogs and the chances we had of winning a shit-load of money. But I wanted that trophy more than money, after all you got to keep the trophy, you can always spend money, as we were soon to find out with Mr Moneybags - the fish man.

It was 8 o'clock on Saturday morning, and by about 9.30 we had to be at Askern greyhound track near Doncaster, about a forty-minutes drive from Hull, on a good day. Kerry had the money that I had collected off the lads from Gipsyville Tavern to gamble on the dogs. We had a hundred quid to play with. I told everyone that would listen that one of my dogs was bang-on. I had a little notebook with names and how much money each one had given me to gamble on me dogs.

The dog I fancied was PFC - Portsmouth Football Club - that was the track name that it was running under. It was bang-on. It was buzzing. It was lean, mean and keen. It had the taste of the dead rabbit. It was ready to repay all that hard work I had put into it, all the love and attention, it was ready to race through a tub of shit!

It's a pity that I never paid the same attention to my wife I hear you say, instead of me putting her through all that shit in life. How she stuck by me for so long I will never know.

Well anyway, we were all singing on our way to the racetrack. We got there just after nine in the morning - the first race wasn't till ten but you had to book yer dog in. Greyhounds have a stamp mark in their ear you know and that's how they tell it's the right dog that is entered in the race. If it doesn't have a stamp in its ear they take a photo of the dog and make a note of all its markings.

There were twelve races that morning, six dogs in each race and a race every 15 minutes. The first ten races were for the dogs that had qualified for the big monthly trophy plus the hundred quid prize money. The six fastest dogs out of those ten races qualified for the final, so four winners were not guaranteed to be in the final, it was all about times. Your dog had to get out of them traps and it had to be 'Jack be nimble, Jack be quick!'

The other two races that morning were open races where prize money could be four hundred quid but those races were for the really top class dogs from around the country. It could cost you a hundred quid to enter one of them races, and in dog racing as in life, one knock and you're out of the race. My dogs were not in that class, I knew that, even though I was only learning this greyhound-racing lark.

I booked my two dogs in, my slower dog was in the first race and PFC my flying machine was in the third race. Askern greyhound track was buzzing, it was just like that bee hive, everybody looking at each other's dogs. Looking for the dog that stood out. But it's not always the best turned out dog that wins the race. It's about the wellbeing of your dog and the fitness and how it's been prepared for that race. Well I'd done my bit. It was now all about a bit of luck. We all need a bit of luck now and again but I believe you make your own luck in life sometimes. We were soon to find out if my luck was in that day. Well I can tell you the fish man sure had some bad luck that day.

Askern greyhound track was known as a compact little track with tight bends and a short run-in to the winning post. From the traps to the winning post was about 450 yards. You had to have a dog that could ping them traps, 'hit the lids' we would say - get a flyer - get out them traps. If you missed the break you were out of the race, also your dog had to have a bit about it to be able to take them knocks at that first bend. The race could be over if you got that bump at the first bend, which is what happened to my first dog in the first race. Askern also had three bookmakers where you could bet on your dog. One of the bookmakers was the greyhound track owner and he was also the judge of the racetrack. The judge's job was to make sure everything was run to order and also if there was a close finish in racing and the photo finish camera wasn't working, it was his job to declare the winner. You couldn't argue with the judge, it was just like life. I've been in front of a few court judges in my time, and you don't argue with them.

If you liked a bet on the dogs, Askern was the place to be that day. The bookmakers would give you odds on your dog to win. And you could even get odds on your dog finishing second or get as much as 10/1 to name the first two dogs home in any race. It sounds simple but you try picking the first and second in a six dog race. It's not easy, as the fish man who came with us soon found out...

The third race was the next race up. I was a bag of nerves but really excited. The only calm thing around us was my dog PFC. We had to parade our dogs in front of the crowd and we could hear a bookmaker shouting the odds for the race. He was shouting 2/1 PFC. That meant that if you put £1 on and PFC won, you'd win two quid, plus your pound back which is £3. I gave Kenny and Kerry the nod to put all our money that we'd collected from the lads from Gipsyville Tavern on PFC. I think Kerry even put her family allowance on my dog, plus I'd given her an extra twenty quid to put on for us.

My dog was drawn in trap one and that was the trap to be in because if it got out quickly it could hug the rails and the other dogs would have to go on the outside to overtake it. A dog could lose a lot of ground going round the outside of this tight little track. It was very rare to get caught if you got to that first bend in the lead. If your dog was fit enough they wouldn't catch it. But all the dogs were fit that day so it was all down to getting out of the traps and getting clear of trouble at the first bend.

As I was putting my dog in the traps I bent down and whispered in its ear, 'Go on my lad show them how it's done, show them all that work I've put into you, show them how it's going to pay off.' I put him in the traps and ran like mad back to Kerry, baby Tammie, Kenny, and the fish man, plus about 300 people that had turned up for a morning's racing at

MALLY - THE REBEL WITHOUT A PAUSE

Askern. It really is a good day out, if you ever get the chance to go to the dogs, believe me you will enjoy it. Well imagine what it was like to own and train your own dog!

It was a big buzz getting that creature to race for you. It's an art, ask any greyhound trainer...

The dogs were in the traps.

The judge was in his box overlooking the winning post, and the starter was waving his little white flag to let him know that all the dogs were ready for the hare. The crowd started to get excited. The hairs on the back of my neck were standing on end. My palms were sweating. The hare was on the move. It whizzed past the crowd, then towards the traps.

'Speed the hare up, my dog will have it before it gets to the first bend!' I shouted.

Oh, I was really buzzing. The money was down, it was now or never.

'Go on my lad, show them how it's done,' I shouted as the hare whizzed past the traps, the lids opened and the dogs shot out like shit off a stick.

Going to the first bend my dog had got a three lengths lead - 6 feet to a length - on the chasing pack. 'Come on my lad, Come on my lad,' I was screaming.

It was pulling away with every stride, the others weren't going to catch him. I could see his little red jacket, he was like a rocket. Coming round the short home run he was well clear, seven lengths in front of the rest. What a buzz I got as he flashed past the winning post.

After all the other dogs had passed the post, I jumped over the track fence, ran after my dog and made a big fuss over him. I don't know who was more excited; me or me dog?

He was mauling the stuffed hare and I had a job pulling him away from his catch. I could just tell the race had taken nothing out of him, he wasn't even panting like the other dogs.

An old greyhound trainer who was the time-keeper of the races told me to put my dog in the van and drive to a nice, quiet spot away from race track.

'Give the dog and yourself a rest because I can't see any dog beating that time today,' he said.

'Never mind hanging around the track, it will upset yer dog.

Give it a little drink of water and wash the sand out of its eyes.
And if that dog gets out like it did in that race again, you've a
great chance of winning the trophy.'

I took his advice and we picked up well over £300 from the
bookies. But the fish man did not back my dog to win, he
thought it would come second.

As me, Kenny, Kerry and Tammie were going to the van to
drive away for a couple of hours to give the dog a rest, we
noticed the fish man.

He was betting at least £30 on each race to try and pick first
and second. He decided to stay at the track and try to win
some money back because after three races he was over £100
down. But there was still worse to come for the fish man - he
got really hooked that day at Askern greyhound track...

We left him and drove to the nearest village and sat outside a
pub having an orange till the two hours passed, and it seemed
like forever.

I kept ringing the track from the pub. I was told we were the
third fastest dog that day but the track record had been broken
in the heats by a dog called Shady Lady. Shady Lady? I've
met a few of them in my time!

Well anyway, we got back to the track and it was still buzzing.
Everyone seemed to have enjoyed themselves, everyone other
than the fish man. He had a face as long as a wet weekend. I
asked him how he'd done and he told me he was now well
over £300 down after 10 races, despite getting a bit back off
Shady Lady's win. And in the early '80s that was a lot of
money.

He said Shady Lady would not get beaten even though the
final was a handicap race and she was giving us 3 lengths start
- 18 foot.

He'd not seen a dog as fast as Shady Lady for a long long time
he said to me, and he said I'd be chucking my money away if I
backed my own dog.

I said, 'You back what you want, you do whatever you want
to do, we have £300 going on my dog. If it wins, it wins, if it
loses, it loses - but the money is riding on the back of my
rocket!'

That's what I'd told the lads in Gipsyville Tavern. If it won its
first race and got to the final, all the money goes on it - and

everyone agreed - we all knew where we stood.

As I was parading my dog for the final I heard a bookie shout, 'Even money, PFC.'

For those of you who don't gamble, even money means that if you put a pound on and it wins, you win a pound plus your pound back, so that makes two pounds, hope you understand. Well, even money and we had £300 to play with. So I gave Kenny and Kerry the nod to bet it all on our dog to win!

Plus Kerry had another £60 on it for her and me - and let's not forget her family allowance money. She refused to tell me how much that was!

Then I heard the bookie shout, 'Even money, both PFC and Shady Lady.'

They were joint favourites and 5/1 the rest of the field. It was a two-dog race in the bookies' eyes and also in everybody else's eyes that were there to witness the clash.

I walked me dog to the traps, buzzing. I gently eased him into trap three this time. He had a little white jacket on and Shady Lady had the red jacket for trap one. She was giving my dog 18 foot start. PFC was giving trap six 24 foot start - and let's not forget the other four dogs were no mugs. This was the race of all races. This was my Grand National. I felt like Ginger McCain, the trainer of the famous racehorse Red Rum, who won the Grand National three times.

I whispered into my dog's ear as I pushed him into the trap.

'Go on my lad, one last effort and you can have two raw eggs for breakfast in the morning instead of one. Go on, show them who's the boss, go on my lad.' As soon as he was safely in the trap I legged it back to Kerry and the gang.

I gave a wave to the judge in his box and shouted, 'Top of the afternoon to you sir, let one's hare go.' With that, over the tannoy came the announcement, 'They're all in.'

The starter was waving his flag. You could hear the noise of the crowd growing with excitement again. I gave Tammie a big kiss and a hug and said, 'Watch Daddy's dog win, love.'

I passed Tammie to Kerry who held her in her arms. I was so excited. The only time I have been more excited is when I sat in that chair on 'Deal Or No Deal' and I had that feeling then that it was my lucky day.

I knew if my dog got out them traps and got past the 4, 5 and

6 dogs before the first bend, Shady Lady, the track record-holder, would have it all on to get round the crowding dogs. But as we know we all need that bit of luck and could Lady Luck strike twice for me in one day? I don't know about Lady Luck, we had another lady who we hoped would have a bit of bad luck, Shady Lady!

Back on the track, the hare was on its way. The noise of the crowd would have put any Wembley crowd to shame. It was banging! We had over £360 riding on my dog PFC. I shouted to the fish man, 'I hope you've 'shovelled' on my dog.'

He shouted back that he had backed Shady Lady. And I gave him that look as if to say, what an arsehole!

Before I knew it they were off.

All the runners crowded at the first bend and a couple of dogs took big knocks. But leading the way by about a length was the dog wearing the white jacket, it was my dog, closely followed by 4, then 6 and then the track record holder, trap 1, Shady Lady. She got a clear run up the inside, avoiding the trouble. Coming to the second bend my dog had gone two lengths ahead of 4 with Shady Lady, closing in fast.

Over the tannoy you could hear,

'It's trap three with one running on well. Coming towards the third bend it's three from the fast finishing one. And down towards the last bend it's three being joined in the lead by one. Everyone around me was jumping up and down for one reason or another but when they were turning for home and you could see the track record-holder loom alongside my dog, I heard the fish man scream,

'Come on Shady - come on trap one.'

I thought you wanker. Then my dog joined Shady Lady again. The voice on the tannoy said, 'It's one and three, it's three and one, it's neck and neck.'

I was screaming, 'Come on my lad, Come on my lad!'

'It's still three and one, it's one and three,' the tannoy announcer repeated.

They flew past the post, neck and neck, nose and nose, nostril and nostril - a cig paper couldn't separate them. The voice on the tannoy said, 'Photo, Photo between trap one, Shady Lady and trap three, PFC, third was trap two, six lengths behind.'

I waited until the other dogs had passed the winning line, then jumped over the rail and ran to get my dog who was fighting over the stuffed hare with Shady Lady. They can't do any damage to the hare or the other dogs with their teeth because they wear muzzles when they race. I shook the hand of the trainer of Shady Lady and said what a great race it had been and he agreed...

The result was a long time in coming and when it did come I was waiting nervously with Kerry, Tammie and Kenny.

I looked up at the judge's box, waiting to hear the result. The judge looked straight at me and gave me the wink and a slight nod. Behind me I could hear the bookmaker say, 'Give even money, Shady Lady to win the photo.'

Well the fish man ran towards the bookie and gave him a wad of cash. I couldn't believe it!

He obviously hadn't seen the judge give me the wink and I sure wasn't going to tell him that I'd got the nod to say my dog had won the race.

No sooner had the fish man - and many others - backed Shady Lady to beat my dog in the photo - than the announcer on the tannoy declared that the photograph machine was not working and the result of the monthly final would go down to the judge's verdict. There was another long pause and the whole place went deathly quiet. The silence was broken seconds later when the tannoy burst into life again with the verdict...

First - trap three - PFC from Hull.

Well, I swear I jumped over that barrier and did a lap of honour, with my dog trotting alongside of me. Oh what a day! I got presented with the big trophy and the hundred pounds first prize, then we collected £720 plus the winnings from Kerry's family allowance bet from the bookie.

Kenny had also backed both of PFC's wins - he was buzzing. We were like big kids with toys we never got for Christmas.

But the poor old fish man was gutted. He looked like death warmed-up. He must have lost nigh on £500 that day. That's probably why he never offered me a penny towards petrol on the way home!

I got loads of pats on the back and even the trainer of Shady Lady came up to me and shook my hand and said, 'Well done.'

We were all in a party mood and just couldn't wait to get back home and go to Gipsyville Tavern and show everyone the trophy and give them their winnings.

We were all singing all the way home, except the fish man. When I told him to cheer up and that it wasn't the end of the world, he said it was worse than that.

He asked me if I could do him a favour and not tell anybody that my dog had won the race. When I asked why, he said someone in Tavern had given him a wad of money to back my dog. If it won its first race he was to put all the winnings on it in the final. But guess what? He hadn't!

I asked who it was but he wouldn't tell me. So I told him there was no way I was going to lie for him!

He hadn't had faith in my dog. He'd stayed at the track and lost a lot of his money. Then he'd backed against my dog. He was cheering home Shady Lady in the final. I called him a shady bastard!

When we arrived back at the Tavern, the fish man went straight home and the rest of us went in to celebrate. We were just in time for last orders and everybody was waiting for the news about my dog. They soon found out when we went dancing in and waving the trophy and the money about.

Everyone was buzzing with us. We shared all the money out to the ones who had given me money to put a bet on, those that were in our little notebook.

After we'd given out all the winnings, I glanced across to the corner of the bar. There sitting in his wheelchair was Terry, a really nice guy, who was loved by all. He never bothered anyone.

He called me over and asked me how the day had gone. When I told him PFC had won its first race at 2/1 and then had won the final at even money, his face lit up!

'That's fantastic,' he said, 'I've got £300 to come off the fish man because I gave him £50 to gamble on your dog.'

'I've got news for you, Terry,' I said, 'He never put the money on for you. He wanted me to come in here and say my dog lost but I just couldn't do that.'

It wasn't much of a consolation but I gave Terry £30 and we had a lock-in at the Tavern that night!

We never saw the fish man for a few months. It just shows you don't it? Be careful who you deal with in life...

MALLY - THE REBEL WITHOUT A PAUSE

That day at Askern in the Summer of '82 led me to build six 'top of the range' dog kennels and a big wire compound in Kenny Grantley's garden. We soon filled our kennels with a few decent greyhounds that I bought for people who paid me to train them and I got to go racing twice, if not three times a week.

I had a couple of 'money-men' who liked a gamble - and what better way than to gamble on your own dog, when you know it's trying its very best all the time...

Kenny's wife Kelly loved the dogs. What another lovely lady Kelly is. She's a dab hand at baking her own bread cakes, and what a treat it was every Sunday morning to go to Ken and Kelly's and get our buttered busters - our nickname for bread cakes - they were that hot the butter just ran down the side of yer mouth. Oh how I miss them. I'll always be grateful to Ken and Kelly for all the help and support they have given me over the years. We're still great friends to this day...

We named the kennels after Kelly and soon had six decent dogs in 'Kelly's Kennels'. We bought four dogs from four different trainers who we'd met at Askern greyhound track, plus the two that I already had. We soon had four people who wanted to own a greyhound and go and see it race twice a week for the cost of three quid a day. Plus they paid the entrance fee for their dog to run and not forgetting a bit for the petrol to travel that 50 miles or so to the dog track. That meant I got my two dogs fed and entered to the races free of charge so to speak, well you don't have a dog and bark yourself, do you?

Things were going well for a while. We had our fair share of winners and losers, we never took the fish man with us racing again but we'd take the owners of the dogs when their dog was running. Sometimes they would follow behind in their own cars. When I knew my dog was in with a good chance I took wheelchair Terry's money to gamble, and we soon had the £300 he missed out on with the fish man when my dog won that big race.

I remember one of the dog owners, Vernon Thorley - god rest his soul - one of Hull's very own legends, you didn't mess with Vernon, he was a very, very hard man. He was a fish merchant, who also gave me a few fish shops where I could sell my fish when I had my fish round. He liked a bet did Vernon. And he was also a keep-fit fanatic.

This one Saturday morning I had his dog 'nailed on' to run a big race but my van wasn't firing on all cylinders and Vernon had just bought a brand new Mercedes car and said he would take us to Askern in it. All we needed were some blankets to put over the seats, which we soon got sorted.

When Vernon picked us up he had Shaun Bristow with him. Shaun co-owned the dog with Vernon, so he came along for the ride and a bit of a gamble. We were travelling first class, me, Kenny, Shaun, and Vernon - and not forgetting Shaun and Vernon's dog, Siddy.

Twenty or so miles into the journey the brand new Mercedes car started to splutter and ground to a halt. We had to stop on the hard shoulder on the M62. And no matter what we tried we just couldn't get the car going again.

Vernon wasn't in the AA at the time and we didn't have mobile phones in them days. If you were lucky enough to have one, it was the size of a house brick and you had to carry a big battery pack with it. You needed a rucksack on yer back to carry the battery for yer phone, how times have changed.

Well as I said, Vernon was into his keep-fit and when we couldn't get the car going he just said to me, 'I'm off!' and he started to jog down the motorway back to Hull with Shaun.

As he set off he said to me, 'Just get me car back when it's sorted Mally, I will send someone out to you when I get back home.' And with that, him and Shaun were on their merry way!

Within thirty minutes of Vernon and Shaun leaving us, someone stopped and helped us to get the Merc going. It was a loose distributor cap. Don't ask me how it makes the car work but it did. Kenny and me drove to the racetrack but missed the race.

You would have thought we had won the lottery when we turned up at the racetrack in the brand new Merc. We even went round Doncaster on the night just driving around in Vernon's brand new Merc, we felt like millionaires, Dell boy and Rodney.

We got the Merc back to Vernon the next day.

He was a great guy was Vernon. Nothing seemed to bother

him and if I can achieve half of what Vernon achieved in his life, I won't have done badly...

I remember when I was training all six of my dogs on the school playing fields. I would have an old bobber's barrow that we used to carry the kits of fish on when we worked on them fish docks. Do you remember them big bobber's barrows, when I worked as that barrow lad, the best barrow lad at that.

On this barrow we had a big battery that we got off a lorry, yes straight 'off the back of a lorry'. From the battery, two cables led up the shafts of the bobber's barrow to an electric motor and an old wooden fishing reel on the top of one of the shafts. On the other shaft was the stop and start button to turn the fishing reel that held about 200 yards of nylon. It really was a clever machine, built for me by a 'gadget man' off the docks. At the end of the nylon would be my rabbit skin that the local butchers used to save me.

I'd have Kenny and his lad Jeff and a few of his mates to hold the dogs. And I'd have the rabbit skin hidden in a towel so that the dogs couldn't see it. I'd place the towel over the rabbit skin about ten foot behind my six dogs, then I would run like mad over them 200 yards to the on and off button on the barrow. When I pressed the on button the fishing reel would spin like mad and pull the rabbit skin from under the towel. It would whiz past the dogs. The dogs would be going crazy. The gang used to let them go at five-second intervals. We soon found out which dog was the keenest and the quickest. We would do that once a week just to keep the dogs on their toes.

One day whilst we were putting the dogs through their paces, one of my dogs, Rabbie, just broke down and started to limp really badly. I took him to one of the town's best known vets and he checked him over.

'Your dog's suffering from a lack of salt and it will need an injection,' he said.

I told him I had another five dogs and asked if he could inject all of them. He said he could, so I asked him how much it would cost? He said it would be £18.

The next day I took all six dogs round to him and he gave them their salt injections.

Then he said, 'That's £18 for each dog - and six 18s is £108.'
'I thought you said it was eighteen quid for the lot!' I exclaimed.
'No, £18 for each one,' he replied.
I only had eighteen quid on me, I thought that was the price for all six dogs.
'Well, if you can't pay the bill, you better leave me your driving licence,' he said.
You had to have proof of who you were when you went to the vets and I only had my driving licence with me. I gave him it or else he wasn't going to let me take the dogs home.
After he'd given the dogs their injections he'd told me to rest them for a week or two.
I followed the vet's advice.But that meant one thing for me! Two weeks on the piss, on the booze, on the tiles, call it whatever you like. And it was while I was on the bender I got into three fights in two days...

CHAPTER NINETEEN
WIDE EYED
AND LEGLESS

When I say 'fights', in the first one I just stuck the nut on an old school friend that was kissing his girlfriend down a dark alley behind Gipsyville Tavern. I'd gone down the alley to have a piss and I swear I didn't see him until I heard a voice say, 'Fucking hell Mally, you're pissing all over my girlfriend's legs. Why can't you just fuck off?' he said.

So I just headbutted him in his face and he fell to the floor!

I did say sorry to his girlfriend though. I was really pissed up that day. I was on the rum again. And I'd also won about two hundred quid on the horses.

I got a taxi to take me the two miles into Hessle. Hessle was a posh place to live 25 years ago. Me and Kerry had our first house in Hessle, down Eastgate.

The likes of Mally Welburn were never welcome in the pubs in Hessle. But I thought fuck em, they ain't going to stop me having a drink in the Marquis of Granby or the Admiral Hawke.

The taxi dropped me off outside the Admiral Hawke pub in Hessle Square. When I staggered in it was late afternoon and there was hardly anybody in the pub apart from these two smartly dressed blokes drinking at the bar. I made my way to the bar but the barman said,

'I'm sorry I can't serve you, you're too drunk.'

I told him to give me a fucking drink or else I'd be over the bar and serve myself. With that, these two blokes that were standing at the bar turned round and said, 'We advise you to turn around and get back to where you came from, or we'll have you locked up for being drunk and disorderly.'

'You and whose army?' I said.

'I will take the pair of you on outside.'

With that, one of them pulled out an ID card and said, 'We're undercover coppers and we are telling you to get on your way or else we will have you locked up.'

As I turned to head for the door I said, 'You look more like Batman and fucking Robin!'

Outside, a taxi was pulling up to drop someone else off at the Admiral Hawke. I staggered to the back door behind the driver who had his window half down and said to him as I was opening the back door,

'Take me to Gipsyville mate, I'll pay you double.'

His reply was, 'Wait until this man has got out first mate.'

Well with that, this bloke in the back of the taxi shouted,

'Wait your fucking turn or else I'll knock your fucking head off!'

'Oh here we go again', I thought.

'Anytime you like mate,' I shouted back as I opened the back door. I thought it was my old man.

This guy was bigger than Giant Haystacks and he seemed to have a half-pint glass, half full of alcohol in his hand. He seemed as though he had been on the piss as well, the way he was shouting to the taxi driver, 'Who the fuck is this clown?' Meaning me.

'Get out of this car and I'll show you who the fucking clown is mate!' I shouted back.

'I'm no fucking mate of yours, you bastard! Fuck off or else I'll kill you,' he screamed, waving his glass at me.

'Get out the car you wanker,' I screamed back at him.

Well as he was leaning to get out of the taxi with his head bent down, I grabbed him. I grabbed a lump of his hair with my left hand and with my right fist gave him uppercut after uppercut, at the same time banging his head, left and right, on the sides of the back door entrance of the taxi. Then I started to slam the door onto his head. The taxi driver was screaming,

'Stop! or you're going to kill him!'

I told the taxi driver to stop because he was starting to pull away with the Giant still half in and half out of his taxi. But the Giant was still screaming,

'I'm going to kill you when I get out of this fucking car.'

I was really shitting it. I might have been pissed but I knew if this guy got on his feet and out of that taxi, I would have had my hands full! So I just kept raining blow after blow, kick after kick down onto this Giant. There was three quarters of him out of the car and when the taxi driver finally decided to speed off, the Giant fell out of the taxi and landed flat out, face up. He was like a big tree that had just been felled. I started to punch his face and bang his head on the floor, all the time screaming, 'You're going to fucking kill me are you?'

There was blood all over the place, his face was well pummelled. His eyes were closed. He was out cold.

The taxi had gone. I remember thinking how quiet everything was. I noticed the two undercover coppers were watching through the window from inside the pub. I stared back at them and yelled,

'Come on then, I'll have the pair of you fucking bastards as well, get out here!' But I knew they wouldn't dare come out. Was I turning into my old man? The coppers were always scared of my old man. And I saw the fear in those two undercover coppers' eyes. They didn't dare come to this man's aid.

There was no way that Giant was getting to his feet that afternoon. He was out cold.

I was an animal - a wild animal at that! It hurts me to recall some of these incidents now. Because I realise what I did, getting drunk, brawling in the street, spending the night in the cells - and lots of things much worse - weren't clever. They're not things I look back on with anything but complete disgust now. But then they were a way of life - my way of life. And I always seemed to come up against the big blokes to fight with. It was a case of lay down and be beaten or stand and fight. And back in them days I can't deny I used to love to have a fight. The big guy that I was fighting was always my old man, it was always his face I saw.

I now know why God gave me two ears and one mouth, it is twice as important to listen, as it is to speak. But back in them days I had a different motto - punch first, ask questions later! The Giant lay in the middle of the road, unconscious.

The traffic had come to a standstill. Women were screaming. A young kid was driving by on his motorbike. I jumped out in front of him and he screeched to a halt. I threatened him, he could either give me a lift or he'd end up like the Giant, flat out on the deck.

He said, 'Jump on, where do you want to go?'

Just get me to Gipsyville, I shouted at him.

I jumped on the back of the motorbike and as we were driving away, I noticed a number of people running to the Giant's aid, including the two undercover coppers who'd emerged from the pub.

I couldn't go home after that incident because I knew a few of the onlookers knew me. And it wouldn't be long before the 'boys in blue' would come a knocking.

I went to a mate Jimmy's flat in Gipsyville and his girlfriend Laura bandaged my cut finger. How I got that cut on my finger I'll never know. I can only guess I got it off the glass that the Giant was wielding at me from the back of the taxi.

I was telling Laura what I could recall. I'd been wanting this taxi and this 'big honey monster' was going to kill me so I battered him before he could batter me. She said I did the right thing and hoped I'd taught him a lesson.

'It will be a while before he picks on anybody else,' I said.

I waited until after it got dark before I went to see Kenny and me dogs because I knew the 'boys in blue' would undoubtedly be out looking for me. Kenny confirmed my suspicions. He told me the coppers had been to his house about an hour earlier and that they'd also been to my house and Kerry had told them the only place I could be was with my dogs. The coppers had informed her that I was wanted for attempted murder and robbery of ten thousand pounds! Yes, robbery of ten thousand pounds that the Giant had allegedly just drawn out the bank. I could understand the attempted murder bit - but I didn't know anything about ten grand!

I went back to Jimmy's flat where Laura re-bandaged my finger. We got pissed up that night. I sent Jimmy out to get the booze including a bottle of Lamb's Navy Rum.

I think they must have thought that I'd got the ten grand because I had the wad of money on me that I'd won on the horses earlier that day.

The next morning I was up and out for six to go see my dogs at Kenny's. He told me the coppers had been back again late on the previous night. They'd told Kenny that if he saw me I had to hand myself in because the Giant was in intensive care and I was wanted for robbery of ten grand. I told Kenny the truth, that I had never seen the ten grand that they were on about. Kenny told me to hand myself in and he would look after the dogs. But I replied that there was no way I was going to do that - the coppers would have to catch me first.

I rang Kerry up from a phone box and she told me the police were looking for me and a cop car had been parked outside our house all night.

I told her I wasn't going home. But I would hand myself in after I had seen her. I told her I'd meet her in the Mermaid pub, which is on Boothferry Estate, at about two o'clock that afternoon.

Just before two o'clock that day I went back to my mate's flat, the one where his girlfriend had done the nurse's job on me. She came screaming at me saying that the bloke that I'd battered and robbed was her Dad, who she hadn't seen for six years! The police had got the kid on the motorbike and he'd led them to her flat.

The pack was closing in. The net was tightening around me. I knew it was only a matter of time before they picked me up...

I went straight to the Mermaid pub to see Kerry as arranged. My brother Richard was also in there with his wife, Mary. They were all worried about what I'd done, so I agreed to hand myself in after we'd had a game of pool - and another drink. One for the road, so to speak.

While I was playing pool with Richard, who is a dab hand at pool, these two builders came in.

They were in high spirits, and came over to the pool table and put their money down. That acted as a marker to say who was on the table next.

That was okay as far as it went, but when these two wankers went and sat next to our wives and started to be a bit too cheeky for my liking, that was their first big mistake!

I didn't like what they were saying to my wife, things like, 'What you doing tonight love?' and 'Would you like to come out with me?'

When Kerry told one of them she was married and told him to leave her alone, he wouldn't take the hint.

So I went across and said, 'Now then arsehole, why don't you do what she has just asked you to do and fuck off?'

He then made another big mistake.

'Why don't you try and make me?' he asked.

Within 30 seconds he was flat on his back after I'd punched him senseless. Then on top of that I was hitting him in the face with the butt of the pool cue. The ladies were screaming for me to stop but I couldn't stop and when I saw his mate run out the pub, I ran after him.

There was a push-bike outside the pub, you could leave yer bike unlocked in them days. Well I jumped on this bike and soon caught up with this other so-called hard-case that was going to fill us in. He was running and crying at the same time. I'd never seen a grown man cry like that before.

As I was pedalling alongside of him I kept saying, 'When you stop running I'm going to kick your fucking head in.' With that, he ran down a long back alley and tried to jump over this seven-foot fence. When he jumped off the top of the fence I heard him cry in pain that he thought he had broken his leg.

When I climbed on top of the fence I saw his leg looked twisted and that he was in agony. But just to make sure he wasn't acting I jumped off the fence and jumped on his leg. He was screaming.

Then I started to punch him in the face, yelling,

'Don't you ever chat my wife up again because next time I'll kill you, do you understand?'

He mumbled summat about being sorry and I just left him crying on the floor.

I started to pedal back to the Mermaid but when I turned into the street I saw there were about six cop cars outside the pub. I knew the coppers were obviously there for me. So I took a different route and headed for Kenny's where my dogs were. When I got to Kenny's he told me the coppers had just been, not five minutes earlier.

With that, the most gorgeous policewoman that I'd ever seen knocked on Kenny's door and asked to speak to me outside. I knew it was time to hand myself over. The coppers knew I would never hit a lady, I never have!

When I stepped outside of Kenny's there must have been about twenty coppers waiting for me, all male, a police van and about six cop cars! The policewoman said,

'Mally Welburn, I am arresting you for the assault on Rob Warton, your friend who you headbutted outside of the Gipsyville Tavern, also for the assault on the Giant in Hessle.

Also for the theft of ten thousand pounds - and finally for the assault on the two builders in or near the Mermaid pub. You do not have to say anything, but whatever you do say may be used in evidence in court at a later date.'

I just put my hands out so that she could put the handcuffs on me. Two seconds later about six coppers jumped on me and threw me in the back of the waiting police van...

'Where's the ten grand?' the coppers kept asking me.

I didn't know what they were talking about.

'Come on, we know you took it, where is it?' they kept asking. When they got me to the police station and I emptied my pockets, some of the coppers' eyes nearly popped out of their sockets. They must have thought that I'd nicked the ten grand off the Giant. But I just kept telling them I didn't know what they were talking about.

Then they asked where had I got the money?

I told them that I had won it on the horses, but they just never believed me. They took my fingerprints and photograph and then banged me up in a cell without my shoes. They reckoned some people had tried - and succeeded - to hang themselves in their cell with their shoelaces. So it was 'Shoes off,' before I was put in the cell. Funny, I always take my shoes off when I visit people's houses, well there's that much dog shit on the pavements nowadays, you never know what you're walking in, especially when it's dark.

Well I sure was in the dark and in the shit from what these coppers were telling me - of what I'd done to four people within the space of just two days. And on top of it all, where was the missing ten grand that the Giant reckoned he had on him at the time of our little 'scuffle'?

He was in intensive care but all he was worried about was his ten grand. He could remember he'd ten grand in a briefcase and that he'd had it with him when he got in a taxi. But the problem was he didn't know which taxi he'd got in!

The police even asked me what the name of the taxi-company was that dropped the Giant off that day? But how the hell was I to know? I just went outside the pub and there it was!

They asked me the colour of the car and what the driver looked like and what age group he was? The coppers were not questioning me about the assaults until they got to the bottom of the missing ten grand.

I was allowed to see a solicitor and I always asked for John Robinson, he was one of the good guys. John always told you what was going on and I never lied to him. I told him how I got into the fight with the Giant and how I was shitting myself in case this guy got out of the taxi. I truly believed it would have been me in intensive care if he had. He was bigger than me Dad!

I told my solicitor all what I could remember and said I admitted to what I'd done and I didn't know why I'd done it. But I was pissed up and on the rum. I know it was no excuse and I deserved all that was coming to me.

My solicitor told me to plead guilty and to hold my hands up to what I'd done and I'd be looking at doing three years, more if we couldn't find out where this ten grand was!

I told my solicitor I didn't know anything about the missing ten grand. But I later thanked John for doing his spade work because after I gave him a brief description of the taxi and the driver, he managed to track the taxi firm down. The driver checked his car and lo and behold, under his seat was the missing briefcase with the ten grand in it.

The taxi driver took it to the police station but that didn't come to light until after I'd been in the police cells for two days. Then, on the third day I was up in front of the Judge to be remanded to prison while the police collected all the evidence and witness statements. I was put on remand in Leeds prison until a court date was available.

While I was in the police cells they charged me with three assaults and attempted robbery. But by the time it got to court the robbery charge had been dropped and one of the assaults had changed to a wounding. Anyway, within three days I was in the back of a police van in a cage on my way to Leeds Prison. These vans were divided into eight little compartments, each big enough for only one person.

During my journey to Armley Jail in Leeds I started to get the 'thinks' on. I started to think about what I'd done wrong. Then I started to think about all the hurt I'd caused to my loved ones. My wife Kerry, my baby daughter, Tammie - and not forgetting my loving Mother.

I started to think what a wanker I was. What a mug I was.

MALLY - THE REBEL WITHOUT A PAUSE

What an arsehole, look what I'd gone and done. Then I started to think what was I doing there? What was I doing in the back of a 'pig van' - on my way to jail?

For what? I only stuck the nut on 'my mate' who was most probably cheating on his girlfriend by going down a dark alley with one of those shady ladies. I think he was on for a course record that night. Picking a woman up in Tavern and taking her down the back alley where nobody goes - well, think about it, you don't take your girlfriend down there, do you?

I only went for a piss, I never saw them, and he made me piss down my pants! He should not have been down there. That's what I was thinking anyway - on the way to Leeds in the back of that van.

Then the two builders. I clouted one in the pub and chased one of them on that bike. I started to put the picture together in my mind of what happened that day because after all I was well pissed. But after three days you start to sober up, and you start to get flashbacks. We were playing pool and these two wankers came over to us, we never went to them. One of them was trying to chat-up my wife. He wanted to fight.

Then all of a sudden the Giant came into my mind and I thought, 'Oh fucking hell, what did I do to him?'

I'd left him on the floor, unconscious and bleeding. I saw the image of his battered face in my mind, over and over again.

Then I just kept seeing this mountain of a man in the back of the taxi. And all I'd wanted to do was to get the fuck away from the pub that I'd been turned away from. But the Giant would not let it go. He was screaming, 'Fuck off or else I'll kill you!'

I just snapped. I thought there's no other man going to hit me like my Dad did. So it didn't bother me how big the bloke in the back of the taxi was.

He couldn't be harder than my old man, could he?

There was no man that could hit you as hard as my Dad did. Maybe I owe my Dad a lot for toughening me up and making me able to stand up to any man. But then again I think, if only me Dad had been there for us when we needed him, if only he could have been that loving Father. And now - look what I was turning into! I was turning into my old man.

'Oh fuck!'

And I was facing three years in nick because of it! Three years, that's what my solicitor had told me.

I was facing three charges. Two were for common assault and one was for the more serious offence of wounding! And the Giant was still in intensive care!

Oh fuck! What had I gone and done?

On the plus side - if you could call it that - the charge of robbery had been dropped. Thank fuck the driver found that briefcase under his seat. Can you imagine if a passenger had found it? They would have had one lucky ride that night.

I often wonder if a passenger had found it, would they have handed it in? And if John Robinson, my solicitor hadn't done the job that the police should have done, to track down the taxi firm and the driver, would the driver have handed the ten grand in, if nowt had been said? I think we can all guess the answer to that one!

While all them thoughts were going through my head, the next thing I remember was getting out of the police van and being led into the Reception in Leeds prison.

There I was kitted-out with my prison clothes and given my prison number. As I was only on remand, I wore different clothes to the men that had been sentenced. I also got to wear my own shoes, with me taking a size 14, they never had any others big enough to fit me.

Next we got a shower and then put the prison clothes on that we'd been issued with. Then we got a bit of grub - which was cold. Then you listened for your name and number. My number was 65573.

There must have been about fifty of us that had been put on remand that day from all parts of the country. We were all waiting for our names and numbers to see which part of the jail we were going to spend our time in.

There were four sections to the prison. Well, when I say 'sections', they were like big corridors and each corridor had four landings. On each landing there was an endless row of cells. It was a massive place from the inside was Leeds prison. And I remember you never got to see the front of it until you were leaving after serving your sentence!

They called the corridors, wings. I was put on D wing and my cell number was D-4-23. So that was the fourth floor and 'bedsit' number twenty-three! Each cell had a small window that was so high up, you had to stand on someone's shoulders to look out of most of them. There was no glass in the window space, just metal bars! I think that was to let the fresh air in because, believe me, it did stink in Leeds Prison when I was there, even more so when it came to slop out time! Slop out was when you emptied your plastic bucket in the morning. The bucket could contain the night's piss from three inmates. And if you were unlucky enough to be in a cell with a bloke who had the shits - a lot more besides!

That was when the cell really did stink! But that was a rarity because most cons never shit in the bucket. They would shit in a newspaper and throw it out of the window - and it would land with a thud near the exercise yard...

In 1983 one of these cells became my home for a month, along with another two inmates who were also on remand. All that was in the cell was one single bed, a set of bunk beds, and not forgetting - the plastic bucket!

It was just like being back at number 11.

I was put in the same cell as a suspected murderer and a child-killer. Although I never knew he was a child-killer until one night when he slit his wrists with a razor blade that he'd managed to nick when the screw wasn't looking.

I could never get a good night's sleep. If it was not my cell-mates that were snoring, I could usually hear the other inmates in the other cells shouting out their windows to their fellow cons!

We were allowed a little transistor radio in our cell but nothing else. It sure was the bare essentials!

The night the child-killer slashed his wrists in our cell, he'd woken me up earlier to tell me he was going to kill himself. When I woke up later, there was blood all over the place.

There was a button on the wall that you pressed in case of an emergency. It alerted the nightwatchman, at the end of the wing.

That night, 'Cloggy' took his time coming to our cell and when he did come, he refused to open the door. He had to wait for other prison officers to assist him. It must have taken a couple of hours.

While we were waiting, the murderer and me wrapped a

pillowcase round each of the child-killer's wrists to help stop the bleeding. When the screws finally arrived to take him away, the murderer and me were taken to separate cells.

At least I got a good couple of hours sleep until seven in the morning when I was woken up by,

'Come on Welburn, the Governor wants to see you to get your story of what happened to this child-murderer.'

'Child-murderer?' I shouted.

'What the fuck are you putting a child-murderer in with me for?'

One of the screws said, 'Come on Welburn, we know you've done it!'

I said, 'Fuck off! The guy cut his own wrists as far as I know - and he'd told us he was in for theft!'

A lot of inmates didn't tell us what they were in for, but *I* wasn't ashamed to tell other inmates what I'd done. I think telling other inmates what I was in for, helped me during my time in Leeds. And telling a little white lie to the screw who I used to sell fish to, helped me even more.

He ended up getting me packets of cigs and a Mars bar or two because I'd told him I was also in for selling stolen fish and that the police were looking into it. I had that screw by the balls, so to speak, but I didn't want to squeeze them too hard. After all, I was only on remand and I knew that once I had been to court and been sentenced, I would be coming back to Leeds prison and he would then know what my crimes were. He could make it hard for me.

When I got to see the Governor, I kept asking him,

'Why did you put a child-killer in the same cell as someone who had killed another man and who was facing life in prison?' And in with *me,* someone who'd battered a bloke all over the place and who was well known for fighting?

The Governor's reply was, 'Lack of bed space, Welburn.'

But as I was led back to my cell by two screws, I asked them the same question and one of them said, 'Work it out for yourself Welburn.'

My reply was that if I'd known what the killer had done to that poor child, I would most probably have held his hand while he slit his wrists. After all, I had a young daughter at home myself.

MALLY - THE REBEL WITHOUT A PAUSE

They then put me in a three-man cell that I had to myself. As they locked the door behind me I shouted,
'If there's a lack of bed space, why am I in a cell that three men should be in, yet I'm on my own?'
'Work it out for yourself, Welburn,' the screw repeated. 'Work it out for yourself.' Then he said, 'Now get your head down.' It really blew my head that time in Leeds nick.

I told my solicitor and when he himself asked why the child-killer had been put in with me, the Governor's reply was again simply, 'A lack of cells.'

Nothing much has changed over the years with regard to lack of cells. But maybe that's because they don't have three prisoners in each cell nowadays - and they nearly all have their own telly and toilet. Some inmates are even allowed to keep their cell door open and the prison officers are like care workers. How times have changed, we used to be banged up in a stinking cell with two other inmates for twenty-three hours a day!

You could get different cell mates almost weekly if one was only on remand for a few days. So you could meet a lot of different people from all walks of life in a short space of time. Every day in Armley started in exactly the same way when the lights came on at 7 am and woke us up. We would then hear the jingle-jangle of the keys opening the cell doors and the screw shouting, 'Slop out!' In a strange way I looked forward to hearing them keys opening the cell doors and the screw's footsteps coming along the landing. Hoping he'd stop at my door and ask if I wanted to go down to the gymnasium or the exercise yard. Or better still, to hand me that loving letter that my Mother or my wife Kerry had written to me.

I sure got plenty of time to get the thinks on while I was in that cell for twenty-three hours a day. And I got the stinking thinking thoughts - thinking stinking thoughts - try saying that three times quickly.

The only way I could keep in touch with the outside world was by letter. I was only allowed to send two out a week but I could receive as many as I wanted. And I was always grateful for the loving letters I received from both my Mother and Kerry and not forgetting the little drawings that my three-year old daughter Tammie used to send me. It really did crack me up reading the letters I received. I can't begin to imagine what life must have been like for my Mother and Kerry while I was banged up, waiting for my court date, so I could get sentenced and get on and do my time.

There's a saying, 'If you can't do the time, don't do the crime.' Well in my case I knew as soon as I sobered up, I'd done wrong. But it's the hurt you do to your loved ones.

I was facing anything up to three years for what I had done - and to try and get that into my head was hard to take - stinking thinking!

Don't get me wrong, I knew what I had done was wrong but I believed it wasn't all my fault.

Where was the help? Where was the help for that arsehole, who when he got on the rum, wanted to fight the world?

Yet nowadays it seems if you get hooked on smack and heroin there is always help available. I agree there should be the help for them poor souls that the devil has got hold of. One little prick, that's all it takes. They tell me one hit and you're hooked. I've seen some really nice people get hooked on smack and heroin and it's very sad to see how they end up.

The devil used to come to me in the shape of a rum bottle, please don't ask me how and why. I've tried working it out for myself and I believe there comes a turning point in your life. Sometimes you see that turning point at different stages in your life but do nowt about it and then it's gone. But I also believe if you want to do something with your life there is only you that can make it happen. You have got to want to do something to make it happen.

There are many different things that happen to you in life that make you want to start thinking of changing it. For me, one of those times was when I was in that cell in Armley. I said to myself, 'I am never coming to a shit hole like this again.'

It really was a shit hole and it stunk like one, what with all them plastic buckets getting emptied at seven-thirty every morning. Then we would queue up for our breakfast and when I say we got porridge - we got porridge, we also got one piece of bacon, one egg and a few beans or tomatoes.

I thought I was at our Trevor's!

I was quite lucky because there were a few lads from Hull in Leeds prison at the same time as me. Two of the guys,

MALLY - THE REBEL WITHOUT A PAUSE

Maurice and Joe, used to work on the serving counter and they would give me an extra dollop of spud - or whatever was going. If you upset the grub-servers, which some did, your belly suffered, so, 'Look after the grub men' was my motto.

I thank Maurice and Joe for looking after me food-wise while I was doing my time in Leeds and later when our paths crossed again in Preston prison.

We got our breakfast on a metal tray that was divided into three sections, one for yer porridge, one for your main meal such as scrambled egg and bacon and the third compartment was for your bread. You could have as much bread as you wanted, but you only got a small dab of butter and a spoonful of jam. But if Maurice and Joe were on the butter and jam, they'd give me three times as much.

After we'd got our breakfast, we had to go to our cell to eat our grub, locked up until dinner time. Then maybe, if the weather was nice we would get an hour's exercise in the big yard, where there would be about half a dozen screws with Alsatian dogs growling at us as we walked past them round the yard in pairs.

It was a bit like the animals went in two by two! Then it was back to our cell until teatime. The same 'get yer grub' routine again, then back to our cell where at about nine on the night, they would come and give us a hot drink in our plastic cup - not the bucket. Then at ten o'clock, it was lights out.

It was the same thing day in, day out when we were on remand. We just looked forward to our grub, our letters, and the visit from our solicitor to let us know what was happening. I used to look forward to that hour's exercise to see if there were any 'newbies' from Hull and to catch up on what was happening in my hometown. We Hull lads stuck together.

I was on remand for about eight weeks altogether. In that time I made a couple of appearances in front of the judge at Hull Magistrates Court, just to get the case adjourned again while they got more evidence and witness statements.

We would travel in the back of the caged van to the court, about eight prisoners at a time. Some never got back in the van. They were dealt with at court and we never saw them again, but some, we all knew, were going to be doing a long stretch.

I never came across the child-killer again. I think after the night he slashed his wrists, they took him to hospital and then back to prison where he was put on a wing called Rule 43.

Rule 43 was the wing where they kept all the child-molesters and other kinds of paedophile and, generally, anybody us other prisoners might not like. They never mixed them with us other inmates. But someone had made a mistake earlier, putting the child-killer in with a murderer and a 'madman', the 'madman' being me! I often wonder if he slashed himself to get away from the murderer and me? Because God knows what would have happened to him if we'd found out what he'd done! And what would have happened to him if the three hundred madmen on our wing had found out what he'd done? I'll leave you to work that out. But I believe I saved his life that night by stopping the flow of blood from his slashed wrists.

Maybe I would have wanted to kill him myself for what that man had done to his girlfriend's baby. He'd murdered a child he actually knew, I later found out. He killed the baby because it wouldn't stop crying, I think it was two years old.

I wonder if he's still in prison, it's over 24 years ago now, so I doubt it! But just think of the pain that poor baby's Mother must go through every time it's the child's birthday. Yet the killer probably gets a cake and a card on his birthday nowadays. You often wonder where the justice is.

I was hoping for justice for what I'd done, when the next day, I got the date for my court hearing...

CHAPTER TWENTY
GUILTY

I got my court hearing date, it was November 3 1983.

About three weeks before my court date I wrote two letters.
One was to the Giant who I found out was out of hospital
within a week of our chance encounter outside that pub. I said
I was sorry for what I'd done to him, he knew I didn't know
he'd had ten grand in a briefcase. All I wanted to do was to get
in that taxi and go back to my local. I told him I feared for my
life, that he'd reminded me of my Father and I thought he was
going to knock 'ten bells of shit' out of me! I also told him I
had a wife and a young child to look after.

But I got no reply.

I found out later that he'd just split up with his wife and he'd
gone to the bank and drawn out all their life-savings and had
been on a bender himself for a few days!

He was even known to be a bit of a bully around Hessle. He
was a big man.

I even found out he was burning ten-pound notes just to light
his cigarettes with.

I'd have liked to have been his mate when he was burning his
cash!

I also found out that the police kept asking the Giant for a
statement and asking if he wanted to press charges against me.
But he never made any statement and he didn't want to press
charges.

So I was going to court on my own admission and the
statement that I'd made.

I was once told, 'Never own up to anything in a court of law
- let them prove it. Let *them* get the witnesses, let *them* get the
statements.'

They also say that about 50% of court cases break down
simply because many people don't want to go into a court of
law. But I sure was willing to go into a court of law over that

baby-killer! I was never asked to attend though. I guess it depends on the severity of the case, whether people attend court or not.

The other letter I wrote was to a 'Judge in Chambers'. My solicitor told me to write to him and tell him what I'd done and that I was sorry and ready and willing to serve whatever sentence I received. I also had to tell him that I needed to go home, even if it was just for a week before my court case, so that I could sort my marriage out - and not forgetting my mortgage repayments that I'd fallen behind with.

If I didn't get things sorted out, my wife and child could be out on the streets - without a roof over their heads.

That was just one of the knock-on effects of what I'd done!

I said I realised what I'd done was wrong and asked to be allowed to go home for a week to sort things out.

There were no computers about in them days and I'm bad at handwriting. I can't do joined-up writing but I made an effort, got a dictionary from the prison library and looked for all the right words to write to my 'Judge in Chambers'. Once I'd found all the words, I wrote down what my solicitor had suggested for me to say and ended my letter by saying that if I didn't get the chance to go home and sort my life out, the future looked very sombre - dark and gloomy. And believe me, my future did look sombre.

I've just looked the word 'sombre' up again because I'm also a crap speller, thank God for spell-check on this computer.

I found out that my brother Richard had been charged with assault on one of the builders in the Mermaid pub. I didn't see our kid clout either of them so it may have been when I was chasing the other builder on that push-bike. Come to think of it, I never got charged with pinching a bike - it might have already been pinched anyway!

Our kid had pleaded not guilty and he was given police bail to attend court on the same day as me.

A week before my court hearing, I was in my cell with another two inmates and we were just swapping our food from one tray to another. I was swapping my pudding for a piece of fish when all of a sudden the cell door opened and the screw shouted at me, 'Welburn, you've got 'Judge in Chambers' - get all your gear together, you're going home...'

MALLY - THE REBEL WITHOUT A PAUSE

Well I gave all my tea to the other two inmates. I was taken to the Reception where I first started my journey in Leeds prison.

I was given my own clothes and released. I had to make my own way to the train station and find my own way home, which I did.

I remember it was a Friday because we got fish on a Friday in prison - and it wasn't salmon by the way. You never know, it could have been some of that fish I used to sell to that screw. I don't think it was though, because the fish I used to sell him was the best that money could buy.

I think the fish we got when we were in nick was from the 'fish meal' place. That's where it was sent when they couldn't sell it on the market or if the fish was rotten and not fit for the fish shops. It was sent to be turned into fishmeal, which the farmers fed to their pigs. But I think that some bright spark might have thought about selling it to the prison service - it definitely smelt like it some days...

When I got home to Kerry and Tammie it was just a case of preparing myself to 'go away' for three years or more. It was going to be one big trip!

I classed going to prison as like going to sea on the trawlers, with regard to the time I spent away from home. But everything else about it was of course very different!

How was Kerry going to cope if I got three years in prison? Would she still want me when I got out? Would she wait for me? Would she have found someone else by the time I got out? Would she be able to pay the mortgage? Would she be able to manage? Would she still love me? Would she write to me? It started me 'stinking thinking' again!

I mean I used to sing to her that Beatles song,
'When I get older, losing my hair, many years from now.
Will you still be sending me a Valentine?
Birthday greetings, bottle of wine.'
And what about my baby daughter? Was I going to lose her, like I'd 'lost' my son, Peter? Would I lose her love? Would she have a new Daddy? How would it affect her?

I could not let this happen!

When you know that you're going to be sent to prison, you realise the hurt it's going to cause for the ones that you leave behind. It was like a death really! It was very, very sombre. That week at home flew by.

I don't think I went out of the house. I just spent the time with my wife and daughter - oh and not forgetting PFC, my favourite greyhound. I decided that it wasn't fair to leave Kenny and Kelly to look after the six dogs but I'm happy to say they went to live with their owners. Greyhounds do make good family pets and both Kerry and Tammie loved PFC.

I rang the mortgage company and they said if we missed more than three month's payments they had the power to repossess the house. We were already two months behind at that stage. I knocked on a good friend's door and borrowed three months payments, hoping it would hold the mortgage company back a bit. But facing three years in the nick, I realised I couldn't hold them back that long!

My trial on November 3 1983 should have been held at Beverley but for some reason was moved to Hull Crown Court. They didn't have a jury that day because I'd pleaded guilty to all three charges. They were two for assault occasioning actual bodily harm and the more serious offence of wounding.

Richard was also up for assault on one of the builders. He had planned to plead 'Not Guilty' but changed it after his solicitor advised him to plead guilty and to expect a fine because he'd been acting in self defence.

No witnesses turned up that day, because no one would come forward. The main evidence the police had was my own confessions from when they'd questioned me in the police station. There was no way I could deny the trouble I had gone and got myself into - after all, the two undercover coppers saw me chop the Giant down - and they were there in court that day. But neither my mate Rob who I'd headbutted or the builders wanted to press charges. Somebody in the Mermaid pub had told the police that it had been the Welburns who were fighting in the pub that day and I admitted to putting the pool cue in one of the builder's faces and punching him and then chasing the other on that bike.

I never saw our kid punch anyone that day and after all, he didn't get picked up for it until a month later! But there he was on one of the same charges as me!

MALLY - THE REBEL WITHOUT A PAUSE

When I met Richard at court he told me his brief had told him that he was getting a 'walk out' and to only expect a fine - but added that I was facing three years!

'Cheers our kid,' was my reply. The Judge had his white wig on. He didn't look a happy chappy.

He looked like the Judge in 'Rumpole of the Bailey', the popular courtroom drama on TV. I think it was on TV in the 70s. The court scene was just like you see on the TV, you had the Judge who sat on his perch all on his own. What do you call it where a Judge sits in the Crown Court, I don't know do you? I know he sits higher than anyone else in the courtroom. The courtroom we were in that day was the one that had the trapdoor in, so to speak - the door that led you down the steps and into the court cells. I think that's where the saying comes from 'send him down'.

There you go again, you learn something new every day. As the saying goes, 'A day without learning is a day wasted.'

Well I sure learnt that if I'd have kept my mouth shut and not owned up to the offences that were put against me, I'd have only been charged with the wounding of the Giant - and he never wanted to press charges and didn't even make a statement!

So I was in court on my own admission, which my barrister pointed out when he was putting my defence to the Judge.

There was no jury that day, all that were in the courtroom were the Judge, the Clerk of the Court, and someone tapping away, ten to the dozen on a little typewriter every time someone spoke - I wish I could type as quick as she did. This book would have been in your hands a lot quicker.

You then had the prosecutor and two of his side-kicks.

Then there was my barrister and a couple of his team and a reporter for the Hull Daily Mail. But most important were the four coppers and two prison screws.

When I was led into the courtroom I was told to stand near the steps that led down to the court cells. Stood near the steps were a copper and a screw! Our kid was stood next to me and sat next to him was the other screw and a copper. And at the back of the courtroom were another two boys in blue.

I knew I was going down, but for how long? That was for the Judge to decide! But you should have seen the Judge's face when the prosecutor started telling the court what that wild madman Malcolm Welburn had done to these three innocent guys - such that all of them had to spend time in hospital and one of them had been in intensive care.

'One victim', the prosecutor continued, 'had suffered a broken leg when trying to run away from this crazed man,' pointing at me, 'who threatened to kill him if he got hold of him. To escape from that madman he climbed on a seven-foot fence and jumped onto a pile of bricks, hence breaking his leg.'

My barrister jumped up and said that his client wasn't mad, it was the effect of the alcohol. And that I didn't break the man's leg - he'd done that himself jumping over the wall. And with regards to the Giant, all I'd wanted to do was to get in a taxi and go home to sleep off the effects after celebrating my lucky win on the horses. But when I went to get into the taxi I was threatened by the Giant and I'd felt I couldn't back down to him. Then my barrister told the court about our upbringing.

How we were beaten up by our very brutal Father. How we witnessed the beatings that our loving Mother used to receive from our Giant of a Father. How from a very young age, we were made to drink rum and whisky, which led to us being put in children's homes for our safety. And then how I was sent to Approved School and Detention Centre and that one way or another my problems had all been caused through alcohol.

My barrister then said that I'd learned the errors of my ways and that when I'd woken up in the police station, I'd realised and admitted I'd done wrong.

The eight weeks that I'd served on remand had made me realise that if I was given a custodial sentence, the future not just for me but for my young wife and baby daughter looked very sombre indeed. And if I wasn't able to work we'd probably lose our house as well. But the prosecutor then jumped up and said,

'He should have thought of what would happen when he was drinking the rum and whisky. We just can't allow this man to be put back on the streets. He should be locked away for a long time and then let him realise that he can't go round headbutting, punching, putting pool cues into people's faces and pulling people out of taxis and punching the living daylights out of them.'

Richard leaned over and whispered to me,

'You're going down for a long time Mally.' He was a constant comfort to me was Richard!

But I knew he was right, even the coppers and the screws started to puff their chests out as if to say, 'Stand by, we've one coming down here, let's be ready in case he kicks off!'

The Judge then said he had heard enough. And that the evidence and the admission of the offences were enough to convict me and he had no option but to impose a prison sentence. Well with that, the prison officers and the police stood up ready to take me down!

The Judge then declared, that for the first offence of assault causing actual bodily harm - that was headbutting my mate - I would serve three months in prison. For the second offence of assault causing actual bodily harm - fighting with the builder - I would serve another three months in prison.

I was stood next to my brother Richard, staring straight at the Judge and when he gave the sentences out Richard tapped me on the arm and whispered, 'No probs Mally.'

Then the Judge looked straight at me and said, 'And now to the third and most important offence of wounding the man in the taxi. I accept that you never went looking for trouble with this man and that he refuses to give a statement and doesn't wish to attend the court today. But you went much too far and we just can't allow this kind of behaviour to be seen on the streets of this City. You are lucky not to be standing in front of me charged with affray and putting fear into the general public who witnessed you acting like a wild animal. For this offence you will go away for nine months - so that's a total of fifteen months. I hope that gives you plenty of time to think about what you've done. Take him away.'

I was taken straight down the steps after giving Richard a hug and whispering to him to look after Kerry and Tammie for me. 'Don't worry about that,' our kid replied.

As they were taking me down I looked round and saw my wife Kerry and Richard's wife Mary at the back of the court. They had both turned up without me knowing.

I didn't even get time to say goodbye, just a split second's eye contact with Kerry - and I could see she was upset.

Well no sooner had I got down them steps and into the court cells than I heard Richard's voice again. He'd been sent down as well. He'd got three months. Yippee, I thought, at least I had my brother coming on the journey with me! As you know, I love Richard to bits and I didn't want him to do time, but if there was one person I'd have wanted with me to do a bit of time, it would have been Richard. I was buzzing when I saw him. But he was gutted, he thought he'd just get a fine.

Then I asked the prison officer, who we called Boss, how long would I have to serve?

He soon worked it out and said, 'You got fifteen months all together but with you doing two months on remand already and with good behaviour you could be out in nine or ten months. So you ain't done too bad Welburn.'

'Thank you Boss,' I said, not really knowing whether I should be happy with what he'd just told me or not.

Richard was told that he'd only do eight weeks, which was a walk in the park compared to what I had to do. But hey, it was a lot better than the three years I was expecting. I thought of it as the equivalent of doing roughly three, twelve-week trips on the trawlers, that's how I looked at it, it didn't seem too bad then!

We were taken back to Armley Jail in Leeds in the back of that caged van, with me in one cage and Richard in another.

On arrival at Reception at Armley it was a different ball game! I knew a few of the lads who were dishing out our prison clothes, so they gave us some decent clothes to wear. Just like the lads on the grub-serving duties they could give you 'more or less'. In the case of the Reception lads, they could give you new stuff or old shirts and jeans and underpants that had been well worn.

Our kid and me got decent clothes to wear. The shirts that we had to wear when we got sentenced were blue and white pinstriped - the same colours that we had at North Sea Camp. They said the blue and white stripes dazzled the flies. I don't know about that but we sure needed our striped shirts when we were 'parcel picking' and at 'slop out' time.

Richard and me were then fortunate to be put in cells next to each other and it was a joy to see him every day for a week or so, until they shipped him out to an open prison.

MALLY - THE REBEL WITHOUT A PAUSE

I think Richard was pleased to go to an open prison because it was more relaxed, after all, he only had a month to do. I also think he was glad to get away from me because every day I used to slip a piece of paper under his cell door with a home-made crossword puzzle on it. He told me only recently that they used to do his head in!

When we were sentenced and did time in prison back in 1983 we were made to do a job to get our pocket money. I think the basic wage then was £1.50 for a week's work but we got more money if we did different jobs like working in the kitchens, serving the food, working in the laundry department, or cleaning the wings with a mop and bucket.

There was no staying in our cell for twenty-three hours a day like when on remand. They had a mailbag sewing department and wood and metalworking departments.

The top job in prison was the gym orderly's job. But that job always went to a long-term prisoner.

With at least three hundred prisoners on each wing we very rarely got to read the daily newspapers that had to be passed from cell to cell. If we were lucky enough we got to read Monday's paper, probably about Thursday or Friday! By then however, there'd only be a couple of pages of it left. The rest had been used for the shit parcels that were thrown out of the cell windows at night...

Well guess what job I got - with a little help from the screw I used to sell the fish to. He came to my cell and told me he'd got me a good job working in the parcel department. I thought it was where all the parcels sent to prisoners on remand used to come in. But I soon found out when I was issued with a pair of wellies, a pair of gloves and a barrow and spade that the job wasn't quite what I was hoping for!

With all my gear, I looked like I was going to the sea-side. Well, I was outside all right - but collecting the shit parcels that had been thrown into the exercise yard the night before! But at least I got to read the papers. And the job didn't bother me. I'd been used to shovelling dog shit up most of my life and cleaning rabbit cages out, way back when at my 'loving home' at number 11!

I soon got to know the guards and their Alsatian dogs that patrolled the yard. But my parcel-picking days didn't last long even though I didn't mind it and the pay wasn't bad, at about £3 a week.

The only time the job wasn't so good was when it had been raining heavily the night before because the papers became unreadable...

I was then put in the laundry department but I really hated my spell in there! I'm sure the civilian screw in there must have related to that one at North Sea Camp! They both got a kick out of making me count well over a thousand pairs of soiled underpants with my bare hands. And if the count was wrong I had to count them all over again!

I had to count them into three piles. You won't guess what they were.

The ones without skid marks, the ones with heavy skid marks and the ones that were just let's say, 'well soiled'. They stunk worse than the parcel-picking job but the money was a little bit more. You'd call it shit money, I suppose!

The socks were easy to count because they were all the same colour but there were some cons with very smelly feet in there!

I'm sure the prison service gave us some of them 'shit' jobs to see if we could take it. Believe me, lots of the cons refused to do the 'shit' jobs and were put back in their cells. They'd then be on about a pound a week and that wasn't even enough to buy a quarter of bacca, cig papers and a box of matches. That little lot cost us £1.30!

Yes we were allowed to smoke and have matches. We'd split a match into four to make them last longer and our tobacco would be rolled into cigs thinner than a match!

I never smoked when I was in prison but I soon found out how to get my Mars bars off the rest of the cons.

With my £3.50 week's wages for working in the 'sweat shop' laundry I would go to the prison canteen once a week. It was the highlight of the week to go spend my hard-earned cash at the prison canteen. We could buy cigs and bacca, cig papers, matches, shampoo, soap, chocolates, jam, butter, fruit and stamps and newspapers.

I would get a half ounce of bacca, cig papers, box of matches, stamps, Mars bars and a bit of fruit every week. We could also put what we didn't spend into a savings account - but not many chose to save their money.

After I had been to the canteen on a Friday, I'd go back to my cell and make about fifty roll-ups as thin as a match stick and split my matches, making four matches out of each one. Splitting a match with your fingernail was a real art.

Then on Sunday when most of the other cons had smoked their cigs, I'd offer them five roll-ups plus five matches for six roll-ups, plus a Mars bar - which they would give me back when they got their next week's ration.

It was my entrepreneurial spirit showing through again!

I soon had my regular clients, in fact I had a list of cons waiting to join up.

The Mars bar would soon get me that extra dollop of tatties and dollops of jam and butter plus I could swap a Mars bar for a read of the newspaper - unsoiled I must stress...

I had my little swap-shop up and running. I'd give five cigs and five matches for six cigs and a Mars bar back, so I got a cig and a Mars bar in exchange for five skinny matches from every deal. Not bad, eh? I did that for about four weeks in Leeds prison before it was time for me to be shipped out to: Her Majesty's Prison, 2, Ribbleton Lane, Preston, Lancs, PR1 5AB. That's the address on one of the letters that my loving Mother sent me.

Leeds prison was over-crowded, even in them days, so they shipped me out further away from home, putting more strain on my visiting loved ones.

Leeds prison was only an hour's train journey for Kerry and Tammie, but Preston was a good three-hour journey and you had to catch two trains.

I just couldn't let Kerry fetch the baby on that long journey to Preston. And I used to worry when Kerry had been to visit me on her own and worried about her getting back home safely.

But nine times out of ten she would meet up and travel with other women who had a boyfriend or husband in the same jail as me, so that eased the worry a bit.

When I left Leeds nick I left my little 'swap-shop business' to a friend who I knew didn't smoke. And I gave my stash of Mars bars away to the Hull lads that were on my wing.

Preston prison was just the same as Leeds prison - with exactly the same rules.

I got to Preston at the time of the Christmas football knockout. The wing I was put on didn't have a goalkeeper until I arrived. But to cut a long story short, our wing won the Christmas knockout on that concrete pitch, with the star of the show, Mally, 'The Cat', in goal!

I recall I even saved a few penalties.

I also got to play in the volleyball team and the basketball team, all within two weeks of arriving at Preston.

Sport really helped me on my journey through prison because if you were into sport there were a few good screws about who helped you with it, be it weight training or circuit training, right through to volleyball.

I soon joined all the night classes for every sport I could, just to get out of my cell and to keep fit.

Christmas is a very sad time when you're in prison and I was pleased to know that Kerry's Mother and Father, Pat and Dave made sure their daughter and granddaughter never went short over Christmas...

I got to work in the laundry again at Preston nick. But unlike Leeds, the guy in charge, I called him Bossman, wasn't a bad bloke - and he put me on shirts and jumpers.

Like me, he was also into sport and supported Stoke City. And when I told him Gordon Banks, the former Stoke and England goalkeeper had been my boyhood hero - and how I'd met him at Elland Road, Bossman took a shine to me and made my life easy.

Bossman was a really nice guy, so much so that when the gym orderly's job came up for grabs, he put my name forward, even though I'd only been in Preston nick for two minutes. And to my surprise I got the top job in the prison.

The three prison officers that worked in the gymnasium were also great guys. I owe them a lot for the help and support they gave me in keeping my mind occupied and getting me super fit! I really was one of the fittest cons in Preston prison by the time I left. From 8 o'clock in the morning till 10 o'clock at night it was almost non-stop exercise and sport.

My first job in the morning was to sweep the big gymnasium's wooden floors with used tea-leaves which helped to stain the wood. They were delivered from the kitchens with a delicious bacon butty, a pint of milk and the odd apple and orange that

MALLY - THE REBEL WITHOUT A PAUSE

one of the cons used to sneak in for me. Well, I needed my calcium and vitamins.

Then I had to get all the apparatus ready for when the cons arrived to do their circuit training, weight training or whatever was on for that particular session.

The day would start with a session for the cons that had disabilities. Even if they only had one arm or one leg they all loved to come to the gym.

I would help them with their training, every hour a different batch of cons would come to the gym. The cleaners, kitchen lads, workshop lads, laundry lads, anyone that wanted to, had to wait their turn to spend their hour in the gym. If the weather was nice we'd go outside to play football on the concrete pitch. A 30ft brick wall surrounded the prison, so there was no kicking the ball over the wall, or that was the end of the game! I used to join in with every session, I loved it. I loved playing volleyball and basketball. Then after tea at about 7 o'clock, the trainee prison officers were put through their paces.

I used to love it when the young and cocky, wannabe screws spewed up after an hour's work-out in the gym. Some of them had a bit of an attitude problem towards the inmates. I would be training alongside of them but would only be working at half my pace. I was ten times fitter than some of them wannabes.

Sport was a real leveller for the screws and the inmates. We should have more sport in schools. I look around me nowadays and we seem to be getting to be a nation of fatties. I blame all the fast food that's about - and the lack of exercise. So if you get the chance to keep yourself fit, do it - and lay off the junk foods.

Saying that, who am I to preach? I love my vanilla slices and Mars bars - and not forgetting my Cadbury's Whole Nut.

I have them as treats nowadays but when I was working out at the gym, like I was for twelve to fourteen hours a day in Preston prison, I needed my Mars bars, milk, fruit and meat. And the only way I was going to get all that in prison was through the 'belly boys' - the kitchen lads! I got to know quite a few inmates that worked in the kitchens. Well, I got to know most lads that came to the gym because I had to have their sannies - training shoes - and shorts and tee-shirts ready.

I got to know what size training shoes they all wore.

The shorts and tee shirts used to be in a big pile in the changing room and it was first in, best dressed, so to speak. But they had to come to me first to hand their working shoes in and ask for their size in sannies. They ranged from size four, right through to size fourteen but there were only a few of us that took a size fourteen!

It really was a mad rush when they came in for their sannies. Imagine twenty inmates all shouting at you - 'Size seven!'

'Mine are eights!'

'Tens please!'

'I want fives, mate!'

'Elevens for me!' - while I was crammed into my little office with all the sannies in little cubby holes.

My office was next to the changing rooms and showers.

I made sure I gave the right sized sannies to the right inmates but I remember one occasion when a new batch of inmates had been shipped in from other prisons and it was their first training session in the gym.

This big Rastafarian guy pushed to the front of the queue for a pair of size nine sannies and shouted at the top of his voice, 'Hey, Blood Clot! Work me da best size nines in da place or else *you'll* sure end up with a blood clot! Get me them now and every time I come in here, I want the same ones!'

'Wait yer fucking turn and don't tell me what to do', I shouted back at him. I then passed him a pair of size six sannies. He grabbed them off me and without checking the size, ran into the changing rooms to get the best shorts and tee-shirt because it was basketball time.

Well, when the gym officer blew his whistle you had to be on the gym floor ready to go. If you weren't ready - you had to do twenty press-ups! And everybody else had to do twenty press-ups as well, so you had to be on your toes.

I was always ready in my shorts and tee-shirt and stood next to the gym officer waiting for the inmates to come onto the 'dance floor'.

The last person out of the changing rooms was the big Rastafarian guy and he was late, stumbling about like one of Cinderella's ugly sisters. He was walking on his toes and looked like a ballerina - all he needed was a tutu!

He looked a right bonny sight as his shorts were too tight for him as well.

We all started to laugh at him when the gym officer called him Cinderella. And with him being late out of the changing rooms, he was told to get down and do twenty press-ups.

But he refused, saying it wasn't his fault and blaming the 'Blood Clot', pointing at me, who had given him size six instead of size nine sannies. He then continued to say what he was going to do to me after the session had finished.

'Oh yeah!' I shouted.

Well with that, the gym officer looked at me and said,

'Go sort him out Welly!'

Welly was the nickname the gym officers called me.

As we were leaving the gymnasium the gym officer shouted, '...with the proper sized sannies, Welly.'

'Yes Boss', I replied.

Well, no sooner than we'd got to the changing rooms, I headbutted the Rastafarian right in his face and as he fell to the floor I grabbed him around the neck with both hands and pulled him back to his feet. He was 'very dazed' and I shouted at him,

'Don't call me a fucking Blood Clot, you bastard! And if anyone asks, you fell over, do you understand me? Or else I'll batter you all over the place.'

He nodded and whispered, 'Yes.'

There was already a swelling on his forehead and it looked as though he was getting a black eye at the same time. He was very wobbly on his feet so I had to half-carry, half-drag him back to the gymnasium. Everyone had started playing basketball but they all stopped when they saw me appear with 'Cinderella'. I shouted to the prison officer that Cinders had slipped and banged his head in the changing room.

'Is that right Cinders?' asked one of the officers.

'Yes Boss,' was Cinders' mumbled reply.

The next time Cinders came to the gym we shook hands and I gave him the best pair of nines I had. He was a brilliant basketball player, especially in the correct sized shoes.

Just after that incident, the gym officer pulled me up and said, 'Be careful Welly, don't spoil yourself.' I took his advice.

When I wasn't in the gym I would be sleeping or playing

darts. Yes we were allowed to play darts, and I even used to get dart magazines sent to me by brother Raymond.

I ended up getting my own cell after a while because of my job. They knew I needed the rest. I worked long hours in that prison but in a strange way I loved it. I got on with doing my time, never bothered anyone, and just got on with my job...

Things were not going so well at home however.

Kerry was having a bad time. The bailiffs were closing in and she did her best to hold them off.

I used to write to Kerry and my Mother every week. And it was one of the highlights of the week to receive letters back from them both.

Another thing I looked forward to was when Kerry visited me once a month. It made me realise what I was missing. She was and still is a beautiful woman - I knew I'd be a fool to lose her!

In prison when we reached the point where we only had a hundred days of our sentence left, we were on what we called, countdown - ninety-nine and a break. That meant you had ninety-nine days and a breakfast left. Breakfast was our last meal in prison and we'd be woken up early, get our breakfast, go through Reception, then be out of the big doors!

When I had twenty days and a break left I was chosen to take part in a seven-day, new pre-release scheme, where we were allowed out into the community. We could go out of the prison to go camping, canoeing, abseiling down cliffs and to do country walks.

I remember one day as we were walking through a village we saw a betting shop and one of the screws who liked a bet as much as I did, asked me to pick him some winners. I think I picked him three winners out of four!

My reward was a lovely ice cream - with a flake in the top - plus he let me ring home.

Whether the scheme worked for everyone or not I don't know but it got me ready for going home. When the day finally arrived I was a little sad to leave Preston Prison because I'd met some really genuine guys and that wasn't just the screws. They say there's honour amongst thieves - there certainly was at Preston. I could leave my cell open without any fear of anyone going in and helping themselves.

MALLY - THE REBEL WITHOUT A PAUSE

Well I was going home, I'd done my time. When I came out I was five times as fit as when I went in. I even had to get some new clothes sent in that fitted me...

Well I hope that gave you an idea of what prison was like back in the 80s. It was July 1984 when I got out. They were taking our home off us.

I had to get work. But the company I'd been with had laid up most of their trawlers. What chance did I have of getting a job?

Kerry and me had even been thinking of moving to Scarborough if I'd have been able to get work on any of the small trawlers that were fishing out of there at the time. But it's all about being in the right place at the right time, and Scarborough didn't work out.

My search for work continued...

The next Chapter's about my efforts to make a living, and of how I lost my house - and my marriage!

Plus another, more unexpected, bombshell...

Take care
Mally

CHAPTER TWENTY-ONE
GREEN DOOR

I was released from Preston prison on July 10 1984.

Oh, I was looking forward to being with my loving wife and darling daughter again. Tammie was just three months short of her fourth birthday. And most of all, I was looking forward to going round to see the 'Pal of my cradle days' - my Mother.

I've just read the letters I've managed to save over the years from my loving Mother and the last letter she wrote to me in Preston prison confirms my release date.

I've always kept my Mother's letters in a 'shoebox full of memories'. Many a time, it was her letters that kept me going during dark times - and as I was released from prison, things couldn't have looked much darker...

After getting home, the first thing I had to do was to find work and pay off the mountain of debt that being in prison had got us into. I tell yer being in prison has a huge, knock-on effect. But there was only one person I could blame for all the debts we had - myself!

Why couldn't I be like normal people, get a proper job and go home to my loving wife and daughter every night?

Well, after I came home from Preston prison I couldn't get a job of any description and I believe it was because of my name and reputation.

At every door I knocked on I seemed to get that knock back! I couldn't even get a factory job.

I think one of the reasons was the charge-hands who worked on the factory floor, I most probably had taken their dinner money off them when we were kids - and there was no way I was going to take orders off them at this stage of my life.

If they'd said to me do this, do that, sweep the floor etc - I'd have most probably stuck the brush up their arse!

No I didn't really want to work in a factory. All the people that worked in factories seemed like robots to me.

MALLY - THE REBEL WITHOUT A PAUSE

They were all ruled by the clock - and I didn't like clock-watching! But I was desperate to find work and prepared to do anything that would pay the bills!

To stand a chance of getting a driving job, I first needed to get my licence back off the Vet. He'd kept it in lieu of payment for my dogs' injections. I still had no money and I'll never forget the Vet's words when he handed over my licence, after I told him it was against the law for someone to hold another man's driving licence.

'Here's your licence, don't ever come back to this fucking surgery again!' he said.

If I hadn't just got out of prison I'd have stuck the nut on him, no matter how big he was. I told him there was no need to swear. He then told me to fuck off again.

So I told him to go fuck himself, even though he was another Giant, bigger than my old man!

My licence didn't bring me instant employment but I was happy to have it back. And a little later I had a stroke of luck, when I applied for a bricklayer's job in Antwerp in Belgium that was advertised in the local paper.

The advert read, 'Bricklayers and labourers required - £10 an hour - must be time-served.'

It also said they preferred a '2 and 1 gang', which was two bricklayers and one labourer. Now I'd never worked on a building site in my life, well, not until I got to Antwerp in Belgium.

I rang the number on the advert and basically 'blagged' the guy on the phone, that I'd be coming across with me Dad and uncle, as a two and one gang. He gave me the job and told me to keep all my receipts and he'd pay my travelling expenses when I got to the hotel.

I was then told which hotel we'd be staying at and what train to catch when I got to Belgium. He also told me another hundred British guys were staying at the same hotel and we'd all be working on the same building site, which was to be a multi-storey car park.

This sounded good with the prospects of plenty of work and plenty of overtime, I'd be able to send over £250 a week home. There'd still be enough money for the digs and a bit of spending money. After all, when I left England, I was on the dole with a wife and a child on about £35 a week.

Whatever happened, I just had to get to Antwerp.

The job was mine and I set off for Antwerp in Belgium on me own. I knew my old man was never a bricklayer. He had fists as big and as hard as bricks, but never for the building game! Looking back, I suppose I was a bit of a bricklayer myself really, cos when we were kids, we used to shit bricks when we knew he was due home from sea.

So there I was, back in 1984, standing at the terminal waiting for the ferry to take me to Zeebrugge. My wife, Kerry was crying her eyes out and handed me my packing-up of bread and jam and some potted-meat sandwiches. I only had enough for a one-way ticket and I had to look forward to sleeping in an aeroplane seat, not a cabin...

I'd no money for boozing on the ferry taking me to Zeebrugge, only my bread and jam and potted meat sandwiches in my carrier bag - and just enough money for the train fare from Zeebrugge to Antwerp, when I got to Belgium. It was a twelve-hour sea crossing and about an hour into the crossing it was announced on the loudspeaker, dinner would be served, in the dining room on Deck Two.

You know what it's like on those big ferries, it can be hard to find out where things are.

I knew I was sleeping in one of them aeroplane seats, which was all I thought I'd paid for, and why I took my bread and jam with me.

I didn't know what was happening until I got to the dining room. I was only going to see if I could get a pot a tea. I then saw one of the stewards, and it turned out I knew him from my trawler days. He'd got out of the fishing industry to be a steward on the ferries.

He spotted me and came over saying; 'Aren't you hungry, Mally?'

I said, 'I'm starving, but I can't afford to pay for a meal at these ferry prices, they're dearer than the motorway cafes.'

He said, 'Do you see all the different meals on them hot plates, Mally? They're all free; they're included in the price of your ticket.'

I said to him, 'I won't be a minute.'

I went onto the deck of the ferry and threw my sandwiches to

181

the mollies. I then went back to the dining room and 'went round the buoy three times', that's a fishing term which means going back for more. I had three different meals and my plate was overflowing, I tried everything that was on offer.

Well you know what they say,

'When you're at your nannies - fill yer face.'

I even took an apple and orange for later. I certainly didn't know where my next meal was coming from and the steward told me it would only be a continental breakfast before docking in Zeebrugge. But I just filled up on cornflakes at the breakfast table. I definitely got my money's worth on that trip and a doggie bag to boot, an apple and orange plus a bit of cheese.

Somehow I got to Antwerp. I don't know whether I took one or two trains. What I do know is, when I got to Antwerp train-station I had to get a taxi to the hotel. The bloke who I'd rung up about the brickie's job told me the hotel was only about five minutes from the station.

The big mistake I made was not to get my thirty quid changed into Belgian money; it was the £30 I'd borrowed off the mother-in-law, by the way. When I got in the taxi and opened my mouth, unfortunately that was it!

He definitely took me for a ride as the supposed five-minute ride took me half an hour. He took me right round the houses. We then pulled up outside the hotel and I asked him what the fare was?

I couldn't understand what he was saying and like a daft tourist I pulled all of my money out and he took twenty quid off me.

'It's fucking dear to live here,' I said, as I got out of the taxi. The taxi driver shouted at me in very good English, 'Have a nice day!'

Well, you should've seen this run-down bed and breakfast place which they called a hotel! It must have been built over the main sewers. All you could smell every day was the stink of blocked-up toilets - I thought I was back at Armley jail. Looking at the hotel, it was like that place in the TV programme 'Auf Wiedersehen Pet', you know, the one with Jimmy Nail. In those days if there was no work at home in England for you it meant going abroad. About 80 different blokes from all over England had come here because they couldn't find work.

There were definitely some Jimmy Nail - Oz characters - a few real hard-cases, but it was all good humoured when you got to know them.

What I'll say is, I got to this shithole of a place and when I went through to the lounge there were about twenty blokes in there. The rest were scattered about in this dump of a hotel which had over 70 rooms.

It was then that the leader of the gang, the boss man, asked who I was and I told him. He asked where my Dad and uncle were?

I told him they'd had to go back home.

He asked if I was a time-served brickie, I said I was, even though I had never laid a brick in my life.

He then asked me where my tools were?

I said my old man had taken them home but I think he could tell I was lying and he asked who I'd done my trade with.

The first name that came to me was Sammy Allon, the local demolition firm. He asked me how well I knew a certain guy who worked there.

I said I knew him well and I was only talking to him last week.

'You must be a clairvoyant then because he's been dead ten years,' the boss man said.

'Look, I've come all this way out here, please don't send me back. I need the money, I'll do anything, and I'll even make the tea,' I said.

He told me he'd see what I was like on site the following day and gave me twenty pounds for my expenses.

'Is that for me taxi?' I asked.

'Is it fuck,' he said, 'that's how much it costs to get from Hull to here!'

'Well the taxi driver has just took me for twenty quid,' I said. He said, 'You'd better go find him, he owes you £18, the fare should have only been two quid, you've been had, my lad.'

'I don't fucking think so,' I thought. 'What's the quickest way to the station?' I asked.

I found out it was on foot and believe me, it was only a five-minute walk. In fact the boss's son, who was about eighteen, said he'd come with me.

MALLY - THE REBEL WITHOUT A PAUSE

We found the taxi driver and I got my twenty quid off him alright, he shit bricks when I put my hand round his neck and he certainly understood English on that occasion...

I had fun working on the building site and soon learned how to carry a hod and how to mix the cement. They say I was one of the best labourers they'd ever had working for them.

The boss was a good man and paid me the same wage as the brickies because I could keep six men going at once. It also meant I was able to send £250 home as promised and I was getting my three meals a day.

You learnt to live with the smell of the sewer and you were amongst your own people even though you were working in a strange country. We all had a good crack, it was definitely 'whistle while you work', and we got paid for overtime, which we never did.

But all good things must come to an end and for me they did after I'd been in Belgium for about three months. The gang were moving on to Germany for a big two-year job and they wanted me to go with them.

It had to be a no because the love of my life didn't like living on her own with my daughter Tammie who had just turned four at the time. So I went home... and fortunately, a letter I sent out produced my next stroke of luck. It was to Ron Faulkner, the manager of Hamlyn's, the company I was with before my spell in jail.

I told him I was sorry for letting the company down but that I'd now done my time and had a wife and daughter to look after - plus a lot of debts to sort out. He sent me a reply and asked me to be at his office at 11 o'clock the following day.

'Will he give me another chance?' I thought.

Why should he? I knew the company only had four, big deep-sea trawlers and they were laying more men off all the time.

There were five or six men going after every job - and not many jobs available.

The skippers would pick their own crew and I knew that not many skippers would want me on their ships because of my reputation.

I was thinking I needed a new pair of shoes for the big 'walkabout'. But fishing was in my blood, it was a way of clearing my debts because I had to send a weekly wage home and on top of that you picked up a fair sum after three weeks on the mackerel boats. It wasn't fantastic money but I'd only need to do about ten, three-week trips to pay my debts off.

Well I got to Ron Faulkner's door for ten forty-five that morning. When I knocked on his door, he sounded like my old headmaster.

'Come in Welburn.'

'Yes Boss,' I said, forgetting for a moment where I was.

I said to Ron, 'I'd thought I was back in prison because that's what we called the prison officers, Boss.'

I think he liked being called Boss instead of Sir.

Mr Faulkner then laid the law down, he sounded more like me Dad. But his bark was worse than his bite so to speak, Mr Faulkner was one of life's nice guys.

He said because I had a bosun's ticket and there weren't a lot of bosuns about, he was prepared to give me another chance. But he also explained that it could be quite a while before anything came up. All the ships were away and as the trawlermen were earning good money, they all stuck to their jobs. But as I was about to leave Mr Faulkner's office his phone started to ring.

I heard him say, 'You want a man to join your ship up at Ullapool in Scotland and you want him tomorrow - I've got just the man for you.' Mr Faulkner looked at me and asked, 'Do you have any sea gear?' I told him I did.

'Good,' he said. 'Do you want to go up and join the St Lorman?'

I knew the St Lorman was the biggest, newest ship they'd just bought - and that the crew were earning anything from one thousand to three thousand pounds a week!

'You bet I do', I exclaimed. I couldn't believe it!

'Go and say your goodbyes,' Ron told me. 'The taxi will come for you at your house at five o'clock.

Now go to the cashier and get two hundred quid and sort your wife out. And don't let me down.'

He then got on the phone to Renee the runner and said, 'Sign Mally on the St Lorman - he joins her in the morning. Get a taxi for him to go home and sort him out some money and any sea gear he's short of. Then order another taxi to take him the two hundred mile journey to Ullapool.'

MALLY - THE REBEL WITHOUT A PAUSE

I couldn't believe my luck. It was like a dream - and one that could solve all my problems.

I was going on the biggest money-earner in England. Put it this way, I could earn a minimum of a thousand pound a week on the St Lorman. It would take six weeks on the stern trawlers to earn that amount of money. But the St Lorman could catch up to a thousand ton of mackerel in one go. Yes, she was the pride of the new type of fishing boats, a super, super trawler that had a trawl net as big as Wembley stadium! It was called a purse net. When you put your net in the water you circled round to pick the trawl net up and pull it in with the big winches and then store the net by hand into the net compound at the back of the ship. The compound was as deep as a cave.

We had to be careful when the net was coming into the compound above our heads because jellyfish could fall out of the loose net. If one landed on your face it could have meant 'a going in job', which meant taking you ashore to hospital. Those jellyfish had a very deadly sting!

The St Lorman had a half-English, half-Norwegian crew. The Norwegians had their heads screwed on, they made sure they got all the easy jobs.

The English were just used so the ship could fish in the British waters.

The Norwegian skipper would be in charge but the ship had to carry an English skipper and an English first mate - plus eight English deck hands. They were just using our tickets and brawn, because it was non-stop work when you saw what was in your net. I remember my very first catch of fish aboard the St Lorman.

We had the net alongside of our ship and we would stick a pump into the shoal of fish that had not escaped our purse net. We would pump all the mackerel into two sea-water tanks that could each hold up to a thousand ton of fish.

Well in just one night we caught nearly one thousand five-hundred tons of mackerel! Yes, in one night, that's three times as much as what the St Jason could catch in three weeks! It was amazing, what other ships were catching in nine weeks, we were catching in one night! And while you're sat there amazed, I should point out that we were only allowed to catch three hundred and seventy tons of mackerel a week!

It would take us a good twelve hours to pump the fish aboard and while we were pumping and filling the tanks, the Norwegians would be in their bunks asleep, lazy bastards! They were on three times as much money as us - yet they did very little work for their money.

When we went across to Denmark to unload our fish we always travelled at night with all our navigational lights off except our one, all round, white mast headlight. This was to avoid the fishery protection boats. To other ships, it looked like we were just a small boat instead of a massive trawler. We never got stopped once.

We sure were the 'mackerel pirates' in them days.

Us Englishmen would not stop work because while we were on our way to Denmark we had to freeze 70 tons of mackerel using four, one ton freezers. The frozen fish had to be boxed and strapped and it was non-stop because you could freeze the fish in an hour. So it was four tons every hour until we'd got our 70 tons quota of frozen fish. It could work out that by the time we'd finished the freezing we weren't far from Denmark. There waiting at the quayside would be fifty 20-ton container wagons waiting to take up to a thousand tons of our illegally caught fish. We called it the ghost train. It was strange - nobody saw the ghost train. But I sure saw it every time we docked in Denmark. I wasn't dreaming. But I sure was dreaming about what to spend the money on that I earned!

We also made sure we landed our 300 tons quota of fresh mackerel in eight stone boxes for the fresh fish market. By the time we'd landed that amount of fish from our tanks, using one ton bailing nets, we were shattered. We sure never got time to sleep but we always made sure we got a shave because the Norwegian skipper had his wife aboard all the time and she was a real stunner!

When we would be landing the fish, the skipper's wife would make us cups of tea.

The Norwegians would always be ashore getting pissed-up. It was the English guys' jobs to discharge the catch.

When we'd discharged the catch we'd sail on the next tide. Sometimes we'd go ashore but it wasn't ever long enough to get drunk - and we knew that within 18 hours we'd be fishing again.

I loved it! It was another paid workout. But I couldn't work with the sly, lazy Norwegians who were aboard the St Lorman.

The chief engineer was a nasty man. He didn't like us English, I don't know why. He had his big German Shepherd dog called Brutus aboard the ship with him. We were never allowed pets aboard a ship. How the chief engineer got away with it I'll never know.

The dog was like the ghost train, nobody ever seemed to notice it. It certainly wasn't a ghost.

It was a big, vicious beast of an animal - but like a pussycat after I got my hands on it.

The dog used to sit outside the chief engineer's berth door at sea and if you went anywhere near the door the dog would show its teeth, growl at you, then bark, alerting the chief. He'd then quickly emerge from his berth and tell you in his Nordic way to piss off and if he clicked his fingers the dog would go for you!

Well, as you know I grew up with German Shepherd dogs and not forgetting the dogs in Leeds prison.

I made my mind up to win this dog over. I'd have it following me like it followed the chief.

I didn't like the way he was treating his dog.

I decided it needed some loving and some fussing over.

So how did I turn this beast of a dog into a lap dog?

Well one morning as I was going up to the bridge to take the English skipper, Eddie 'Woolbags' a pot of tea I had to pass the chief's berth. The dog was in the berth panting.

I noticed the chief engineer with a pair of pink rubber washing-up gloves on and he was giving the dog a quick 'flick of the wrist'.

Yes, that's right, he was giving the dog a quick 'ham shank' - and I don't mean the meat on the bone type. No, he was playing with the dog's mating tackle! The Alsation's legs were shaking. And I'm sure I saw the dog smiling.

It never growled at me and the chief said in broken English, 'It has to be done, he ain't had a bitch for months.'

'No probs, Chief,' I said with a grin.

No probs all right!

The next time I saw the dog, I put a pair of pink washing-up gloves on and in front of all the lads I said, 'I bet I can get Brutus the dog to sit on my lap.'

I think I took about two hundred quid in bets.

Well when the chief came in for his grub with his trusted shadow, the dog, we all sat at the same table to eat. Even the skipper's wife sat at the same table.

When the dog passed me I gave a little whistle to get him to look at me and when he did I gave him the flick of a wrist sign with my pink rubber gloves.

The dog just turned round and within a second or two it had its two front legs wrapped round my leg and he was off at ten to the dozen, as though he was mating with another dog. By, he had a tight grip! And the grip got tighter as I stroked his balls with my foot. My heavy woollen socks really seemed to do the trick.

You could see it in the dog's eyes that he loved it. He was smiling again! I know how he felt. It was just like I'd feel after being away for weeks on end.

The chief was not a happy engineer. He clouted the dog really badly that night.

I nearly got into a fight with him. If it hadn't been for the other English lads I'd have been on my way home! And at the back of my mind were Ron Faulkner's words,

'Don't let me down.' But I couldn't see a man hitting his dog. After that the dog never growled or barked at me again. And every time I saw the dog the chief would let me stroke it. So it wasn't all that bad.

Pity the skipper's wife wasn't into the rubber gloves. But saying that, she did wear them to wash the dishes. Not the same gloves that the chief or me wore. But every time I saw the skipper's wife put them gloves on I felt how the dog felt. I'm sure she wore them on badness...

I did ten weeks solid work on the St Lorman, backwards and forwards to Denmark, loading that ghost train up.

I remember the time I 'chucked my hand in' and refused to work aboard the St Lorman.

We were on our tenth week at sea and we had landed not far off 15,000 tons of mackerel when really we should have only landed 3,000 tons!

MALLY - THE REBEL WITHOUT A PAUSE

The fish had moved from off the west coast of Scotland down to the south coast of England. Or had it all been caught?

The skipper tried fishing for herring in the North Sea but he only managed to rip the net.

There was a huge amount of damage to the net and it was the only one we had. It would take three weeks to mend it.

So it was decided to take the ship into port in Norway.

When we docked in this lovely little fishing port the English members of the crew were told to mend the net.

We then saw all the Norwegians going home for them three weeks. They were told the English would mend the net. They thought we were daft enough to let them go home for three weeks while us silly twats mended this net in sub-zero temperatures with our bare hands. I saw them Norwegians laughing at us. Even the dog was waggling its tail when it left us.

I thought, 'Frig this, what's good enough for them is good enough for me.' But I was the only one that went up to skipper Eddie to say, 'Get me a plane home skipper, let someone else have a go mending this lot. I've got what I wanted out of the trip!'

Within forty-eight hours I was at home with Kerry and Tammie. The twelve thousand pounds I picked up really came in handy. We paid our debts off and had a lovely Christmas.

It made up for the ones I'd spent away from home, be it through prison or being at sea...

I knew I had to get some good walking shoes again because when you jumped a ship there was no way you'd be working for that company for a very, very long time.

I needed to get out of the fishing game but it always called me back. But I never went on any of the Hamlyn's ships again because within two years they'd sold out to the government.

Their ships were either scrapped or used as standby boats to the oilrigs. I think we all knew we'd over-fished the seabeds. Greed, that's all it was, man's greed.

Within those two years, on August 2 1985, my second daughter, Keelie Marie was born.

Also within that time we moved from our house in Hessle and went to live in Devon Street in Gipsyville.

We were soon on the move again though. We sold the house

in Devon Street and the money we made on the sale we used to pay cash for one down Malvern Avenue, Cecil Street, off Hawthorne Avenue.

The house needed some work doing on it but we got a builder to build an extension and I helped to do all the labouring work to keep costs down. And within a year, the house we'd paid five thousand pounds for was worth twenty-five!

It was also the time I started to keep racing pigeons. I built a little pigeon loft in our small back yard. I even kept some of my pigeons in Tammie's wooden 'Wendy' house which I'd moved onto the top of the kitchen and bathroom extension. Well, it had a nice flat roof, the kitchen and bathroom extension, that is.

When Tammie wanted to play in her 'Wendy' house, I would carry her up the 12ft ladder to get onto the roof of the extension, but she soon lost interest in her 'Wendy' house after seeing some of my pigeons in what used to be her little sanctuary. I had started keeping pigeons as another hobby because I just love birds.

Later on I started to get serious about this racing pigeon lark. I could send a racing pigeon 500 miles and get it to land back on me hand out of the sky for a peanut.

There's so much to tell about my pigeon days. I met some really nice people. When I started I even believed that all pigeon people were nice people because they care about their birds. And if you care about the birds, you have to be a nice person don't yer?

On the other hand though, I've also known a few pigeon fanciers that used their birds to cheat other true pigeon fanciers out of their hard-earned cash. I believe if you cheat at any sport, be it greyhound-racing, pigeons, football, even tiddlywinks, you're an arsehole and an arsehole is full of shit and I don't mix with that type of person!

I've met a few arseholes in the pigeon world. I even had a so-called mate who cheated to win a race and a nice trophy, which you got to keep for life. A trophy that he wasn't even bothered about! No, he was more bothered about stealing money off honest pigeon fanciers.

I believed what he told me. Of how he'd won the race, fair and square. But they caught him out and I was glad. He was nowt but a cheat and you don't cheat at sport.

Don't get me wrong, I've cheated, but not in sport! I've cheated in life with other men's wives. But it wasn't while I was married to Kerry. I never once had an affair with another woman all the time I was with her - when we spilt up, yes - I played the field. I even got revenge on my 'mate' who cheated at pigeons. I slept with his 'wife to be'. Now she was worth cheating for! Well anyway, I'll tell you everything you need to know about pigeons in Part Three...

Malvern Avenue had promised to be a fresh start. But from 1986 until 1990 I was the biggest dickhead walking! My life still just revolved around boozing!

I stayed out drinking until all hours. Sometimes I didn't go home at all. I treated Kerry with utter disrespect! And worse still, I just didn't realise what I was doing to my lovely wife and children. I realise now the pain and suffering I caused them and I hold my head in shame.

My oldest daughter Tammie recently told me she used to have her clothes folded, ready to grab and run out of the house to a women's refuge centre.

Her Dad was turning into her granddad because of the booze, but without the violence, I must stress! She told me she slept with the light on. And when she heard me screaming for Kerry to come down the stairs at two in the morning to cook me something to eat, it used to really frighten her. Night after night she would cry herself to sleep.

How that hurts me now to think of the fear and heartache I caused my daughter. I'm so truly sorry Tammie.

Keelie my younger daughter told me she couldn't recall ever being frightened - she just remembers playing with all the other kids at the women's refuge centre.

Do you know, I once broke into my own house after Kerry had left me and locked me out. I robbed the gas meter so I could go out 'on the piss' and have another bet on the horses!

In 1986 I started working on the fish docks, unloading the containers full of cod and haddock that came across from Iceland. Maybe it was their ghost train?

We'd work in gangs of ten and I was the leader of my gang. For that I thank the legend that is Ray Beharrell.

He gave me the chance to do some hard graft. He always said

I was his number one and that I was the best grafter on the docks. Ray, and Dave Lilley were the best two blokes to work for when it came to unloading containers.

Don't worry, I soon had a 'ghost train' of my own going. You don't think I was going to graft my balls off for a tenner a container, do you?

Each one could take two hours to unload and you had to do six containers a night. The Icelanders wouldn't miss a few fish would they? And after all, it was the Icelanders who'd put a 200 mile exclusion zone around their little island.

That meant we weren't allowed to fish in the rich fishing grounds off Iceland. Game over!

No Hull trawlers fishing off Iceland!

No, they were all laid up! And here we were unloading Icelandic fish, caught in their waters and shipped across here because the demand was always very high for fish in England. It's like everything else nowadays, we've become a nation of importers!

Well between you and me, I was getting some kind of revenge on the Icelanders with my little ghost train and I used to get more than a tenner a container. It sure was hard graft though. I remember one week when I did six containers every night for five nights, sometimes doing 16 hours graft in a shift!

Well on my last night of that particular week, I'd started on the Thursday evening and I got finished about 6 on the Friday morning.

I told Kerry to wake me up at one o'clock on the Friday afternoon so that I could go for my wages.

The next thing I remember was Kerry saying, 'Mally, wake up it's three o'clock!'

When I asked her why didn't she wake me at one o'clock, she said it was three o'clock - on Sunday afternoon! She couldn't wake me and I'd slept right through! After all, it was back-breaking work on them containers. But the money we got plus our bit off the ghost train soon straightened your back up when you put your wedge of money in your back pocket. Shoulders back, here we go, back on the booze!

That's what it was like. If I had a pocket full of money I would not go home until I'd spent it all on booze or the horses! Sometimes I'd go home without a penny and Kerry would have to go to borrow money from the next door neighbour.

I did go away fishing a few times, including the two trips on the Arctic Corsair, which I explained in Part One. But the money was never enough to pay for my booze...

Not surprisingly the day finally arrived when Kerry had had enough of this dickhead! She was fed up of all the running. Fed up of always dragging the kids away. And early in 1990 she asked me for a divorce.

I said no! But the Judge told me to leave my house and he gave immediate possession of the house and all its contents to Kerry.

I said, 'You can't do that!' But he screamed at me to get out of the court and to sort my divorce out.

I went to see a solicitor and it was agreed to put the house up for sale and split the money we'd get for it.

Kerry didn't want to stay in the house. She moved all over the place with me sometimes banging on her door, pissed-up, asking her to come back and demanding to see my daughters. Kerry never once stopped me from seeing my daughters.

She's the best Mother any child could have wished for.

The house was quickly sold and Kerry and me got ten grand apiece out of it.

I sorted my daughters out. I put some money in a trust fund for when they were 18 and I'm glad to say they both got something on their 18th birthdays.

Then I went on a bender with the rest of the money.

It was party time!

Kerry had left me, she had filed for divorce.

So I was at a party most nights...

Fortunately, me and my pigeons weren't homeless for long because Billy Hames, the former owner of 'Ken Kabs', heard I had nowhere to live or to keep my birds. He was also a pigeon man, in fact in his day he was one of the best 'pigeon fanciers' around.

'Come and put your birds in my pigeon loft and there's a spare bedroom here for you,' he suggested.

Better still, after my accident with the frying pan in the 'Ken Kabs' flat, Billy insisted on just one house rule - 'No Fires, Please!'

I could hardly believe Billy's offer and I moved straightaway into number 27 Priory Grove, Gipsyville, which was a council-owned property.

What more could I have asked for? A place for me and the birds - and my Mother only two minutes away in the next street. She would come round every time she went to the shops and if I was in, it was a quick pot of tea, then I'd go 'on road' with her. Quality time, arm in arm, with the 'pal of my cradle days'.

I walked proudly around Gipsyville with my dear, loving Mother. She was starting to look 'worn out', bless her, and it still brings a tear to my eye to think what my Mother went through in her life. Yet she always had a smile on her face and never had a bad word for anyone, not even my Dad!

'It's with him losing his job on the trawlers,' she'd say.

I could see what she meant but there was still no way she deserved all them beatings.

Well the time spent with my Mother was short-lived because I found out that the trawler company Marrs wanted a fisherman with a bosun's ticket to go in one of her new ships, the Westella.

I didn't need asking twice.

The Westella could catch a thousand ton of fish in ten days. And I could earn three grand as a bosun for ten days work. The English skipper was the daddy of all daddies, Arthur Ball, and he signed me on.

I had to do three trips on the trot.

That was like doing eight weeks away because when we'd caught our fish, we went to Holland to land it and the Dutch would unload it for us. There wasn't a need to return home between trips - and of course a couple of nights in Amsterdam and visits to the 'red light district' were always welcome...

So, what went on behind the 'Green door' in Amsterdam when we had two days off after landing our mackerel in IJmuiden? Well, first it used to be 'shower, shave, and shifted', which meant getting 'scrubbed-up' and putting our 'going ashore clothes' on. Then it was like going on a mini two-day holiday. We would all get an advance on our wages - anything from £50 to £100 - which was a lot of money back in 1990.

Can you imagine what it was like for us after being away for three weeks on the trawlers?

Most of my shipmates were single blokes, the testosterone levels were high, and mine were sky high! I was going through my divorce at the time of going behind the Green Door. Did Shakin' Stevens sing about this Green Door? Because there sure was a whole lot of shakin' going on behind the Green Door that day.

With me being an officer, the skipper would give me the gypsy's warning, 'Don't let me down and make sure all sixteen of yer stick together, and that there's no trouble.'

'Yes skipper,' I assured him as I signed for my £100 advance. Well, when we were sightseeing along the narrow streets of a certain part of Amsterdam, the contents of shop windows were certainly a sight to see, there was a woman in every window! And believe me, it didn't matter what 'type of bloke' you were, there was a woman that would catch your eye as you went window-shopping. There really were some beautiful women tempting us to taste the 'forbidden fruits' - which a few of us did.

One of my shipmates didn't realise that the 'she' was a 'he' until he had handed his money over!

Well, when sixteen hairy-arsed Hull fishermen were let lose on them canal streets of Amsterdam, it reminded me of the children let loose in 'Willy Wonker's Chocolate Factory'.

We all waited for one shipmate until he'd been up to see the Mae West look-alike who tempted him with the words,

'Why don't you come up and see me sunshine?'

But then he told us it had been a waste of twenty quid! Just a simple 'dip and fill'...

The streets we went down were packed with visiting tourists from all over the world - it was like a beehive - and the places we visited were open 24/7.

The Dutch people do a lot of riding, on their bikes that is, so we had to be careful we didn't get knocked over. All we heard were their little bells on their bikes. Well, a couple of the women in them windows really rang *my* bell that day!

There were people coming up to us and giving us leaflets and urging us to visit all the different strip joints. One of the more tempting ones was behind the Green Door, where, for a small entrance fee of only £5, you could drink 'as much as you wanted in an hour' all free! Yes, drink as much as you wanted for an hour - absolutely free!

Well, most of us were up for that! So the more adventurous of us went up to the Green Door, which had about ten Frank Bruno-sized guys vetting who went in and who didn't.

We had to get an 'invisible stamp' on the back of our hands, and we couldn't rub it off.

When we got behind the Green Door the place was massive inside, there must have been another 500 men and women in there! The music was very loud and the atmosphere was banging! The punters were about ten deep at the fifty foot long bar, all queuing up to drink as much as they could in their 'free hour'. Ten topless girls served us. They were on top of the bar, so you had to look up to them.

Once I'd worked my way to the bar, one of the girls served me my drink and then with a nice smile asked me in broken English, if I wanted her to do a 'bar show'. Well, for ten quid I got a show that I'll never forget!

She did things with a ping-pong ball and a tennis ball that I'll have to leave to your imagination. But I'll tell you, not even John McEnroe in his prime would have returned one of her serves! And what she did with a cigar and how she blew smoke rings, I'll never know. Talk about Johnny Cash and his song, 'The Ring of Fire'?

After she'd finished the 'bar show' I was given a gold ticket and told to go up a flight of stairs. At the top there was a big dance floor with another 300 or so men and women being entertained by a disc jockey - and twenty blindfolded men chasing ten scantily-clad beauties around the dance floor.

The game was simple. If one of the blindfolded men could catch one of the beauties, which one did, he got to take her up to the third floor, where the 'love rooms' were. I'm sure you can work the rest out for yourselves!

Well, as we joined in to watch the twenty 'blind mice' to see how they ran, the disc jockey welcomed us by asking, 'Has anyone got a gold ticket?'

Well, nine other men and me shouted, 'Yes!' and stepped forward to the sound of the cheering crowd.

It was now our turn to catch the lady of our choice, 'Without the blindfolds on,' said the disc jockey. I was thinking to myself, that's easy!

The beauties were dancing about ten feet in front of us. But this time there were only six of them - and ten of us - and I wasn't sharing!

With that, the disc jockey shouted, 'At the count of three all you have to do is catch your birdie, and you'll have an hour upstairs with her, it's as easy as that!'

I thought again, that's easy, as I made eye contact with a Brazilian beauty!

All my shipmates were egging me on, the disc jockey then shouted,

'ONE'.

My Brazilian beauty was giving me 'that' smile.

'TWO'.

She was waving at me, giving me the wink and beckoning me to chase her. I was ready but then in-between the count of two and three, the disc jockey suddenly shouted,

'The first man to drop his trousers and underpants down to his ankles and then catch the girl of his choice is the winner!'

'TWO AND A HALF - THR!!!!!!!!!!!!!'

Well, by the time he got to 'EE' my jeans and underkegs were round my ankles and I was waddling towards my Brazilian beauty like a love-struck duck! I was followed closely by another four guys who had also dared to drop their pants and give chase. But I could hardly believe what happened next - the 'Benny Hill' music started! Oh, it was funny - we were pushing each other around trying to reach our chosen girl - it was like being in the sack race at school!

After a good ten minutes chasing the beauties around the dance floor I finally managed to touch my 'Miss World' look-alike. The disc jockey immediately declared me the winner. And my Brazilian beauty led me to the 'love shack' on the third floor.

I shared a jacuzzi with her and another beauty - I thought I was in heaven, it was every man's dream I thought. And again, you can work the rest out for yourselves!

After my hour was up, I was totally shattered but as I came down the stairs to rejoin the 'madding crowd' I couldn't help noticing everybody was cheering and clapping me.

I soon realised they'd seen everything that I'd got up to with them two beauties.

Little did I know that everything I did in the 'love room' had been filmed. The crowd had seen me performing in the 'love shack' - in full colour and on every screen in the place!

A few seconds later, a guy appeared and gave me a video of all the action that taken place on the dance floor and in the 'love room'. I then saw that one of my shipmates was blindfolded on the dance floor, ready for the next chasing game. He ended up grabbing a Dolly Parton look-alike. And not long after he disappeared upstairs, we saw him on the silver screen as well!

We were behind the Green Door for about seven hours that day and we all spent up because after that first hour of free drinks we had to pay top whack for our drinks.

When I rounded everybody up, ready to leave, the Frank Bruno look-alikes wouldn't let us go because the stamps on the backs of our hands gave the time and date we'd gone behind the Green Door! And when they scanned our hands under ultraviolet light, it came up on a machine that we had to pay a pound for every minute over the free hour! So, six hours at a pound a minute worked out at £360!

Me and my shipmate who'd grabbed the Dolly Parton look-alike were lucky, we didn't have to pay because we'd been part of the 'entertainment'.

We were free to leave but we had to go straight back to the ship and tell the skipper that the rest of the lads needed bailing out from behind the Green Door. One of the lads was called Stevens - he sure was a Shakin' Stevens that day!

It's a good job it was our first trip of three, landing our fish in IJmuiden. At least it gave the lads who had been taken for £360 a chance to earn some more cash before they went home. I didn't go behind the Green Door again. But some of the lads did - those who could afford another visit!

And I'm telling yer, just be careful when you go to Amsterdam, because they sure do play it hot behind the Green Door - and I've now let you in on the secret they're keeping!

My second trip on the Westella was also one I'll never forget, but for a very different reason.

Skipper Ball was having a trip off and in charge was another daddy, skipper Trevor Doyle.

MALLY - THE REBEL WITHOUT A PAUSE

Skipper Doyle was asking me how my Mother was and how she was the most beautiful woman on Hessle Road. He even told me that he once fancied my Mother but was shit scared of my Dad.

Skipper Doyle told me some stories about my Dad. And I told him some stories about what my Dad had done to my loving Mother. He admitted he knew what my Dad had done but said nobody dare do anything about it in them days.

Well it was halfway through our fishing trip and we were heavy fishing and when the fish was there, we'd work four hours on and four off. It was easy work really, but we soon learnt that when our head hit that pillow after four hours graft, we went out like a light.

I was in dreamland when my berth door opened and the light came on. There standing in the doorway was skipper Doyle, crying his eyes out.

'I've got some bad news for you, Mally,' he said.

'Don't tell me skipper, I know,' I replied.

I could tell what he was going to say.

I'm filling up now just recalling it.

Skipper Doyle just stared at me and said, 'Your Mother has passed away and we're taking you into port, Mally. There'll be a taxi waiting for you in Penzance and that will take you to the train station.'

I asked him how long ago did my Mother pass away? He told me it had been two days earlier. I started to ask why had it taken so long to tell me?

He said, 'Someone in the office forgot to pass the message on, I'm very sorry.'

Skipper Doyle was in tears. I was in tears. And my cousins Pete and Andrew who were stood behind Skipper Doyle were also in tears. Big, hard men - all in tears.

This next bit is going to be hard for me to write or tap. But it must be done - it's for my loving Mother - the 'Pal of my cradle days...'

This was the saddest time of my life. The love of my life had gone. I never got to say ta-ra. I never got to have that last pot of tea with her. I'd promised I'd take her out to get her hair done and buy her some hair-spray and some new stockings.

That's all she wanted. That and her sons' love. And she got it off all my brothers.

This is hard to write. This period of my life sent me right off the rails again. What else was there to live for?

My wife had left me. She'd taken my kids away. And now the 'pal of my cradle days' was gone as well.

I'm glad my twin Trevor was there. He was a Giant amongst men was my twin Trevor. He sorted all my Mother's funeral out and arranged everything.

My brother Trevor was the star. He was my hero.

We stood side by side as we pushed my Mother's coffin into the furnace...

CHAPTER TWENTY-TWO
PAL OF MY
CRADLE DAYS

The train journey home was one of the longest of my life. It seemed to take forever and don't forget I never had a mobile phone way back in 1990.

My loving Mother had passed away in her sleep on the night of Monday, September 17 1990. When I asked my Dad when was the last time he'd seen my Mother alive he told me she'd gone to bed on the Monday night about nine o'clock and when he tried to wake her on the Tuesday morning, she had left us. So that's the date the undertakers took my Mother away.

Tuesday September 18 1990, that's the date they gave for my Mother's passing.

The date - 18 - how strange it was that the number 18 kept cropping up during my life.

18 - the date of my Mam's passing.

18 - the number of the box I had on the hit TV show 'Deal Or No Deal' and it had the jackpot in it. My Mother would have loved 'Deal Or No Deal'. I would have taken her to meet Noel Edmunds and all the gang and I know they'd have made her feel like a Queen - because my Mother *was* my Queen. Was my Mother watching over me when I went on 'Deal Or No Deal'?

And 18 - the number of kisses she put at the bottom of the very last letter she ever sent to me. I received it just before I was due to get out of Preston prison in July 1984. In the years that followed, up to her death in 1990, she couldn't write to me on my fishing trips anymore. The trawlers I was on operated by themselves and so getting mail using other trawlers wasn't possible.

Here's my Mother's final letter then, exactly as she wrote it...

PAL OF MY CRADLE DAYS

Tuesday July 2nd 1984
1.30 afternoon
Dear Mally,
Thanking you once more for your lovely welcome letter, well, this will be the last now as you will be home a week tomorrow. So when you get this letter, which should be about Friday, you will only have a few days left. I think it has passed these last few weeks but then I have been busy so that's why I was late in answering your letter last time.
Yes, the kettle will be on for a cup of tea, it will be for Kerry and Tammy as well, not forgetting the old man.
He has just gone round to Harrys, he is building him a shed, so I am having a nice rest from the teapot for 3 or 4 hours, you know what he is like for tea. He has just got over flu and sickness, he has been in bed for a couple of days but he is alright now thanks to the Lemsips, them flu things that you take in water.
Well, Michel was in Hull last week but he never came to see us, and we wasnt out. Mary, Richards wife, told me they were in Mermaid pub with Raymond and Moira.
I think Micheal and Nancy thought we were away at Scunthorpe at Mr Feves Roy Feves dads. we told him we might be going but we are not going now as Dad has too many Rabbitts to see to.
Well, Raymond now has Rabbitts he has 5 they are lovely, We was round yesterday.
When I see Ray again I will tell him you dont want any more Darts Magazines but he knows you are coming home I told him he said Very Nice.
Well it will be very nice going to Scarborough to live one thing is you will be in a Sea Side town it isnt like this in Hull

and you might get a little job I hope you do.
Yes it will be nice a little Holiday for Dad
and me when you get Settled over there but
you know Dad he won't go nowwhere only
on Road to Post office and Harrys he thinks
too much about his Rabbitts.
Yes Tammy is lovely she has lovely hair and
like you said just like Kerry nice looking
well I think Tammy is like you Mally so you
are a Bonny Man.
Well I have a little job to do while Dad is out
clean the fire place out again as we had a
fire last night for Hot Water, so untill I see
you Mally (BE GOOD) and not long now a
Week.   so Look after yourself
Lots of love and kisses
Mam and Dad
XXXXXXX
XXXXX
XXXXX

I never found out why my Mother put eighteen kisses at the bottom of that final letter. It was so spooky - she hadn't put eighteen on any of her other letters. But I did find out about what my brothers were doing on the night of my Mother's passing - fighting amongst themselves!

My youngest brother had a pop at my eldest brother, then they say Trevor had a pop at one of my other brothers. Then Raymond tried to stop it. And finally they were all popping at each other - all in the living room at number 11.

Then one of my brothers had his say to my Dad, and it all kicked off again!

They told me that the coppers were called that night but no arrests were made.

Where was I? Stuck in the Irish Sea, aboard a trawler! That's where I was! Looking back now I'm glad I was. I'd have preferred to be anywhere that night, rather than in the front room with all my brothers!

Because I was angry. I was burning up inside. Why was I the last to know about my Mother's passing?

PAL OF MY CRADLE DAYS

I blamed the trawler owners for not getting in touch with the ship straight away. I didn't get home until very late on Friday September 21 - three days after my Mother had passed away! Friday September 21 was my Mother's birthday. She would have been 63. I'd promised her a big treat for her birthday. All she ever wanted was a little treat so that she could get her hair permed. My Mother loved her hair.

I've just been looking at a photo of my Mother with her hair rollers in. She had that happy smile - that smile that always greeted you, every time you met her.

I'm in tears now as I tap this. It really hurts when the one you love is taken away from you without a goodbye. Without that kiss. She always gave me a big kiss and a hug when I met and left my Mother. Oh how I wish she was still here.

The good Lord took the wrong one in my eyes. He must have needed an extra angel or a good 'cup of tea maker'.

Oh how I miss those cups of tea in them cracked cups and the odd dog hair floating on the top of yer tea.

If you pulled a dog hair out of your cup of tea my quick-witted Mother would usually say something like, 'Oh, that must be the cup I used to rinse all the soap off the dog when we bathed him last night.'

Also my Mother's timing was spot on. After you'd finished your cup of tea she'd stand up, blow a raspberry and say, 'More tea, Vicar?' as she took your cup for a refill.

Oh, she was funny.

I was heart-broken at the news of my Mother's passing. And I'm still heart-broken today, tapping this book out on my computer.

I'm in tears looking at these photos of the 'Pal of my cradle days'. I've just received them off my brother Mike's wife, Nancy. I can assure you there's some tears in these pages...

At the time of my Mother's passing it was a job to get all my brothers to attend her funeral.

After that first night when all my brothers had met at number 11, emotions were still running high.

I think each of my brothers was letting their anger out against each other - and don't forget there were seven of them!

A lot was said that night but I guess I knew how each and every one of my brothers must have felt.

MALLY - THE REBEL WITHOUT A PAUSE

I'm sure I felt the same way. But we had to pull together for our Mother. We had to make it a special time. My Mother was a special lady. She deserved the best send off any Queen could expect. It was her lads' duty to make sure she got that big farewell. But let me tell you now, that if it hadn't been for my twin Trevor taking charge and sorting everything out, it would have been a farce. Trevor organised everything right down to the last detail of pushing my Mother's coffin into the furnace at the cremation.

He had it in his head that the coffin would be opened and her wedding ring would get nicked. I shared his concern - and I helped him to push it into the furnace.

Trevor would not leave the crematorium till he saw my Mother's coffin blazing away.

I saw his point that day but I couldn't understand why two of my brothers said they weren't even going to their own Mother's funeral.

One of them, my oldest brother Johnnie, told me what had happened on the night of my Mother's passing. How it all got out of control and that he couldn't be doing with any more hassle because he'd had a heart operation and 'wasn't the man he used to be'. But I pleaded with him and told him he was the head of the family and it was his duty to lead the way.

I explained to Johnnie, who used to be in the army and who even stood on guard outside Buckingham Palace, that Trevor had arranged eight black cars to follow behind my Mother's hearse.

Johnnie was to travel in the first car, then it would be brother David in the next car, then Raymond, followed by Mike, then Richard, then me, then Trevor and finally in the eighth car, the baby of the family, Bobby, who is two years younger than me. Bobby took my Mother's passing very badly - he was in a really bad state. He was going round in a daze wearing my Mother's pinafore that she always wore. The passing of my Mother really hit Bobby incredibly hard. He had been the last to leave home at the age of 16. He'd been the last to get away from my Dad.

He's told me stories recently that I never knew. Things that he'd been through living at number 11 West Grove, Gipsyville. And some of them, were as upsetting as the harrowing times I'd been through. After thinking it over, Johnnie said he would go to the funeral. He would be in the first car.

I then spoke to all my other brothers on the Saturday, two days before the funeral, be it on the phone or going to their houses or meeting them in Gipsyville Tavern, to make sure they were all going to be there.

Trevor had everything arranged. He even arranged for me to go see my Mother at rest on the morning of the funeral at Garton and Sons funeral parlour in Gipsyville.

The funeral took place on Monday, September 24 1990, at 1.30pm. But before the funeral, we were also having trouble trying to convince brother Mike to come to his Mother's funeral. He said he unfortunately couldn't cancel his holiday that had been booked and paid for.

I pleaded with him on the phone not to go on the holiday but he said he couldn't let his wife and young kids go alone.

I said he could always go on another holiday, but he only had one Mother! I said I expected to see Mike in car four on the day of our Mother's funeral. But he said again, he would not be there. I told him in no uncertain terms that he'd regret it for the rest of his life and that he'd pay the price for not going to his Mother's funeral.

Then I wished him a shit holiday, put the phone down on him and never talked to him again for well over ten years. I just couldn't understand why Mike would not be at his own Mother's funeral. And for the sake of what? A holiday!

The ending of this book is dedicated especially to my loving Mother. On the Saturday morning two days before my Mother's funeral I got on the phone to the Hull Daily Mail and put my thoughts in the Bereavements column. You can read what I wrote, on the back cover of this book alongside my Mother's photograph.

On the Saturday afternoon I went down to the dock to pick up the money I'd earned while I'd been away before my Mother's passing. I got a thousand pound advance.

I then went straight back to meet my brothers in the Gipsyville Tavern to finalise some of the last-minute funeral arrangements. They all turned up apart from Michael. As we were discussing a few last-minute details, someone came over and told us that there was a horse running that afternoon in the 3.40 race at Ayr called 'At Peace'.

It was 8/1 to win the race so we all chipped in and put £500 on it. If 'At Peace' had won, we'd have collected £4,500! We believed the name was an omen. And that we couldn't lose, could we?

Well my Mam was at peace wasn't she? Was it a sign? She was watching over us, we had to back it, didn't we?

It came eighth out of more than 20 runners!

We believed she couldn't have been at peace after all. But we just carried on drinking. Then would you believe it, another regular came into the pub and said, 'You'll never guess what's just won the 4 o'clock race at 33/1?

'No!' we all shouted at once. 'What was it called?'

His reply was spooky, to say the least.

'It was called - Seven Sons,' he exclaimed, as he gazed at the seven of us.

Yes, Seven Sons had won at 33/1. If we'd backed that horse we'd have collected £17,000!

Seventeen thousand pounds!

I guess our Mother had been watching over her seven sons who were due at her funeral after all.

I don't think Seven Sons ever won again. So it was particularly strange that it won at 33/1 - and on the day seven sons were planning to lay to rest their most loving Mother.

So I do believe there's someone watching over us.

So never give in. Never give up hope.

Hope - the last thing in Pandora's Box.

Two days to go before I got to see my Mother in her coffin. I had to see her. I had to give her that last kiss goodbye.

It's all flooding back now...

Kerry, who was filing for divorce, got in touch with me to see if I was ok. She asked when did I want to see my daughters? I said, 'Let me get my Mam's funeral out of the way first.'

Kerry was also very upset about the loss of my Mother because Kerry used to go down and take Tammie and Keelie to see their Nana. Kerry knew what they meant to my Mother. The day of the funeral soon came round. I arranged to meet some of my brothers at the funeral parlour to pay my last visit to my Mother. I went in to see my Mother on my own.

My Mother looked like an angel. Although she looked as though she'd lost a lot of weight - I just saw an angel.

As I bent over to kiss her forehead, two tears fell silently onto her cheek. My Mother was at peace.

I said my goodbyes to the 'Pal of my cradle days'.

It was tough to walk out of the room and leave my Mother.

I knew it was something I'd never do again.

As I left, I informed the Funeral Director that there was one thing I wished to be placed in my Mother's coffin - the treasured trophy that I'd won greyhound-racing at Askern...

All my brothers barring Mike met at number 11, to wait for the undertakers to arrive with my Mother's coffin, so we could all leave together for the last time.

Trevor had organized our family and friends into the eight big black limousines with about six people in each car.

I don't know who got in my car. I was in a sort of a daze.

But I know there was one brother in each of the eight cars - barring car four of course - and I think my Dad was in Johnnie's car.

My Mother had a brilliant send off. All the street were out, paying their respects to a lovely lady. Most of Gipsyville turned out for my Mother. It was the saddest yet the proudest day of my life.

Sad that my Mother was leaving us but proud of the respect the people of Gipsyville were paying her. And proudest of all of us was Trevor, he'd done a great job. He was the man that day and I was very proud to be his twin brother.

When we arrived at the crematorium there was a large crowd waiting for us. Waiting to pay their respects to a lovely lady who had lived to care for her kids.

A lady who had always done her best. A Mother who really did try to look after her eight sons - and after losing her only daughter in a fire. And a wife, who I believe my Dad always loved - but he sure had a strange way of showing it at times. How my Mother coped I'll never know...

My brother Bobby led the way into the crematorium chapel.

I didn't see much that day. It was just a blank. But I know it was 'standing room only' after our family took up all the seats that were available. There were that many people there from all walks of life that day. I think I sat on the front row next to

MALLY - THE REBEL WITHOUT A PAUSE

Trevor on one side and Richard on the other.
They carried my Mother into the crematorium chapel to the sound of, 'Please paint a rose on the garden wall, so mama won't leave me now.' I don't know who sang it. Trevor picked the songs.
After the Vicar had said his bit, which just went straight over my head, I didn't hear him, all I could hear was people breaking down and crying. My brothers and their wives and girlfriends were all either crying or close to tears. And when Trevor started to cry, I put my arms around him and cried too. But when the song, 'Pal of my cradle days,' by Ann Breen started to play, I nudged Richard and Trevor and we all stood up and started to sing along.
And within a few seconds everyone was stood up and singing! It brought joy to my heart seeing everyone singing along...

PAL OF MY CRADLE DAYS (1919)
Recorded by: Ann Breen

What a friend, what a pal, only now I can see,
How you dreamed and you planned all for me,
I never knew what a mother goes through,
There's nothing that you didn't do.

Chorus:
Pal of my cradle days, I've needed you always.
Since I was a baby upon your knee,
You sacrificed everything for me.
I stole the gold from your hair.
I put the silver threads there,
I don't know any way I could ever repay,
Pal of my cradle days.

Greatest friend, dearest pal,
It was me who caused you
Every sorrow and heartache you knew,
Your face so fair I have wrinkled with care,
I placed every line that is there.

Repeat Chorus: End

Singing that song at the end of the service was one of the proudest, yet saddest, moments of my life.

I looked around the packed crematorium chapel and nearly everyone was crying.

The curtain closed in front of my Mother's coffin. But Trevor refused to leave until he'd actually seen his loving Mother put into the furnace.

Not until then would Trevor himself be at peace.

The Vicar took us through to the back where the furnace was but a shocking sight greeted us!

There, stacked on top of four or five others, was my Mother's coffin. And sitting on top of the pile, wearing scruffy jeans and trainers and smoking a quick cigarette, were two council workers.

Their job was to put the coffins in the furnace and get the loved ones the ashes when the job was complete. But they were just sat there, doing nothing!

They were soon knocked off my Mother's coffin by a couple of Trevor's quick karate moves.

Just as quick as when I'd hid behind the bathroom door and scared him half to death when we had the fire in our flat.

Well our kid scared the two workers half to death that day when he gave them both a quick chop-chop!

You'd have thought they'd seen a ghost.

Trevor screamed at them not to sit on his Mother's coffin and then told them to get my Mother in the furnace.

They didn't need telling twice and the Vicar was quite shocked to see these coffins piled up.

It looked as though they were waiting for so many coffins before they would then have one mad burning session.

Which led me to think about whether the ashes you get are actually the ashes of your loved ones?

Because there's no way of getting your loved one's ashes until they've cooled down. But how many coffins did they burn before they let the ashes cool down?

Trevor then insisted that he wanted to put my Mother in the furnace himself.

He wanted to make sure the job was done 'right'.

And if it wasn't for Trevor, we might never have known if it was my Mother's ashes we received!

MALLY - THE REBEL WITHOUT A PAUSE

I helped Trevor to lift my Mother's coffin into the furnace.

And I can assure you, he made certain that they *were* our Mother's ashes that we took away, and he's still got them to this day!

Naturally, the wake was held at the Gipsyville Tavern that afternoon. But first the eight cars took us back to number 11 West Grove. That was when I asked my Father the questions...

Why? Why did you beat my loving Mother?

Why? Why did you beat ten bells of shit out of us?

And why were you always so hard on us? Why?

My Father couldn't answer any of the questions.

He just sat there, crying his eyes out.

For a moment I almost felt a little sorry for him. But that changed seconds later when there was a knock at the door and the old man jumped up immediately to answer it.

I was disgusted when Pete Maltby walked in with two big bags of rabbit food.

My Dad had it delivered every Monday and had made sure he was back at home for 3 o'clock, Pete's usual delivery time.

My old man never failed to amaze me with the heartless things he did - and not even the fact that it was the day of his own wife's funeral changed that!

I left my Dad's house and got a taxi down to Gipsyville Tavern.

I'd earlier put five hundred pounds behind the bar so that nobody went without a drink that day.

When I got there, the booze was already flowing and the 'party' was in full swing. It was a 'happy' wake and it was three cheers to our brother Trevor - and not forgetting our 'baby' brother Bobby who was still in a daze - and still wearing Mother's pinafore! He didn't take it off all day.

My Mother would have been proud of seven of her sons behaving themselves for once.

I'm sure she'd have forgiven my brother Mike for going on holiday. But I was left with the thought that it was Mike who had to live with the fact he didn't attend his own Mother's funeral. And I'm sure it must eat him up at times.

I also couldn't help but think that my Mam was now on a well-deserved 'holiday' of her own. I knew that every day for the rest of my life I'd miss her - but that her pain was over.

PAL OF MY CRADLE DAYS

My Mother was finally at rest... but I certainly wasn't, not yet.

I hope you can understand what it was like in them days and I hope you won't judge me too harshly on what you've just read.
I was living in hope. Hoping my wife would take me back. Hoping I could carry on fishing and hoping I could keep out of trouble. It didn't work out like that at all though and in Part Three, I'll tell you about how I was accused of mutiny - but not on the Bounty - on the Westella! It was that little incident that led to me getting out of the fishing game for good.
I'll also tell you about what I now think was the most important turning point in my life, when I met a very special lady who managed to get me to change in a way I never thought was possible. Nobody who knew me thought it was possible either, but I'll share the secret in Part Three. I'll tell you about the birds I've raced and chased, of both varieties, and I'll take you inside the secretive world of pigeon-racing, something I really got hooked on. You'll also come with me into the difficult world of business, something I'm still trying to understand. Yes, I'll tell you some very odd stories, one of which was how a tin of glue got me out of a run-down flat and into a luxury three-bedroomed house.
And I'll tell you what happened when my Dad died in May 2007 while I was writing this book that you're reading now. It was a very sad death and not one that you would want for yourself. I wonder if Mam and Dad are now reunited?

My first book was about all the pain inflicted on me and my brothers. This book we're at the end of now has been about all the pain *I* inflicted on others - and my third book will be all about how I turned pain into pleasure.

Take care of yourselves and keep smiling. As my Mother always told us, 'Never worry until worry worries you ...'

See ya
Mally

P.S.

To see more photographs of my family and read more of my Mother's letters, visit my website:
www.mallywelburn.co.uk

Oh and by the way, it would be best if you didn't lend this book out to anybody - let them buy it, like you did -
or you'll have me banging on your door!

Cheers,

Mally